IBN KHALDUN, LIFE AND TIMES

IBN KHALDUN, LIFE AND TIMES

✦ ✦ ✦

ALLEN JAMES FROMHERZ

Edinburgh University Press

Edinburgh University Press Ltd
22 George Square, Edinburgh
www.euppublishing.com

Typeset in JaghbUni by
Servis Filmsetting Ltd, Stockport, Cheshire, and
printed and bound in Great Britain by
CPI Antony Rowe, Chippenham and Eastbourne

A CIP record for this book is available from the British Library

ISBN 978 0 7486 3934 2 (hardback)

CONTENTS

ACKNOWLEDGEMENTS AND PREFACE

Ibn Khaldun credits a long list of teachers in his autobiography. The detailed mini-biographies he wrote for each of his mentors demonstrated the highly personal nature of education for the fourteenth-century North African scholar. The life of twenty-first century scholars may seem more dependent on Google, email and jstor.org than on the type of face-to-face contact with mentors that Ibn Khaldun received. Nevertheless, scholarly debate, discussion and traditional mentorship survive for a lucky few. I have been fortunate and inspired by a long list of mentors and scholars in History and Middle East Studies.

It was Professor Gene Garthwaite at Dartmouth College who first introduced me to the *Muqaddimah* of Ibn Khaldun. I was pursuing a Classics degree at the time and may have ended up as an investment banker, not an assistant professor, if it were not for Gene's encouragement. Dartmouth Professors Dale Eickelman and Kevin Reinhart have similarly maintained contact and offered welcome advice. My Fulbright Research Scholarship to Morocco in 2003 launched a serious interest in medieval North Africa. It was during the Fulbright scholarship that I met and worked with Professor Abdesselam Cheddadi, one of the world's leading experts on Ibn Khaldun. Professor Hugh Kennedy, my Ph.D. supervisor at St Andrews University in Scotland from 2003 to 2006 kept me focused on the primary sources of North African History even as he taught the careful application of theory. Robert Hoyland and Ali al Ansari in Middle East Studies at St. Andrews similarly encouraged me to expand my research in new, interdisciplinary directions. My research on Ibn Khaldun as a nationalist symbol was funded by the American Institute of Maghribi Studies (AIMS) and was greatly aided by my friend and colleague Larry Michalak, director of the AIMS institute in

Tunis. I also received a summer grant from the Georgia State University History Department. My colleagues at Georgia State University inspired me to write more intelligently about the world system and the fourteenth-century context in which Ibn Khaldun lived. My research assistant Edwin Bevens provided tireless, professional advice and effort beyond the call of duty. My family, my mother Robin and my father Allen, as well as my sisters Amy and Becky provided encouragement and support as I wrote this book.

By way of a preface, most transliteration symbols are avoided for ease of reading. The Arabic letter ʿayin is indicated with ʿ. All Hijri dates are converted into Gregorian dates unless indicated.

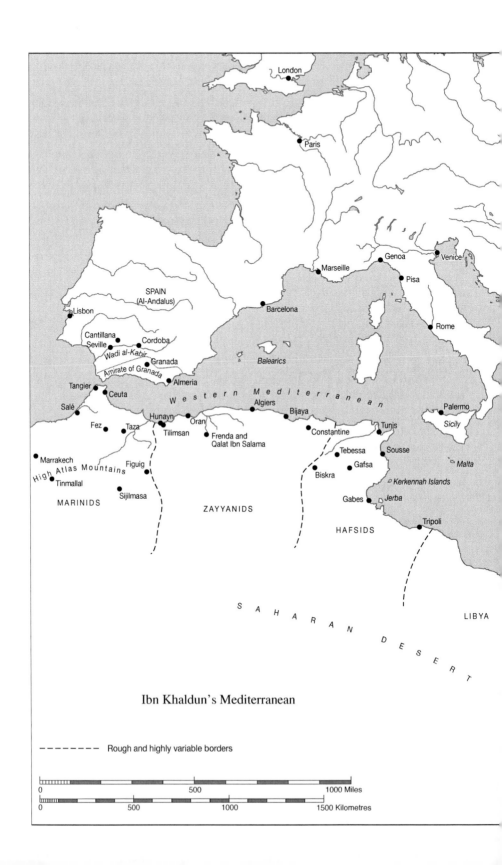

Ibn Khaldun's Mediterranean

– – – – – – – Rough and highly variable borders

| 0 | | 500 | | 1000 Miles |

| 0 | | 500 | | 1000 | | 1500 Kilometres |

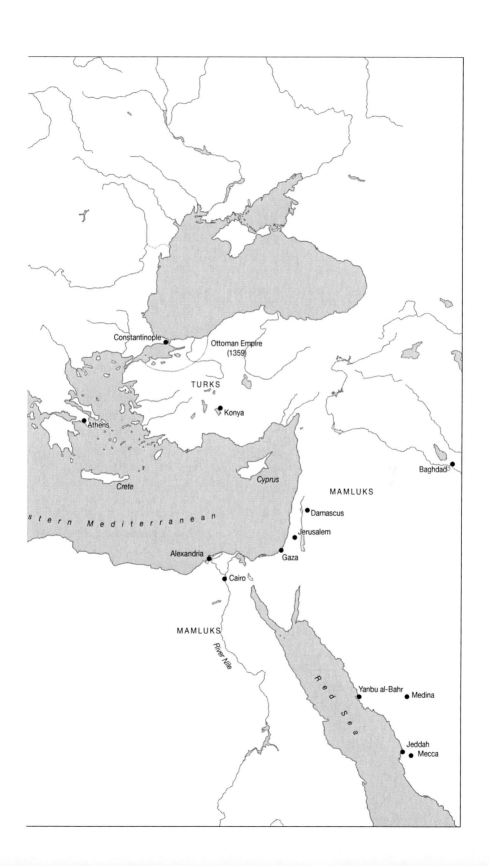

TIMELINE

Early eighth century   Khaldun family migrates from South Arabia to Carmona, a city situated between Cordoba, Seville and Granada. They move from Carmona to Seville.

Late ninth century   Kurayb, Ibn Khaldun's ancestor, revolts against the Umayyad amir, establishing an autonomous government in Seville. Kurayb was killed in 899 AD.

Mid-eleventh century   The Khaldun family regains prominence in Seville. Along with other powerful families, they gain control over most political activities in the city.

1057–8   Abu Muslim Ibn Khaldun, a renowned scholar, dies in Seville.

c. 1230   Ibn Khaldun's ancestor gives a slave girl to a member of the Hafsid dynasty in Tunis, cementing blood ties between the Khaldun and the Hafsids for centuries.

1230s   Increasingly threatened by the encroachment of Christian armies into Al-Andalus and Sevillian territories, the Khaldun family leaves for North Africa.

1248   Seville falls to King Ferdinand III of Castille.

1283   Abu Bakr Muhammad, Hafsid financial minister and great-grandfather of Ibn Khaldun, is killed during a revolt.

May 27, 1332   Ibn Khaldun is born in Tunis.

1336–7   Ibn Khaldun's grandfather, a humble deputy doorkeeper who devoted his life to pious studies, dies.

1348–9   Ibn Khaldun's father, mother, and many of his relatives and teachers die in the plague.

1347–57   Threatened by Marinid expansion, Hafsid rule virtually disappears, only to return in the 1370s.

1347   Abu al-Hasan, Marinid ruler of Fez, conquers Tunis in an attempt to reunite all of North Africa. He was repulsed from Tunis by Arab tribes at Kairouan.

1352   Ibn Khaldun becomes official calligrapher to Ibn Tafragin, effective ruler of Tunis. He leaves Tunis that same year.

1354   He accepts an invitation from Abu ʿInan to come to Fez and study among a distinguished group of scholars.

1354–62   Ibn Khaldun remains in Fez. He marries the daughter of a famed Hafsid general.

February 10, 1357   Shortly before his furtive conquest of Tunis, Abu ʿInan imprisons Ibn Khaldun for conspiracy because of his relationship with a Hafsid, Abu ʿAbd Allah.

1357   Abu ʿInan, patricidal son of Abu al-Hasan, attempts to conquer and hold Tunis where his father failed.

1358   Ibn Khaldun is released from prison after the death of Abu ʿInan on 27 November.

1359   Ibn Khaldun supports the succession of Abu Salim as Marinid ruler. He is appointed *mazalim*: a judge in charge of non-religious legal matters.

1359–62   Muhammad V, amir of Granada, lives as a fugitive in Fez. While in Fez, Ibn Khaldun conspires to help Muhammad V regain his position in Granada.

December 1362 Ibn Khaldun arrives in Granada.

1364 He directs a diplomatic mission to Pedro of Seville. Pedro offers Ibn Khaldun his ancestral lands but Ibn Khaldun politely refuses.

1365 Ibn Khaldun leaves Granada to accept the position of prime minister for ᶜAbd Allah, the Hafsid amir of Bijaya in what is now Algeria. Ibn Khaldun is sent out to forcibly collect taxes from Berber tribes in the surrounding mountains.

1366 ᶜAbd Allah dies. Ibn Khaldun transfers his loyalty to a rival Hafsid: Abu al-ᶜAbbas of Constantine, but quickly falls out of favor with the amir.

1368 Ibn Khaldun refuses an invitation from Abu Hammu II of Tilimsan. He sends his brother Yahya Ibn Khaldun in his stead.

1370 He is captured by the Marinid ruler of Fez ᶜAbd al-ᶜAziz during an attempted escape to Granada.

1374 After a period of great political turmoil in Fez Ibn Khaldun flees to Granada, is extradited and returns to North Africa.

November 1377 He completes the first draft of the *Muqaddimah* after taking up residence in a remote tribal fortress, the Qalᵓat Ibn Salama. He is protected as a guest of the Awlad ᶜArif.

December 1378 Ibn Khaldun is reconciled with the powerful Hafsid ruler Abu al-ᶜAbbas and returns to Tunis. He is denounced by the influential jurist Ibn ᶜArafah al-Warghami (d. 1401).

1382 Ibn Khaldun asks permission to go on the pilgrimage, probably to escape court intrigue and his obligations to Abu al-ᶜAbbas.

1383 Instead of heading to Mecca, Ibn Khaldun settles in Cairo, the capital of Mamluk Egypt. He develops a relationship with the Mamluk ruler, Al-Malik al-Zahir Barquq (d. 1399).

March 1384 Ibn Khaldun is appointed professor and gives the inaugural lecture at Qamhiya College.

August 1384 He is appointed chief Maliki judge of Egypt.

October/November 1384   Ibn Khaldun's wife and four daughters are killed in a shipwreck on their way to join him in Cairo. His two sons survive.

1387   Ibn Khaldun goes to Mecca on the pilgrimage and returns eight months later.

1389   Barquq is temporarily overthrown after a revolt. Ibn Khaldun claims he is forced to sign legal opinions against Barquq.

1390   Barquq regains the throne. Ibn Khaldun loses his lucrative position as president of a Sufi scholarly institute. He regains his judgeship nine years later, however, after being restored to favor under Faraj.

1399   Faraj, son of Barquq, becomes ruler after the death of his father.

September 1400   A rival for the Maliki judgeship replaces Ibn Khaldun.

1401   Ibn Khaldun visits Damascus just before its plundering by Timurlane.

January 10, 1401   He is lowered over the walls of the city of Damascus to meet with Timurlane. He remains with the world conqueror until the end of February.

1401   While fleeing from brigands who attacked his caravan back to Egypt, Ibn Khaldun boards a ship to Gaza and meets a representative of the Ottoman sultan, Bayezid I.

March 1401   Ibn Khaldun returns to Egypt and is appointed judge, but then relieved of his position and appointed again several times.

March 17, 1406   Ibn Khaldun dies. He is buried at a Cairo Sufi cemetery.

1

HISTORIAN MEETS HISTORY

. . . [M]an is not born every day. He was born with a specific historical setting with specific historical priorities.

Carl Jung[1]

On January 10, 1401, a world historical figure and a world historian were seated across from each other in a Mongol tent pitched outside the city walls of Damascus, Syria. Ibn Khaldun, one of the greatest historians of all time, and Timurlane the Conqueror, one of the most powerful, and most vicious, rulers in history, had a civilized discussion about the underlying patterns of human history.

Ibn Khaldun described his visit with Timurlane in his detailed memoirs, an extraordinarily rich autobiography for the period. Although justifiably afraid of the terrible conqueror, Ibn Khaldun wrote about Timurlane with the wide-eyed fascination of a scientist who has just discovered a seemingly conclusive piece of evidence that proved a life-long theory. In order to avoid detection by the besieged citizens of Damascus who still refused to surrender, he was lowered over the city walls in the middle of night and made his way to the conqueror's tent. After showing deference to the great Sultan, Ibn Khaldun exclaimed rather cryptically, 'May God help you sir! It has been today thirty or forty years since I have hoped for this encounter.'

Obviously puzzled and intrigued, since Ibn Khaldun could not have known about him so long ago, Timurlane asked, 'For what reason?'

'For two reasons,' Ibn Khaldun responded, 'The first, is that you are the Sultan of the world, the King of the earth; I have never known a king since the creation of Adam who is comparable to you.'

Already we can detect in Ibn Khaldun's words the refined and highly developed art of flattery for kings, an art he had practiced many times over since the first of his many government appointments as a counselor for the ruler of Fez, Morocco some fifty years earlier. Nevertheless, given the rapid and seemingly unstoppable advance of the Tartar armies, and given that he was seeing this terrible, charismatic, enigmatic figure face to face, it is conceivable that even Ibn Khaldun, who had both experienced and read so much history, could have actually believed that this lame and brutal man was the greatest of kings since Adam. Although he admitted to being frightened by the great Muslim conqueror, we are left not knowing what he was really thinking behind his mask of flatteries.

He continued, 'I do not base this observation on something out of thin air for I am a man of science.'

The fact that Ibn Khaldun saw himself as 'a man of science,' not merely in the typical sense of religious sciences, as almost all 'science' was studied at the time, but of science in the sense of logic and philosophy and observation as they were known by the ancient Greek philosophers, is very important here.[2] This bold self-proclamation by Ibn Khaldun of his superior knowledge in front of a brooding and skeptical tyrant shows just one example of why Ibn Khaldun was such a great part of Muslim intellectual history. Ibn Khaldun the scientist, the polymath, the thinker who thought outside the box was not a typical man and he knew it.

Timurlane was himself fascinated by history and his own sense of destiny. During his conquests he even brought along a coterie of Uyghur and Iranian writers who transcribed his every word. Although the Tartar ruler was illiterate, Timurlane listened to recitations of historical chronicles with rapt attention. Timurlane, the amateur historian, must have been pleased by Ibn Khaldun's words and curious to hear the illustrious Ibn Khaldun's explanation of his own power.[3] Ibn Khaldun explains Timurlane's power not simply through reference to the divine, but through reference to his own logically developed ideas about the origins of political power:

> Here is the explanation. Power does not exist without tribal solidarity (*ᶜasabiyya*). Power is at its greatest extent among mainly tribal peoples, those whose lives are mostly governed by tribal solidarity. Men of science are agreed on the fact that the two nations most tribal on earth are the Turks and the Arabs. You know of the great power of the Arabs after they were united by the religion of their prophet [Muhammad]. As far as the Turks, their [successful] rivalry against the Kings of Persia is sufficient witness to their power . . . No King on earth, neither Chosroes, nor Caesar, nor Alexander nor Nebuchadnezzar had at their disposal a sense of tribal solidarity such as theirs . . .[4]

It might be easy here to accuse Ibn Khaldun of overlooking the destructive and bloody nature of Timurlane's rule. Timurlane and his followers left burnt cities and massive pyramids of skulls in their wake. And it was not only Timurlane's mass killing of settled populations that would have set off an alarm, his next destination for his destructive conquests was Mamluk Egypt, the very place Ibn Khaldun was representing as envoy. Ibn Khaldun served off and on for many years as chief judge of Cairo.

Egypt was not the end of Timurlane's ambitions. He also planned to vanquish North Africa, including Tunis where Ibn Khaldun was born and spent his early life, an area of the Muslim world he could conceivably call home. Yet, despite his obvious personal fear of Timurlane as an imminent threat to the world in which he lived, Ibn Khaldun saw Timurlane primarily as a phenomenon to be studied and understood. In his discussions he even assisted Timurlane and his plans for the conquest of North Africa, describing the geography and the peoples of North Africa. Perhaps Timurlane, a Muslim conqueror with large stores of tribal solidarity at his disposal, represented for Ibn Khaldun a new opportunity for Muslim unity and revival. Besides, the constant history of chaos, revolt, division, and power struggle in North Africa and Egypt may have made Ibn Khaldun pine for some strong man representing order. And what scientist is not thrilled when their predictions go according to plan?

In Ibn Khaldun's view, Timurlane and his Mongol followers were a culmination of Ibn Khaldun's theory that tribal solidarity, or *ᶜasabiyya*, was the primary explanation for the rise of empires, rulers, and dynasties.[5] For Ibn Khaldun tribal solidarity was the key to understanding the Near East. No matter how magnificently arrayed in their latter stages, empires and dynasties, according to Ibn Khaldun, arose out of simple tribal beginnings. Like a rider taming a wild horse, the potential power of intense group affinity that existed within a disorganized collection of tribes could be harnessed and unified by charisma, religious prophecy, or simply the circumstances of history to spectacular effect. As Ibn Khaldun explained to Timurlane, Timurlane and his followers had successfully harnessed the tribal power of the Mongols and the Tartars. The incredible loyalty, the sense of being one tribe, one body, one force out of many, so exemplified here by Timurlane's horde, was *ᶜasabiyya*. For Ibn Khaldun, *ᶜasabiyya* was the driving force of history. This idea, that the rise and fall of dynasties is fundamentally linked to *ᶜasabiyya*, is a primary thesis of Ibn Khaldun's famed book, the *Muqaddimah*, or introduction to history. *ᶜAsabiyya* is still shaping the Near East. *ᶜAsabiyya* can be found today in the form of tribal politics in Iraq, the rise of the Taliban in Afghanistan, the rivalry between tribes in Darfur, and even in the secretive decisions and negotiations of the elite hyperwealthy tribes of Dubai, Abu Dhabi and other Gulf states. Although many tribes have settled, and many attempts have been made at establishing formal institutional structures that recognize the individual over the tribe, the ties of *casabiyya* and their influence on the course of events has certainly not gone away.

For this reason the *Muqaddimah* and Ibn Khaldun's articulation of the central role of tribal solidarity in social and historical change has inspired Western historians ever since its rediscovery by Europeans in the early nineteenth century. It had been buried deep, hidden from European view, in an Ottoman archive, even as important Ottoman scholars studied it. Since then, Ibn Khaldun's theories have caught fire among intellectuals of both East and West far outside the medievalist and orientalist community. Ernest Gellner, one of the most influential intellectuals and anthropologists of the twentieth century, used Ibn Khaldun's ideas as one of his primary inspirations.[6] Arnold Toynbee, that icon of historical writing, called Ibn Khaldun the greatest historian of all time. Many thinkers, political scientists and theoreticians have practically adopted Ibn Khaldun as one of their own, as a contemporary, as a modern, or even postmodern thinker. Hundreds of books and articles have been written about Ibn Khaldun. If only these accounts of Ibn Khaldun's thought are read, it could seem as if Ibn Khaldun were an orphan of his own time, a lonely and exiled modern mind removed from history.

IBN KHALDUN: A MODERN IN THE ROUGH?

The temptation to identify Ibn Khaldun as a modern mind, however, ignores the direct relationship between his times and his thought. In fact, serious scholars of Ibn Khaldun have long argued that he should be seen in 'his own time,' although no authoritative biography has yet appeared to accomplish this.[7] Even though he was not a typical thinker, and even though some of his ideas have modern scientific relevance, Ibn Khaldun was still very much a product of the late medieval Islamic world. This fact is clearly seen in Ibn Khaldun's second, stated reason for proclaiming Timurlane the greatest king since Adam. It is a reason that should annihilate the temptation to falsely view Ibn Khaldun as some sort of orphaned, modern thinker. Immediately after referring to his hypothesis about the origins of dynasties and empires in tribal solidarity, again, a hypothesis that many thinkers, historians, and even modern pundits find compelling, Ibn Khaldun presents a second thesis to Timurlane that seems less useful to the modern mind, but that is still incredibly useful for understanding the world in which Ibn Khaldun lived: 'The divine predictions of the saints of North Africa: this was the second reason why I hoped I would see you.'[8]

Ibn Khaldun made what he would certainly have thought was a smooth transition here between what seems to the modern ear like a cosmic shift from independent, logical explanation to the divine and fated explanations of the saints. To Ibn Khaldun there was no easy divide between the truth of his logic and the divination of saints or mystics, such as Ibn ᶜAbbad of Ronda (1332–90), a famous Sufi predictor of events at the Qarawiyyin university, the ancient center of learning in Fez, Morocco.[9] Mystics such as Ibn ᶜAbbad influenced Ibn Khaldun while he was in Fez. Modern writers, however, often inadvertently impose a false and anachronistic separation onto Ibn Khaldun. This is seen even in the very way that the *Muqaddimah* is typically published. The *Muqaddimah* is a massive book and is difficult to publish in full for wide distribution. Those parts of Ibn Khaldun's famous *Muqaddimah* that are most often translated and published and most often cited in papers and books about Ibn Khaldun are those parts that refer to Ibn Khaldun's logical and innovative explanations of history. These are the parts that seem most attuned to the modern ear. In contrast, there is little mention in the massive collection of books and articles about Ibn Khaldun's obsession with diviners and saints, with magical books written secretly for the Prophet Muhammad that foretold the entire history of the world. Nor is there much mention of Ibn Khaldun's obsession with numerology, astrology, magic, and a whole cornucopia of seemingly strange and fantastic 'ologies' that fill his voluminous *Muqaddimah*. It may be easy for cash-strapped publishers and modern readers to dismiss these sections of the *Muqaddimah*, yet this deeply non-modern aspect of Ibn Khaldun's thought, especially his Sufism, his use of the predictions of spiritual saints who were a major part of the Arab and Berber North African life, reveals compelling clues about Ibn Khaldun the man, and about the society from which Ibn Khaldun emerged.

Perhaps the best way of approaching Ibn Khaldun biography and his thought is to abandon the tempting adjective 'modern' when describing him. Certainly, as this book will illustrate, Ibn Khaldun introduced bold and new approaches to historiography, sociology, geography, and even economics and linguistics, many of which happen to parallel modern thinking. However, thinking of Ibn Khaldun and some of his ideas as modern in a sea of premodernism creates categories and conflicts that were simply never a part of his worldview. Although he knew many of his ideas were original, Ibn Khaldun did not see himself as separate from his age.

Anachronistic thinking only obstructs the more fascinating story of Ibn Khaldun's life and times, the story about how his many unique and continuously inspiring ideas emerged out of a period of turmoil, plague, and rapid political change. This is not to say that Ibn Khaldun's ideas should not be considered relevant and useful to the modern world. To the contrary, the late medieval period was, for Islam, a time of great division, a time that has many similarities with today. By identifying Ibn Khaldun's ideas with his particular historical circumstances and biography reveals a much more accurate vision of the incredible importance of tribal dynamics in a period of failed states and governments, a period that, in this last respect, was not so different from our own.

THE FOURTEENTH-CENTURY WORLD

The fourteenth-century world of Ibn Khaldun was a world of political disintegration, unpredictability and pestilence. It was also, however, a world characterized by the maturation of Islamic social institutions and the diversification of Islamic culture in a variety of distinct regions. Despite the increasing regionalization of Islamic culture, however, Ibn Khaldun still represented a more universal cultural system. As a historian, a polymath, and a philosopher, Ibn Khaldun was influenced by events and trends far outside his immediate field of action or experience. He was, for example, much more informed about the rise of the Mongols in central Asia and the specific biography of the Mongol founder, Genghis Khan, and immensely more curious about the larger context than any of his more provincial political patrons, or even most of his colleagues in the intellectual circles of the fourteenth century.[10] It is only appropriate, therefore, to begin this brief introduction to Ibn Khaldun's historical context in the broadest possible way.

From Classical to Medieval Islam

Western scholars often impose categories such as 'classical' Islam and 'medieval' Islam as they frame Islamic history according to events in the Western world. Despite this seemingly orientalist imposition, there is still some utility in the categorization of Islamic history into 'classical' and 'medieval' eras. Just as historians defined the beginning of the medieval period in the Latin West by the loss of practical hope for the political re-integration of Latin Rome, decline in hope for the political re-integration of the ᶜAbbasid caliphate similarly characterized the beginning of the medieval period in Islam. There was a sense of the beginning of an end of times, of foreboding and doom among Muslims when the Mongol chief, Hulagu, executed the last, and largely powerless caliph of Baghdad, Al-Mustasim, in 1258. The ᶜAbbasid line was not completely extinct, a descendant of Al-Mustasim reappeared under the protection of the slave rulers of Mamluk Egypt, but it was severely compromised. Alleged descendants of the ᶜAbbasid caliph would be shuttled over to legitimize Egyptian dynasts. Later the Ottomans claimed the Caliphate, just as Western rulers such as Charlemagne claimed the title of Holy Roman Emperor. Yet after 1258 the notion of the caliph as an independent political power in Baghdad was effectively extinguished.

The classical world in the West is often said to end in the year 476 AD, the year the Germanic chief, Odoacer, deposed the last, and largely insignificant, Roman emperor, Romulus Augustulus. The much-weakened late Roman Empire, that last, languid breath of the Western classical imperial rule, represented little more than the pretense and memory, but still the hope of unified political power in the Latin world. So, too, did the much weakened ᶜAbbasid caliphate still represent the memory and the hope for a unified political unity in the Islamic world.

The office of caliph, a word that literally meant 'successor' to the Prophet Muhammad, founder of Islam, signified the pretense of Islamic political unity. This political unity was, according to the original example of the Prophet and the first four, rightly-guided caliphs, supposed to be fused with the spiritual unity of the Muslim community or '*umma.*' Ibn Khaldun was keenly aware of the fall of the prestige of the caliph. He made clear his near obsession with ideal perfection the office of the caliphate, especially during the life of Muhammad and his first four successors. While Ibn Khaldun described most non-caliphates, most normal governments in perpetual flux and decay, the caliphate was, in his view, an ideal, the only true government, one based on the correct practice of *sharia*, Islamic law. In fact, Ibn Khaldun structured his book so that his chapter on the caliphate came at the end, at the tip of a pyramid of various governments of varying virtue. As the scholar H. A. R. Gibb observed, Ibn Khaldun would 'culminate' his description of various forms of society 'with the Caliphate.'[11] Nevertheless, Ibn Khaldun was fully aware that the caliphate in the fourteenth century was little more than a shadow of an ideal. There was little or no power left in that institution when Ibn Khaldun was writing. The ideals of the caliphate, although the Mamluks claimed the institution, were effectively nullified.

Late Medieval Islam: Social Continuity and Political Disruption

Hulagu, the Mongol conqueror of Baghdad, killed the last ᶜAbbasid caliph, Al-Mustasim, by wrapping him up in a carpet and crushing him under the foot of an elephant. Despite this ignominious end, hope for an overarching political stability and unity under a renewed Caliphate, the continuity of Islamic civilization itself was not crushed. In fact, by the year 1258 AD the spiritual, religious, social, and cultural consensus of most Sunni Muslims had matured significantly, often at the expense of political unity and the authority of the caliph. Great Sunni jurists and *ulama*, such as Ibn Hanbal (d. 855 AD), and his successors, successfully resisted the attempts of powerful caliphs to control the interpretation of religious law.[12] Likewise, in the West, Latin culture, language, and norms were maintained in the institutions of the Catholic Church, institutions that, as Edward Gibbon famously argued, could develop at the expense of Roman political power. By the late medieval period, Islamic law, custom, and society had matured even as the political structure of the Islamic world fractured. Who was specifically in power was becoming less relevant. Muslim society had developed and matured to such an extent that it could exist in a state fairly independent of political variables. The caliphate, representing the perfect fusion of religious, social, legal, and political views had not become irrelevant, it was still an ideal to which Muslims aspired; it was simply defunct. As Marshall Hodgson described the centuries from 1250–1450 AD in *The Venture of Islam*, 'We come to a society which – however unstable it was in its political expressions – was relatively stable (as citied societies go) in its underlying expectations and expressions of social and cultural life.'[13]

This stability and continuity in society, if not in politics, after 1250 was produced by three interrelated social and intellectual developments in religion, education, and law. In the religious arena there was a burst of Sufi mysticism, a great spiritual awakening of sorts that grew almost unchecked throughout the Islamic world. Tilman Nagel, historian of Islamic theology, called this new era 'die neue Frömmlichkeit,' the era of a new religiosity.[14] The shrines of Sufi saints not only channeled the emotional and spiritual needs of Muslims throughout the Islamic world, the descendants of saints who managed the shrines negotiated settlements between rival clans, encouraged pilgrimage and provided a type of informal stability in the countryside and on crowded, politically volatile, urban streets. Sufis within a religious order communicated with one another across important political and geographic boundaries, regularly traveling to other members of the same mystical order or *tariqa*. In religion the institution of the *ulama*, or learned Muslim jurists and scholars, preserved and applied the *sharia*, the corpus of Islamic law, with the benefit of centuries of precedent. Al-Ghazali (d. 1111 AD), often called the greatest Muslim since Muhammad, systematically integrated Sufism and Islamic law and orthodox practice, thus closing the circle. Al-Ghazali's wildly popular writings provided a stable theological basis and worldview, a worldview upon which medieval Islamic society was built. Politics in the medieval Islamic world, however, was another matter entirely.

Although Marshall Hodgson described the centuries after 1258 as the beginning of a new era of continuities and consolidations, it would be inaccurate to assume that the political disunity of the late medieval period inevitably led to an opposite reaction of dull and changeless conformity in all cases, to less cultural or economic vibrancy, to changeless social characteristics in every corner of the Middle East and North Africa. In many cases, political disunity and fragmentation led to increased cultural creativity and vibrancy, not only as different, neighboring dynasties rivaled each other explicitly, but also more subtly as distinct geographic regions solidified their own, particular cultural characteristics.

A multitude of political centers at various levels of cultural vibrancy, tied, however tenuously, by important cultural and religious continuities of the *ulama* and the Sufis, characterized the late medieval Islamic world. The late medieval Islamic world had two symbolic bookends: the fall of the ᶜAbbasids in 1258 and the beginning of major Ottoman expansion with the conquest of Constantinople in 1453. The Ottomans would eventually come to dominate both Mesopotamia and the eastern and southern Mediterranean, reviving the legacy of the ᶜAbbasid Empire and the golden age of Islam. Ibn Khaldun would never live to see this resurgence of Islamic unity. Living from 1332 to 1406, Ibn Khaldun's life was in the very middle of this politically fractured, if formative period of Islamic history.

The Mongols: Scourge or Hope of Unity?

The political fragmentation of the late medieval Islamic world after the Mongols was not inevitable. In China the Mongol incursion managed to actually reintroduce a period of stability and prosperity under the Yuan Dynasty, established by Kublai Khan, the son of Genghis Khan. The Muslim world, in contrast, experienced no such post-Mongol reprieve of political unity. The Mamluks, or slave-rulers of Cairo who had taken outright control of Egypt from their former Shiite Fatimid owners, used their superior cavalry and mercilessly trained ranks to become a bulwark against Tartar and Mongol expansion. By stopping the Mongols from entering Africa, the Mamluks became a wall of trained military efficiency, a bastion of military supremacy fed by the riches of the Nile. Thus, the Mamluk solider-rulers, trained and steeped in the ethos of war, ended up being more effective than the wall of stone that separated the Chinese Son of Heaven from the Mongol hordes. The Mamluks had stopped the Mongols at two major battles: they defeated them at the battle of Ain Jalut when an initial wave of Mongols was crushed; and the next great defeat happened shortly after Ibn Khaldun visited Timurlane. By proving to be a stubborn blockade against Mongol expansion, the Mamluks of Egypt effectively separated the Western Islamic world in Africa and the Levant from the Mongol and Tartar dominated the Islamic world in Asia. While China was united under the Mongols, the Islamic world never fully submitted. Although they were formidable the Mamluks never managed to wield effective power further east into the lands of the Ilkhans or further west into the lands of the powerful Berber Amirs of Tunis, Tilimsan and Fez. With the Islamic world divided between Mamluks and Mongols there was little hope of the revival of a centralized Caliphate until the re-emergence of the Ottomans decades after Ibn Khaldun's death in 1406.

Even where the Mongols had conquered and established their rule in Asia they did not unite the populations of the Middle East as they had done in China.

Instead, divided and feuding Mongol dynasts and Mongol Muslims called Ilkhans controlled fragments of Muslim Central Asia. A man that some consider the Ibn Khaldun of Central Asia recorded the history of these Ilkhans and the earliest Mongol invasions in Persia: the scholar, historian, and polymath Rashid al-Din (d. 1318). It was not surprising that Ibn Khaldun identified Timurlane as a possible unifier of the Islamic world.[15] Knowing of the achievements of the Mongols in China, wanting to assuage the tyrant in order to save his life, and realizing that Timurlane had submitted the Ilkhans to his rule, he may have been completely earnest when telling Timurlane of his eventual success.

West of Central Asia, the rest of the Islamic world was similarly beset by dynastic divisions clustered around geographically similar regions. In late medieval Anatolia small and politically divided Turkish states dominated the scene even as *ghazi*, or *jihadi*, warrior chiefs, Osman, Orhan, and the early Ottomans began to sow the seeds of what would become the Ottoman empire and the next great hope for Islamic unity since the fall of the ᶜAbbasids. The political situation was no better in the western North African regions of the Islamic world, or the Maghrib. After the fall of the once-powerful North African Almohads, weak Berber emirates that will be discussed in more detail below maintained a light grip on power. The only place of relative political stability and continuity was Cairo, the capital of Mamluk Egypt where Ibn Khaldun would spend the last decades of his life. Despite his awareness of the importance of Central Asia and the Middle East, Ibn Khaldun's most formative years were spent in the western Mediterranean. It was the political and social history of the western Mediterranean that shaped Ibn Khaldun's thinking most profoundly.

Medieval North Africa and Al-Andalus

The North Africa of Ibn Khaldun was divided, if by no means completely severed, from Asia by centuries of political distance from the divine rule of the ᶜAbbasid Caliphs of Baghdad. North Africa and Al-Andalus (Muslim Iberia) had developed as independent and self-sufficient social, economic and cultural zones. Even while the eastern Islamic lands from Baghdad to Bukhara were being de-urbanized by Mongol invasions and the decline of agricultural productivity, archaeological evidence from northern Moroccan coastal cities, ports of western Mediterranean trade, showed less decline and even some increase in urban development from *c.* 1200 to 1458 AD.[16] A boom in trans-Saharan to trans-Mediterranean trade during the medieval period resulted in a great deal of urban development and economic activity in northern ports such as Nul Lamta and Badis as well as so-called 'desert ports' such as the famed caravan city of Sijilmasa on the Moroccan edge of the Saharan desert.[17] North Africa, of course, was not the only, or even, in some cases, the primary beneficiary of this trade. The crown of Aragon, centered in Barcelona, had fully established its primacy in North African trade by 1300 and Barcelona even took an active role in the conflicts between North African powers. Aragon often decided the fate of North African sultans.[18] Also, while some urban development may have been maintained or even expanded through trade, the agricultural situation in North Africa and Al-Andalus was, according to Ibn Khaldun's own reckoning, worsening.

Although his writings should by no means be equated with modern environmentalism, Ibn Khaldun seemed acutely aware of the consequences of the overuse or abuse of environmental resources. Ibn Khaldun witnessed, for example, how the overexploitation of the land in Granada was leading to an increased use of expensive fertilizer. This drove up the prices of basic foods stuffs, leading to unrest in the population. He placed most of the blame on the luxurious activities of dynasts and rulers.[19] He indicated that there was a lack of investment in agricultural infrastructure in North Africa and in parts of Al-Andalus. Springs, irrigation canals, and wells not dug up and maintained had become dry 'as udders that are not milked.'[20] Political instability, disintegration, and resulting tyrannies also had a direct impact on the productivity of the land and the ability of North African society to support surplus labor either for armies or for cities. Amirs and unscrupulous rulers taking land away from their subjects and the increase in land taxes to pay for petty, dynastic wars led to a dramatic decrease in agricultural production. Landowners fled their tax burden and moved to the overpopulated cities. This overtaxation and appropriation of rural, agricultural land may be, in fact, one explanation for the increase in settlement in mid-sized, and then larger cities noted by archaeologists of medieval North Africa.[21]

The North African Political Context

It was the famously complex political machinations of the Italian city-states that shaped and informed the thinking of Machiavelli, writer of *The Prince*, a cynical guide for rulers. Likewise, the complexity of North African politics, dynasts, and rivals allying in a dizzying array of coalitions, coups, false allegiances, deceit, family rivalries, rebellions, and even the low promises by some Muslim rulers to convert to Christianity in order to gain support from Christian states against fellow Muslim rivals: all of this influenced Ibn Khaldun. The political situation was such that it seemed impossible to map who was against whom in thirteenth- and fourteenth-century North Africa without a diagram.[22] Perhaps ironically, this very complexity made the political environment of medieval North Africa ripe for Ibn Khaldun's generalizations. In such chaotic times, mere prestige or appearance of authority could not shield a ruler or a regime from bad decisions. If he had lived in more stable times, Ibn Khaldun may not have noticed the importance of securing allies in the countryside or the mutability of loyalty and power.

Forbidden from cutting into the body, ancient surgeons benefited from observing human remains on the battlefield. Similarly, Ibn Khaldun could autopsy the corpses of those dynasts and desperate power schemes strewn about the North African historical scene. He had direct and immediate exposure to the failure of attempts at political unity in the fourteenth-century Maghrib. In Fez he worked for the Marinid ruler Abu ᶜInan, who, like his father Abu al-Hasan, had ambitions to unite North Africa; ambitions that led to disaster. In Tunis, he worked for the Hafsid Abu al-ᶜAbbas who also had ambitions to unite North Africa, ambitions that similarly, and, it seemed, inevitably failed. As a powerful, active witness to history Ibn Khaldun repeatedly saw the cycle of rise and fall over and over again. As both prisoner and chamberlain to North African sultans and tribal chiefs, he experienced power and the consequences of power in all its forms. While every detail of fourteenth-century North African politics cannot be covered in this section, a general overview of the historical roots of the political situation in fourteenth century North Africa, a history for which Ibn Khaldun is himself often the most trusted and cited primary source, is not only thrilling but necessary in order to understand Ibn Khaldun's life and work.

Except for an interlude in Al-Andalus, the first five decades of Ibn Khaldun's life, from his birth in Tunis in 1332 until 1382, when he left for Cairo, was spent living in North Africa or in the service of North African sovereigns. North Africa, or the Maghrib, 'the land of the setting sun' in Arabic, was dominated by three major tribal dynasties in the fourteenth century: the Marinids to the west in Fez (Morocco); the Zayyanids in the center in Tilimsan (Tlemcen, Algeria); and the Hafsids to the east in Tunis (Tunisia). The Hafsids, Marinids and Zayyanid dynasties were all remnants of the Berber-dominated Almohad Empire that controlled all of North Africa from *c.* 1150 to 1230. Yet unlike the Almohads, who based their authority on religious inspiration, and the promised transformation of society, none of these three successor states, states that dominated North Africa during Ibn Khaldun's life, were based on an original system of beliefs or social practices. ᶜ*Asabiyya* and tradition, not ideology or religion, was the main social and political glue of fourteenth-century North Africa.

From Almohads to Hafsids

Although the Almohads only ruled over all of North Africa from approximately 1147 until 1230, their legacy and influence would remain an important factor in North Africa even after Ibn Khaldun's death in 1406. Most importantly, the Hafsids, essentially an Almohad successor dynasty that ruled out of Tunis, maintained important symbolic aspects of Almohad doctrine and institutions well after the collapse of the Almohad North African capital of Marrakech.[23] Under the Almohads North Africa became, for the first and only time in its history, a concrete and unified political and historical expression. By securing the High Atlas Mountains, that great spine of nearly impenetrable peaks looming over the North African landscape, the Almohads had made usually centrifugal forces of North Africa's geography centripetal. For most dynasties, the Atlas Mountains were a den of rebellion; even the Ancient Romans did not penetrate them. For the twelfth-century Almohads, the Atlas Mountains were a natural fortress. The Almohads were the first dynasty to unite this mountainous spine of North Africa. They subdued virtually all of the Atlas Mountain Berber tribes, from the Anti-Atlas of Morocco, through Northern Algeria to Tunisia, as well as a great number of desert tribes. In addition to these geographic advantages, an explosive combination of religion and tribal solidarity was the basis of Almohad power.

The founder of the Almohad movement was the infallible Mahdi Ibn Tumart (*c.* 1080–1130). In Islamic tradition, the Mahdi, the rightly-guided one, proclaimed the end of time. By preaching in Berber, upending fruitless, horizontal feuding between clans, enforcing a new vertical hierarchy of tribes, and proclaiming a new doctrine that was specifically relevant to the powerful Atlas Mountain Berber tribes, the charismatic leadership of Mahdi Ibn Tumart inspired the Almohads to burst out of their Atlas strongholds and conquer the major urban centers of North Africa and southern Iberia. Although it would be Ibn Tumart's successor, the Caliph ʿAbd al-Muʾmin who would conquer Marrakech in 1147 AD and unite all of North Africa to Tripoli by 1160 AD, the memory and doctrine of the infallible Mahdi and his miraculous deeds would continue to inspire the loyalty of the proud and powerful Atlas tribes, a loyalty that demanded the sacrifice of local, clannish *ʿasabiyya*, for a wider, more comprehensive *ʿasabiyya*, a group feeling and solidarity based on loyalty to the doctrine and infallible guidance of the Mahdi. In order to make this wider group feeling viable, Ibn Tumart and his successors created a complex hierarchy. At the summit of this hierarchy were councils of ten, fifty and seventy. There were also the memorizers, those who had learned Ibn Tumart's doctrine by heart, and the scholars, those qualified to spread and enforce the doctrine throughout the mountainous realm. Then there were the tribes themselves. Remarkably, tribes became pseudo-bureaucracies. Institutionalized, tribes ranked into roles in the hierarchy according to when they joined the cause. In the highest reaches of the complex Almohad hierarchy, in the council of ten prominent tribal sheikhs who advised the Almohad Caliph, was an important and powerful Berber chief whose descendant would later form a close relationship with the Khaldun clan: Abu Hafs al-Hintati, or Faska u-Mzal Inti in Berber.[24]

Ibn Tumart changed Faska's Berber name to Abu Hafs: the same name as one of Muhammad the Prophet's closest companions in the seventh century. In fact, the fashioning of Berber names and identities into an Islamic, Arabic scheme was quite prevalent during the initial stages of the Almohad movement. Abu Hafs was chief of the powerful Hintata tribe of the Anti-Atlas, south of the Sous valley in what is now Morocco, whose warriors Abu Hafs commanded in battle against the ruling Almoravids, great enemies of the Almohads. Unlike other sheikhs, who were assigned to the ranks of tribes other than their own, he was one of the few sheikhs allowed to command his own tribe into battle. It is doubtful that the seemingly unstoppable Almohad wave against the Almoravids would have arisen as quickly without the military support of the large and unified Hintati tribe, or without the leadership and unshakeable loyalty of Abu Hafs.[25] The Hafsid family remained consistently loyal to the original Almohad doctrine of Ibn Tumart. This loyalty led to their complete independence from the western Maghrib. The grandson of Abu Hafs, Abu Zakariyya b. ᶜAbd al-Wahid, broke away from the Almohad Caliphs in the main power centers of Seville and Marrakech when, by 1230 AD, the Almohads had rejected the doctrine of the Mahdi Ibn Tumart. The Hafsids were horrified when the Almohad caliph, Al-Maᵓmun, famously proclaimed that the Mahdi was Jesus, son of Mary, not Ibn Tumart.[26] Reacting against this sacrilege, Abu Zakariyya founded the Hafsid dynasty in the region of modern-day Tunisia, making Tunis his capital city. It was to this Abu Zakariyya, the founder of the independent Hafsid dynasty, that one of Ibn Khaldun's ancestors sent their favored slave girl as a gift from Seville. This slave girl would eventually became the wife of Abu Zakariyya and the ancestral mother of subsequent Hafsid caliphs, including the irascible and powerful Hafsid Abu al-ᶜAbbas, the patron of Ibn Khaldun's first edition of the *Muqaddimah*. Abu al-ᶜAbbas came to power in 1370. Before 1366 and the success of Abu al-ᶜAbbas against his rivals, the Hafsid territory had been divided, with local governors and tribal chiefs taking control of their own affairs. This period of disunity and chaos was sparked by the death of the Hafsid ruler, Abu Bakr, in 1345 and bitter rivalry between his heirs. This allowed the Marinid ruler of Morocco Abu al-Hasan to invade and place his own son, Abu al-Fadl, as governor of Tunis. However, the people of Tunis successfully revolted against Abu al-Hasan and Abu al-Fadl. In 1350 a strongman named Ibn Tafragin declared himself regent and installed the young brother of Abu Bakr as ruler of Tunis. Yet Ibn Tafragin never controlled much territory outside the city of Tunis. It was in this complex and delicate political brew that Ibn Khaldun started his political career as a low level bureaucrat for Ibn Tafragin. It was little wonder that Ibn Khaldun left Tunis for Fez. He would not return to his city of birth until Abu al-ᶜAbbas reunited the Hafsid realm. Like many of his ancestors, Abu al-ᶜAbbas longed for the recreation of the Almohad Caliphate across all of North Africa. His constant, and ultimately fruitless, military campaigns against his western neighbors, the Zayyanids and Marinids, were all legitimized by this desire to recreate Almohad imperial success. This desire to unite the Maghrib, in fact, has extended to the present times. There have been several stalled national-ist efforts to create a Greater Maghrib union of Morocco, Algeria, and Tunisia that would roughly reflect the borders of the Almohad empire, sans the Iberian Peninsula. As the Moroccan scholar Abdullah Laroui aptly stated: 'There is no better indication of the importance of the Almohad Empire than the fascination it has exerted on all subsequent rulers of the Maghrib.'[27]

The Hafsids were the Almohad successor state that most held onto the original doctrine of the Almohads, maintaining the institution of the 'Sheikh of the Almohads' as jurist and as the most important functionary at court, and by continuing to mention the Mahdi Ibn Tumart in the mosque.[28] In many respects, the Hafsids did not see themselves as successors of the Almohad Empire but as a continuation of Almohad rule, if over a smaller geographic area around Tunis. As will be discussed later in the book, Ibn Khaldun's understanding of the Almohads and Almohad traditions had a profound impact on his historical theory, a theory that was designed with the interests of his patron, the Hafsid Caliph Abu al-ᶜAbbas, in mind. Yet Ibn Khaldun did not only work for the Hafsids, he also first worked for their rivals in the region. His first significant position was as a functionary for the most powerful Hafsid adversary: the Marinid Sultan of Morocco, Abu ᶜInan.

The Marinids

Unlike the Hafsids, who explicitly traced the legitimacy of their desire to rule all of North Africa to indisputable Almohad roots and the exalted doctrine of the Mahdi Ibn Tumart, the basis of Marinid rule in the former Almohad homeland of Morocco was far less religious or prophetic. A Mahdi or a prophet did not inspire the Marinids. They did not emerge to impose a new form of doctrine or to lead the purification of Islam. Instead, they relied almost entirely on ᶜasabiyya: a rough tribal solidarity formed without significant religious or prophetic inspirations. As the historian of the Berbers, Michael Brett, noted, the Marinids were intensely proud of their tribal identity, making honor, not religion, a central part of their lit-erature: 'The Marinids were a self-consciously Berber dynasty whose official his-tories fall in the category of *Mufakhir al-Barbar*, or "Boasts of the Berbers."'[29]

Although they had no charismatic prophet or Mahdi the Marinids simply took advantage of a power vacuum caused by the break down of Almohad authority. As discussed above this breakdown was caused by a split between the Almohad caliphs, who grew to reject the doctrine of the Mahdi, and the original Berber sheikhs, who resisted attempts at centralizing power in the caliph's administration, rather than in the traditional tribal Almohad hierarchy. The Marinids, or the Banu Marin, the founding Marinid tribal confederation, originated in the region surrounding the improbably remote oasis village of Figuig.[30] On the border between modern Algeria and Morocco, about 400 miles south of the Mediterranean coast and hundreds of miles from any major, urban centers, Figuig remains an extreme destination for travelers to this day. A common Moroccan phrase for something impossibly far and remote is 'until Figuig!' The approach to Figuig is astonishing. After endless hours of seemingly dead and monotonous desert land, Figuig appears as a vast, emerald mirage. Remoteness, however, had a certain advantage. In contrast to the forbidding, but also protective, surrounding desert, Figuig was, and still is, unusually well supplied with water and springs, allowing for extensive settlement and date palm growing. It was also an important stopping point on a trade route between Sijilmasa, that rich desert port of the gold and salt trade to the south and Tilimsan and other Mediterranean ports to the north. Despite some settled agriculture in the oasis, most Marinids, like almost all members of the larger Zanata Berber confederation of which they were a member, engaged in pastoral activities on the surrounding mountains, moving seasonally between Figuig in the south and the Mulwiyya basin.[31]

During the high point of Almohad rule between 1147 and 1212, the Banu Marin, unlike other Zanata Berbers who joined the Almohads in their victorious march across North Africa, consciously maintained a great deal of independence and autonomy from the Almohad government. Although a Marinid chief named Muhyu joined the Almohads at the battle of Alarcos against Spanish Christians, the Banu Marin were never as closely integrated into the Almohad system as other surrounding tribes. Sensing the weakening of Almohad authority after the Almohad defeat at Las Navas de Tolosa in Spain in 1212, the Marinid chief, Abu al-Haqq, son of Muhyu, led a wave of rough and ready Marinid tribesmen hundreds of miles over the mountains, occupying northern Morocco from 1214 to 1217. Although they were repeatedly expelled from the region by various Almohad Caliphs such as Saʿid, they always returned in full force, occupying Fez, Taza, and Meknes in 1248. By 1258 Abu Yahya, then the leader of the Marinids, had occupied almost all of Morocco. With the capture of Marrakech in 1269 AD, his brother and successor, Abu Yusuf Yaʿqub (d. 1286), finally snuffed out Almohad power everywhere but in Hafsid Tunisia. The Hafsids, once only governors in a vast Almohad empire, were now rulers over the last loyal bastion of the doctrine of the Mahdi.

Lacking any unifying doctrine, launching campaigns against Christian Castile in Iberia was one main source of legitimacy for Marinid rulers. Abu Yaᶜqub Yusuf (d. 1307), successor of Abu Yusuf, repeatedly went on *jihad* against the Christians across the straits of Gibraltar. Ibn Khaldun's account of the formation of the Marinids stressed both their tribal dynamic and their ability to rally the disparate and diverse people of the Maghrib around *jihad* in Iberia.[32] In 1294, Abu Yaᶜqub, rallying his forces around the restoration of Al-Andalus, began an ultimately fruitless campaign to reunite the entire Maghrib as their Almohad rivals had once done more than a century earlier. Similar campaigns to unite North Africa, revive the Almohad empire, and restore lost Muslim lands were launched by the Marinid Abu al-Hasan (d. 1351) and his son Abu ᶜInan, Ibn Khaldun's patron in Fez. In each case these would-be conquerors entered Zayyanid and Hafsid territories to the east with short-lived tactical victories, securing the cities and important ports but failing to secure the countryside and the *ᶜasabiyya* of tribes. When he invaded west toward Tunis in 1347, for example, Abu al-Hasan briefly appeared to have united the Maghrib. He even received embassies of congratulations from sub-Saharan rulers. Almost immediately, however, he was faced with rebellions by Arab and Berber tribes. In 1357 Abu ᶜInan captured Tunis, only to be forced back to Morocco by his own troops.[33] Unsupported by any feeling of loyalty, religious inspiration, or by tribal *ᶜasabiyya*, the campaigns of these Marinid sultans bore little fruit. Ibn Khaldun not only started his political career working for the powerful Marinid sultan Abu ᶜInan, he also dedicated a large portion of his *Kitab al-ᶜIbar* to their history.[34] The repeated failures of Marinid ambitions only confirmed his central thesis that securing the *ᶜasabiyya* of rural tribes was the key to imperial and political success in the Maghrib.

Ibn Khaldun was in an ideal position to model his history and theories on the Banu Marin. He held the position of junior 'minister to the tribes of the Banu Marin.' Although the exact nature of this position remains somewhat obscure, Ibn Khaldun was essentially an official, designated negotiator between the dynasty in power in the city of Fez and his family and tribal relations still practicing nomadism hundreds of miles away. As his predecessors in the position must have done, Ibn Khaldun took advantage of this position and even rode out to call the Banu Marin back to Fez during a dynastic dispute. Perhaps because his autobiography has not long been translated into English, Ibn Khaldun's special position as tribal negotiator has hardly been remarked upon by modern commentators on his *Muqaddimah*. Nevertheless, it was in the context of this essential role as a connecting agent between city and tribe that Ibn Khaldun would spend almost his entire career in the Maghrib. As a tribal negotiator, Ibn Khaldun was certainly motivated to emphasize the power of tribes and tribal *ᶜasabiyya* in the *Muqaddimah*.

For Ibn Khaldun the multiple failures of the Marinids exemplified the ephemeral nature of power unsupported by *ᶜasabiyya*. That even the ruler Abu ᶜInan's most loyal troops sensed almost immediately that support for the sultan would not last despite his 'conquest' of the city must have been especially revealing. How more obvious would it have been for Ibn Khaldun, a functionary in Abu ᶜInan's court and a participant in his campaigns, that true power was found not in the cities but in the countryside where the prospect of rebellion and revolt, but also reform, constantly lurked. In fact, Ibn Khaldun would make one of his first bold moves as a young functionary when he left the city walls of Fez to meet the Marinid tribal chiefs in order to secure their support for a successor to Abu ᶜInan. Also, the Zayyanids, existing as a comparatively weak but stubborn buffer between the ambitions of Hafsids and Marinids, only exasperated any attempts to unify the Maghrib.

The Zayyanids

Without the Zayyanids sitting between them, controlling the area around the strategic city of Tilimsan on the western coast of what is now Algeria, it may have been possible, if still unlikely, that some especially capable and skilled Marinid or Hafsid ruler, perhaps the Marinid Abu al-Hasan, or Abu ᶜInan, or the Hafsid Abu al-ᶜAbbas, could have overpowered their main rival and restored something approaching the might of the Almohad empire. The Zayyanids, although less powerful than the Hafsids or Marinids, constantly used their geographical position to play their more powerful neighbors off against one another. They also used the revenue from economic opportunities with Europe, discussed below, to prevent long-term domination. Without the Zayyanids, Ibn Khaldun may have personally witnessed the rise of an empire. Instead, his experience in North Africa was colored by the futility of any attempts at large-scale unified rule of the region.

As Ibn Khaldun informed his readers in the *Kitab al-ᶜIbar*, the Zayyanid dynasty, like the Marinids and the Banu Marin tribal confederation, was built on the *ᶜasabiyya* of a powerful Berber tribal confederation: the Banu ᶜAbd al-Wad. In fact, the Zayyanids were also called the Waddadids. They controlled a large region around Tilimsan in northwestern Algeria. They were relatives of the Marinids, and were linked to them through the super-confederation of Berber tribes called the Zanata. Like the Hafsids and the Marinids, the Zayyanids built their independence and their power on the ruins of the Almohad's empire.[35] In 1228 the Almohad caliph, al-Maʾmun, famously rejected the doctrine of the

Mahdi Ibn Tumart and usurped power with the help of Castilian mercenaries. The governor of Tilimsan at the time, Ibn ᶜAllan, continued to be loyal to the original doctrine of the Almohad Mahdi. In 1230 the Almohad Caliph, Al-Maᵓmun, managed to replace Ibn ᶜAllan with Jabir ibn Yusuf, the chief of the ᶜAbd al-Wad confederation who was loyal to Al-Maᵓmun despite his rejection of the doctrine of Ibn Tumart. Unlike Ibn ᶜAllan, a representative of an imperial doctrine who had little tribal support from the surrounding countryside, Jabir ibn Yusuf could rely on the support of his clansmen. Also, with the Almohad caliphs, his symbolic overlords, occupied in the Maghrib, Jabir ibn Yusuf was able to assume a high level of independence. In 1234 power was transferred to the Banu Zayyan clan, a section of the ᶜAbd al-Wad, after a tribal revolt against the brother of Jabir. Eventually, a strong and charismatic ruler named Yaghmurasan came to power in 1236. Yaghmurasan was a remarkable ruler not simply because of the force of his character but because of the sheer length of his reign, a true rarity in the tumultuous political environment of late thirteenth-century North Africa. After several decades as ruler, Yaghmurasan captured the vital desert trading port of Sijilmasa in 1263 and expanded east at the expense of the Maghrawa tribe. The main motivations for these conquests were new and profitable commercial relations with Aragon, established around 1250 and made official with the remarkable visit of Ibn Baridi, the Zayyanid envoy, to Barcelona in 1277. In this agreement, the Zayyanids stated that an independent consul, called *alcayt* in Catalan, could govern European traders living in the Zayyanid realms. Yaghmurasan realized that the capture of the door to the Sahara, Sijilmasa, would allow him to stabilize the gold and slave trading corridors between Sijilmasa and the coast. Although he lost control of the town in 1274, he made up for it with an expansion to the east that extended Zayyanid power all the way to Bijaya, threatening the Hafsids on their western hinterland. Abu Hammu I, the grandson of Yaghmurasan, consolidated Zayyanid power and established the first Maliki, orthodox madrasas in Tilimsan. The city grew to about 100,000 inhabitants; a large city strategically placed on high land not far from the sea that easily rivaled Fez and Tunis, the capitals of the Marinids and the Hafsids. It was Abu Hammu II, ruler of Tilimsan, son of Abu Hammu I and descendant of Yaghmurasan, who would force the reluctant Ibn Khaldun into his service as he ambitiously attempted to expand further into Hafsid territory in the middle of the fourteenth century. As a sign of the changing political landscape, Ibn Khaldun reminds his readers with unveiled satisfaction that Abu Hammu II was able to escape the revolt of one of his sons only by stowing ignominiously on a Christian Aragonese ship.

Before the fourteenth century, it was possible for North African rulers to rely on domination of the sea to shore up their power against the threat of revolt from the countryside and from their rivals. The changing economic and political dynamics of the Mediterranean, however, especially the rise of Christian powers as serious threats to geographic control of the western sea, had begun to close even that option.

Ibn Khaldun and the Mediterranean

In the words of the French historian, Fernand Braudel, 'The whole Mediterranean consists of movement in space.'[36] Controlling, encouraging and profiting from this movement across and through space was essential for any power that happened to hug the Mediterranean shore.[37] Ibn Khaldun similarly realized the importance of the Mediterranean.[38] He traveled regularly on the Mediterranean,[39] and had an intimate knowledge of its seaports, of the nature of its currents and of its potential perils, especially after the death of his family in a shipwreck in the hazardous and unpredictable waters between Tunis and Cairo. He was, however, also aware of the historic importance of the Mediterranean as an avenue of power. According to Ibn Khaldun, there was once a golden mythical era of Muslim maritime power, in the eighth and ninth centuries, when Muslims ruled the Mediterranean virtually uncontested. Control of the Mediterranean was a conduit of empire, important not only for the goal of defeating the Christians but also for the goal of reuniting the Muslim world. By the fourteenth century, Ibn Khaldun lamented, Muslim powers have largely turned away from the sea, becoming vulnerable to cycles of rise and fall in land-based Bedouin dynasties: 'The Muslims [once] gained control over the whole Mediterranean. Their power and domination over it was vast. The Christian nations could do nothing against the Muslim fleets, anywhere in the Mediterranean. All the time, the Muslims rode its waves for conquest.'[40] As Ibn Khaldun put it, the Christian nations were sent cowering into the islands of the Aegean and useless and isolated northern shipping lanes: 'The Muslim fleet had pounced upon them [the Christians] as eagerly as lions upon their prey. They covered most of the surface of the Mediterranean with their equipment and numbers and traveled its lane.' Finally, in a fit of hyperbole Ibn Khaldun claimed: 'Not a single Christian board floated on it [the Mediterranean].'[41] Even in the late twelfth century under the Almohads Muslims possessed a definite naval edge over Europeans. Naval control of the western Mediterranean, according to Ibn Khaldun, was a crucial reason for the success of the Almohad empire. The power of the Almohad fleet was so renowned that Saladin once pleaded unsuccessfully for assistance from surplus Almohad ships in his campaigns against eastern Christian crusaders.

The situation was much more dire for Muslim navies in the fourteenth century. After the fall of the Almohads, 'Maritime habits were forgotten . . . The Muslims came to be strangers to the Mediterranean.'[42] By this time Muslim shipping was in tatters. Although the office of the admiralty still existed in Hafsid Tunis in the Zayyanid court and in the Marinid realm, Maghribi shipping activity was largely reduced. Ibn Khaldun, however, did not lose all hope. Foreshadowing the rise of the Ottomans, he predicted the rise of a great, new Muslim naval power, a power that would conquer all the lands of the European Christians beyond the sea according to the 'books of predictions.'[43]

It would be extreme to say that by the fourteenth century the Muslim east–west axis of Mediterranean trade had disappeared completely. However, a north–south, European axis was becoming more prevalent as the Northern European market became an increasingly important trading partner for Iberian merchants.[44] According to some scholars, this north–south axis eventually enticed European merchants into the Atlantic world and the age of discovery. It would be a mistake, however, to assume that no Muslims or North Africans were engaged in the north–south scheme, that the rise of European hegemony in trade was a result only of European initiative and Jewish middlemen. Despite the disillusion of the Almohads and a consequent decline in the North African admiralties, Muslim trade, commerce, and travel, as Ibn Khaldun's work richly attested, was still bustling in the fourteenth-century western Mediterranean. According to the scholar Abu-Lughod's influential book on economic and world history, *Before European Hegemony: The World System AD 1250–1350*:

> Too often, European writings view the medieval Italian maritime states as 'active' agents operating on a 'passive' Islamic society. The Italians are credited with introducing enormous and innovative mechanisms for transport and trade into a presumably less competent region. That argument, however, illustrates . . . reasoning backward from outcomes . . . Although it is true that the 'West' eventually 'won,' it should not be assumed that it did so because it was more advanced in either capitalistic theory or practice. Islamic society needed no teachers in these matters.[45]

Abu-Lughod was referring mainly to Islamic society in Mamluk Egypt and European traders from Venice and Genoa. However, her conclusions, and her attempts to apply 'world systems theory' (the argument that the world has shifted between dominant economic trading spheres or hegemonies), can also be applied to the much-neglected sphere of western Mediterranean.[46] North African commercial relations with Aragon, Italy, and France mirror, although in distinct ways, the Mamluks' relations with Venice and Genoa. Up to the Black Death and the middle of the fourteenth century North African amirs were very much equal partners with their European counterparts. After the fall of the crusader state of Acre to the Mamluks in 1291, the Pope attempted to ban all trade with Muslims and the Barbary coast of North Africa. Ignoring this, the Venetians continued trading with the Hafsids and North Africans. In 1273, the Genoese complained that their archrival, Venice, was revitalizing the infidel, forgetting, of course, their own long history of trade with North Africa. Charles II of Sicily proposed that the true crusade must be an 'economic crusade' against the Muslims. Learned friars submitted several proposals to the Pope in Rome. Fidenzio of Padua and Raymond Lull suggested a fleet of police ships to enforce the blockade and encircle the Barbary coast: 'source of the revitalization [of Muslims] in the Levant [Holy Land].' [47] Although none of these proposals were effectively implemented, they reveal a great deal of discomfort in the Christian West with the amount of profit the Muslims were gaining from commerce. Rather than seeing North Africa as a helpless and easily dominated market, there was an obvious fear among Christians that trade was actually more advantageous to the Barbary pirates. The sins of greed and commerce, in this theory, killed the crusader dream. In a way this fear of trading with the enemy was comparable with American paranoia toward the purchasing power of oil-rich sheikhdoms and their affiliates.

Another sign of the active role that North Africans played in the trading system was their ability to frequently capture Christian slaves, who became powerful negotiators for their masters. Hilal le Catalan, a high-ranking Muslim minister born into slavery in Granada, overthrew the Zayyanid amir of Tilimsan in Algeria, Abu Hammu I, in 1318 and put a ruler named Tashfin in his place. Representing Tilimsan, Hilal, that defiant son of Christian captives, said to King John II of Aragon, 'If you accept our conditions there will be peace between us. If you have need for our supplies of gold we will make them available, but only if you give us guarantees. But if you reject our conditions all negotiations will be broken between us!' [48] Clearly, it was not the Aragonese who dictated all the terms of economic exchange in North Africa. The ability of North African wazirs like Hilal to dictate the terms of Mediterranean trade, however, was beginning to decline. As the fourteenth century progressed and the effects of the plague ravished North Africa and Egypt, however, the economic situation began shifting, if very gradually. The fruits and profits of this trade were being increasingly shared with Christian kingdoms and Italian city-states. It was for this reason, along with several other complex economic, political, and societal shifts, that the era of European hegemony described by Abu-Lughod began to emerge only around 1350. [49]

For the scholar Abu-Lughod, as for Ibn Khaldun, the plague was a major factor in changing the course of history. What Ibn Khaldun did not see, however, was the way that the plague came to incrementally favor European economic domination. Europe, with its vast tracks of undeveloped and virgin lands could support the flight of urbanites and even gain some benefit from the plague. In

Egypt and North Africa, however, the situation was more constrained. 'Although it [the Black Death] did not 'kill' Egypt immediately, it so undermined its basic strength that even the continued infusion of wealth made possible by Egypt's monopoly over the sea route to India and China was barely enough to support her.'[50] In Egypt, Venice came to increasingly dominate the market, dumping refined fabrics and textiles onto the Syrian and Egyptian economies.[51]

Trade was also becoming less advantageous for North Africa. Aragon, centered in the port city of Barcelona, began to import mainly raw materials from Hafsid Tunis and Zayyanid Tilimsan, and export mercenary troops, which were used at great cost, by North African amirs to defend their cities. Castile, a Christian kingdom with its capital in Seville on the Guadalqivir, claimed the Marinid region as its zone of influence and trade in an almost pre-colonial fashion. Castilian mercenaries, in fact, had become a regular feature of west North African history since the Almoravid period centuries before. Marseille, a port city in southern France, had extensive, profitable ties with North Africa. Similarly, Italian city-states such as Pisa and Genoa had mercantile interests in North Africa. Venice had traded with the Hafsids until 1332 when, after facing raids by pirates from the North African shore, it periodically forbade all trade with the 'King of Tunis.'[52]

Sensing great commercial opportunities on the North African shore and realizing that Venice had gained a near monopoly over Mamluk Egypt, Aragon, the kingdom in control of Barcelona, attempted to push rival Italian cities out of the North African market and monopolize trade with both the Hafsids and Zayyanids. James the Conqueror of Aragon sent militias to Zayyanid emirs in exchange for mercantile advantages for Aragon. He was even able to extend his protection over Jewish traders as far away as the desert 'port' city of Sijilmasa.[53] Although Ibn Khaldun hardly mentioned encounters with Jews, Aragonese, or Christian merchants in his autobiography, it is clear that the large Jewish merchant population in Barcelona was intimately connected with Jewish merchants all along the trade routes to Africa. Yet even in these cases of intense Aragonese involvement in the affairs of North Africa, there was still a need for a North African partner, for intense North African involvement in the profitable trans-Saharan trade. Even at the height of Aragonese intervention in Maghribi trade in 1286, the North African Zayyanid Amir still kept 50 percent of all trade tax revenue going north.[54] Also, despite attempts by the Aragonese to dominate trade and threaten different amirs with the withdrawal of mercenary support, North African rulers also managed to play major European partners off against one another. Pisa, Genoa, and Venice revived their trading pacts with the Hafsids and Zayyanids throughout the fourteenth century. Indeed, instead of seeing the rise of a north–south European trade as causing the disappearance of Mediterranean east–west trade, many scholars have spoken of a new triangular system, a combination of north–south–east–west, with ships traveling from North Africa to Italy, to Spain and the Near East, not simply from Al-Andalus directly east along the shores of the Maghrib.[55] The situation was similar in Egypt and the eastern Mediterranean.

Fernand Braudel, the theorist of the Mediterranean world, described how Egypt, Ibn Khaldun's home from 1382 until his death in 1406, oriented itself away from the eastern Mediterranean and toward the Red Sea and Indian Ocean, just as Europe was newly oriented toward the Atlantic in the later fourteenth century. Yet Mamluk Egypt, even in the late fourteenth century, remained a central player in Mediterranean trade.[56] Just as the opening of Atlantic trade to North Europe did not eradicate east–west trade in the Mediterranean, opening the door of trade with the Red Sea and the Indian Ocean to the south, a trading route that Ibn Khaldun saw first-hand during his pilgrimage from Cairo to Mecca in 1387, did not necessarily close off contact with the north and the east. The coming of the Mongols and Timurlane at the turn of the fifteenth century, the end of Ibn Khaldun's life, appeared to suspend relationships between Mamluk Egypt and the Khans of the East. Yet even this major political interruption did not end Cairo's central importance as a portal between the Mediterranean and the East.[57]

Whereas east to west corridors and Muslim shipping may have dominated the Mediterranean world of the Almohads and Fatimids (in the east), Ibn Khaldun's fourteenth-century Mediterranean was a much more triangulated, complex place. Migrations from Iberia after the conquest of Muslim Al-Andalus and the expelling of a Muslim and Jewish elite around the southern and eastern Mediterranean had a profound impact on the society and culture of North Africa, where many of these Andalusi exiles landed. The flight of Ibn Khaldun's ancestors from Seville in Al-Andalus to Tunis in the thirteenth century was one example of these changes. Prominent artisans, craftsmen, and political leaders fleeing from Al-Andalus all influenced the character of cities and courts from Fez to Tunis, leading to a growth in economic and cultural vibrancy in North Africa. The gold trade and trade in silks, fruits, and exotic items remained strong in the Maghrib.

Eventually, however, as the Black Death took a disproportionate toll, the Maghrib failed to achieve any effective political unity despite several attempts by ambitious Hafsid and Marinid rulers, attempts so well chronicled by Ibn Khaldun. Both Arab and Berber tribes became more sophisticated in avoiding taxation and pressing their demands from urban rulers, and as mercenary payments caused revenue to exit North Africa at an accelerated rate, the Maghrib, like Egypt, became susceptible to European and then Ottoman Turkish incursions.

For Ibn Khaldun, however, the east–west axis and the network of Muslim trade and shipping from Granada, along the coast of North Africa to Alexandria, Egypt and onwards to Lebanon or the Red Sea, fragmented by Christian incursions on some strategic beachheads, was still important. The rise of Europe as the dominant western Mediterranean power, even the ultimate success of the Christians in the struggle for Al-Andalus, was in no way fully evident to Ibn Khaldun. In his letters to his friend Ibn al-Khatib, the influential prime minister for Muhammad V, ruler of Granada, a Muslim emirate in southern Iberia, Ibn Khaldun spoke triumphantly about the success of Muslim sorties deep into formerly Muslim territories. Rejoicing in a positive battle report from Ibn al-Khatib, Ibn Khaldun believed the Muslims were profiting from the 'wind of victory.'[58] Indeed, the Marinids and the North Africans were not shrinking violets when it came to warfare and the use of technology. The scholar L. P. Harvey describes how the Marinids troops used cannon for the first time in the Iberian peninsula during their defense of Algeçerias against Alfonso XI in 1344.[59] Some scholars have even cited Ibn Khaldun as proof that firearms were invented and in the hands of North Africans before Christian Europeans refined the technology.[60] Ibn Khaldun did not know that these gusts of Muslim victory would only be short-lived, just as he did not know that Timurlane would ultimately fail to conquer and reunite the entire Muslim world. From the perspective of Ibn Khaldun, there was reason for hope that Islam might once again dominate Iberia, that crucial Mediterranean and Atlantic peninsula. Ibn Khaldun's patrons shared hope and ambitions for a restoration of political unity to face Christian advances in the western Mediterranean. Ibn Khaldun was constantly moving between the courts of ambitious rulers, be they Hafsid, or Marinid, or Zayyanid, who saw their mission as the restoration of Almohad domination. Even, Timurlane, as terrifying as he was, seemed to promise the possibility of an all-out conquest and reunification of the Mediterranean as a Muslim sea. From Ibn Khaldun's perspective, the fourteenth century was a period of severe disruptions and false hopes, plague, dynastic disputes, and the constant cycle of history: decline and fall dominated his worldview. The severe political and social disruption inside the world in which he traveled, a world which was still dominated by strongly tied Muslim social institutions and practices, was never for him an indication of some inevitable rise of the West. Ibn Khaldun's own life voyage, his movement from the Hafsid court in Tunis, to the Maliki madrasas of the Marinids, to the court of Pedro of Seville, to the Mamluks of Egypt, and finally to Damascus where he met with Timurlane, representing the deepest corners of Central Asia, exemplified the dynamic, uncertain power struggles and changes that characterized the fourteenth-century Mediterranean world.

The Northern Shore

Despite the increasing ability of Christians to penetrate into Muslim lands and trading networks, the internal political situation of the Christian world in the fourteenth century was no better, and in some respects, worse than in the Islamic world. It was a 'calamitous fourteenth century.'[61] Jean Froissart (d. 1410), the French historian of the Hundred Years War and contemporary of Ibn Khaldun, believed that little hope was left in Europe: 'A third of the world had died.'[62] Considering the sheer scale of calamity in Europe, the Hundred Years War, the decline of the papacy, even the flagellant movement with masses of people throughout Europe spontaneously whipping themselves in despair, Jean Froissart had at least as much reason to be pessimistic as Ibn Khaldun, his fellow historian across the Mediterranean.

Yet Froissart had little interest in the intellectual life of North Africa, despite his first-hand experience in the Maghrib. He recorded the Christian incursions and the siege of Mahdiyya, Tunisia in 1390 but knew little of the intellectual and cultural importance of the area. Ibn Khaldun, in contrast, had heard about the advance of the sciences in Europe and found them relevant enough to comment. In a remarkable statement he noted that Europe was beginning to emerge out of the darkness of war and plague to excel in the philosophical sciences:

> We further hear now that the philosophical sciences are greatly cultivated in the land of Rome and along the adjacent northern shore of the country of the European Christians. They are said to be studied there again and to be taught in numerous classes. Existing systematic expositions of them are said to be comprehensive, the people who know them numerous and the students of them very many.[63]

The health of the philosophical sciences did not necessarily equate, for Ibn Khaldun, with a prediction of the political rise and domination of Europe. Ibn Khaldun, understandably, did not foresee the true extent of European power. By the end of the fourteenth century Europe was on the cusp of the age of exploration, the rise of the nation-state, and world domination, but such a future would have seemed unfathomable even by most Christian Europeans themselves.[64]

Besides, rumors about northern Europe as a place of scholarship seemed to be exceptions: they contradicted some of Ibn Khaldun's basic prejudices about the nature of civilization and its relationship with geography. Ibn Khaldun divided the world into geographic zones; those living too far north, in Ibn Khaldun's estimation were incapable of sustained civilizations. According to Ibn Khaldun's classification of humanity along latitudinal climatic zones, the Slavs, inhabitants of the extreme northern climate zones, had, because of their cold climate, qualities of 'character . . . close to those of dumb animals.'[65] Ibn Khaldun's equal disparagement of both white northern Slavs and African blacks can only be understood in the context of the multiracial institution of slavery in Al-Andalus and North Africa. In Ibn Khaldun's worldview the 'Slav' was as much the quintessential slave as a sub-Saharan. In fact, the English word for slave comes from Slav.[66] Since, for Ibn Khaldun, the middle zone was the zone most conducive to humanity and civilization, a slave could just as easily be from a barbaric north as from a barbaric south. Since their extreme climates made both groups 'close to animals' their slavery was, in Ibn Khaldun's mind, as it was in the mind of his contemporaries, justified. The climate not only affected culture, it made both the white and the black, sub-human. In Al-Andalus, Slavs were so numerous that they become their own sub-group in society and would play a significant role as mercenaries and power brokers in Andalusi and Iberian history, as would sub-Saharans, despite their remote origins.[67]

Even though much of Ibn Khaldun's experience of the Christian world came from his visit to the relatively prosperous realm of the Christian king in Seville, Pedro the Cruel, most of fourteenth-century Europe was mired in a vortex of political, environmental, and economic troubles. Politically, the Hundred Years War tore Europe apart. Unlike the twelfth and thirteenth centuries when Europe was able to amass large crusading armies and abandon internal rivalries, the long war turned Europe against itself. The last crusader state had fallen in 1291. Reflecting the desperation of those who still hoped for Christian unity and the defeat of Muslims in the Holy Land, one French author, Pierre Dubois, composed a tract for King Philip IV in which he proposed sending beautiful and 'personable' young French women in droves to the Holy Land to entice Muslims to convert to Latin Christianity.[68] When it came to recapturing the crusading states, Europe seemed to be running out of workable options.

Environmentally, overpopulation had denuded the forests and had made cultivation untenable throughout the once fertile valleys of the north. Disease and pestilence wiped out swaths of city dwellers.[69] Economically, the powerful banking houses of Florence, the Bardi and the Peruzzi banking system, that provided nourishment to the roots of Renaissance cultural vitality, were ruined by a series of profound credit crises, similar, in fact, to the banking crisis of 2008.[70] Although the banking system would eventually recover, entire monarchies, powerful kings and noblemen, such as Edward III of England, simultaneously defaulted on their loans. Despite the advances in Europe since the twelfth-century Renaissance, the Islamic world, with trade routes connecting the Mamluks to the rich markets of Asia through the Red Sea and the North Africans to West Africa through the Saharan desert, still maintained a significant, if dwindling, economic advantage over Europe. This advantage was maintained throughout most of the turbulent thirteenth and fourteenth centuries.

Muslim rulers may have seemed to still have the upper hand, especially in the eastern Mediterranean. In 1187, Saladin captured Jerusalem and expelled most of the crusaders. Successive waves of crusading were consistently defeated, first by Saladin and his successors, then by the Mamluks and the Ottomans. Symbolic of Europe's fruitless eastern campaign was King Louis IX of France, later canonized Saint Louis, who twice failed disastrously in his bid to capture Cairo. In 1250 the Ayyubid Egyptian army captured him. The ransom for his release was set at almost twice the state revenue of France. Beset by disunity and challenged by the power of the Mamluks, Europe was unable to hold its possessions in the Levant. Acre fell to the Mamluks in 1291 after a fierce and bloody siege. Even after the capture of Christian Acre, the Mamluks continued to harass the Lusignan monarchs of Cyprus, descendants of the crusaders. Although powerful, the Italian city-states were not a serious threat to the Mamluks. The Italian cities jockeyed for trading privileges from the Mamluks. Even as the Venetian thalassocracy expanded into the Adriatic, the Mamluks reigned supreme as gatekeepers to the Red Sea and India. If anything, the rise of Venice and the sacking of Christian Constantinople during the debauched Fourth Crusade had seriously weakened the Byzantines, a prominent foe of the Muslim world.

The fractured Muslim dynasties of the western Mediterranean were less successful at repelling Christian advancement. Although the decisive conquest of Granada, last bastion of Muslim power in the Iberian Peninsula, would not occur until 1492, the situation seemed balanced in favor of expansion by Christian kingdoms. In 1291 the Christian kingdoms of Castile and Aragon, long locked in war and distracted from their expansion into Muslim lands, had decided on a truce. In a move that would prefigure the colonial divisions of Africa centuries later, Marinid western Maghrib was established as the sphere of influence for Castile, and Zayyanid and Hafsid North Africa as the sphere of influence for Aragon.[71] Even so, Christian expansion did not go unchecked. Aragon and Castile remained often-bitter rivals. The Marinids frequently interfered in Al-Andalus, pushing against Christian expansion and recapturing Gibraltar from the Castilians in 1333. Similarly, Muslims recaptured the beachheads of Jerba and the Kerkennah Islands off the coast of Tunisia in 1335. The fact remained, however, that Christian pirates could continuously harass and attack the North African shore almost with impunity. Tripoli, the major city on the Libyan coast, was captured by opportunistic Genoese in 1354 and only ransomed after the payment of 50,000 pieces of gold. Similarly, before its liberation the island of Jerba was forced to pay Aragon a massive 600,000 pieces of gold. Christian brigands even briefly captured Salé, the important port on the Atlantic coast of Morocco.[72]

A major reason for the maintenance or even expansion of Muslim power in the East under the Mamluks and Ottomans and the decline of Muslim rule in the West was access to loyal mercenary troops. Whereas the North African amirs only really had access only to Christian mercenaries, with dubious loyalties, or the fickle support of tribal *ʿasabiyya*, the Mamluks of Egypt, whom Ibn Khaldun would serve the last decades of his life, developed a way of training both effective and loyal mercenary support. Ibn Khaldun was certainly aware of the importance of these mercenary or slave troops. Mercenary troops have a crucial role in Ibn Khaldun's science of history.

Slaves, Soldiers and Sultans: Mamluk Egypt

In pre-modern North Africa the notion of a citizen army, or a group of willing volunteers from the cities and the countryside signing up and fighting for some national ideology did not exist. This left a fundamental problem for any ruler attempting to maintain power and order in his realm. Raising an army could happen in one of three basic ways: through outright payment of mercenaries; through promise of booty to rough and ready tribal warriors; or, in Ibn Khaldun's view the most legitimate way, through religious inspiration, a compelling message that, supported by fate and by God, united tribes to volunteer to fight for greater ends. Both Muhammad the Prophet and the Arabs and the Mahdi Ibn Tumart and the Berbers achieved this legitimate path to power. In normal times, however, religious inspiration was not present, and sometimes undesirable as it could lead to radical imbalances and was very rarely successful, if spectacular when it did succeed. The choice for most rulers was thus quite limited: either rely on foreign mercenaries who could be trusted because they were paid directly and they did not have any ties to the local population but who could easily abandon you, or rely on the fickle support of tribes and tribal coalitions from the countryside. It was either dependence on the fickle *ʿasabiyya* of tribes or the bought *ʿasabiyya* of mercenaries. The way different governments in different regions of the Islamic world recruited and used their mercenaries or recruited and used surrounding tribes had a profound impact on the future shape and viability of government in those regions.

The ʿAsabiyya Option

According to Ibn Khaldun's theory of the rise and fall of dynasties, a new dynasty must first secure the loyalty and solidarity, the *ʿasabiyya*, of a group of tribes living far outside the city gates. Although religious inspiration can make a dynasty initially more powerful, it is not necessary. It is the power, the group cohesion, and even the natural virtues and fighting abilities of the rural tribes that makes them successful. After conquering the cities of the previous dynasty, the ruler of the new dynasty governs and enforces his will on the population though the use of tribal contingents and the loyal service of those whom he had convinced to follow his cause. Tribal solidarity, or ʿasabiyya according to Ibn Khaldun, was more important than any of the other reasons he listed, including luck, provisions, number of troops, even 'celestial intervention' for victory in war and the maintenance of power: 'The fact proven to make for superiority is . . . ʿasabiyya.'[73]

Ibn Khaldun insisted that the most effective form of warfare must involve the establishing of a line of retreat, a base camp that should be populated by the wives and children and relatives of the fighters. Instead of seeing the line of followers, the women and children and dependants of a tribe, as a stumbling block, Ibn Khaldun praised such a line formation as the font of loyalty, bravery, and honor.[74] Troops will be more vigorous when they are united willingly and fight to defend their women and families. In fact, Ibn Khaldun viewed holy warfare, *jihad*, as justified, even against other Muslims, but only when it was supported by, and involved, society as a whole, not simply a mercenary, or rebellious contingent. He quoted the Qurʾanic verse 'God never sends a prophet without military support provided by his people' (Sura 17:107–10). Religious movements could not have long-term success without political support.[75]

For Ibn Khaldun, just war, or *jihad*, needed the support of ʿasabiyya, a strong sense of social solidarity, not only to be effective, but also to be right. Mere religious preaching was not enough if it was not supported by society as a whole. With characteristic bluntness he even listed false prophets and reformers who attempted to launch *jihad* without a strong and overwhelming ʿasabiyya as among the 'stupid.'[76] With success comes divine justification. (Or, in the strict sense of ashʾari theology, with divine fate comes success – even if it simply appears otherwise.) Ambush and retreat and guerilla tactics, the method practiced by Bedouin since before the coming of Islam, were acceptable as long as these tactics were supported by the a commitment of the entire tribe or group of tribes. This 'social warfare' the type of warfare where entire tribes put themselves at risk was the only appropriate tactical and strategic method, Ibn Khaldun tells us, of the first Muslim warriors and of almost all successful campaigns since. Cities and dynasties that sent only paid soldiers into battle were doomed to fail when faced with entire tribes supported by the social network and a vigorous sense of solidarity. The fall and the death of a dynasty were near when the ruler began hiring outside mercenaries and raising taxes from the population and his originally loyal followers.

The Mercenary to Slave-Elite Option

In Mamluk Egypt, however, the situation was different, and, in many ways, more sustainable: the mercenary became the ruler outright. The ironic and elaborate particularities of the Mamluk system, a system in which slaves were ordained as rulers, were established to find a way around the limitations of both tribes and mercenaries. Whereas the governments of North Africa relied heavily on either fully trained adult, Christian mercenaries, or the ʿasabiyya of tribal collations such as the Banu Marin, the Mamluks the 'slave soldiers' of Egypt had circumvented the inherent weakness of both of these approaches, by themselves becoming the government. Instead of relying simply on lineage, the Mamluks used a complex system of patronage, a system that touched all classes, to maintain control.[77] Unlike the Zayyanid amirs or the late Almohad Caliphs who used independent Aragonese and Castilian mercenaries, forcing them to relent to interference by Christian powers and even the establishment of Christian institutions on Muslim soil, the Mamluks trained and indoctrinated young boys. The Mamluks relied on Genoese slave merchants who established trading bases in the Black Sea to capture fair-skinned Circassian youths who converted to Islam, learned military discipline and replenished the Mamluk army.[78] In order to avoid conflict of interest, descendants of slaves could not technically work for the army and were relegated to work and management of landed estates that supplied the Mamluk elite. Merit was ideally the only basis of promotion. In practice, however, several Mamluk rulers attempted to make their own sons their successors. Nevertheless, the Mamluks deliberately avoided recruiting the rank and file, as well as important officers, from the local population of Egypt. Training youths and assuring their loyalty to the Mamluk system seemed to be much more effective.

The Mamluk dynasty began with a slave coup. In 1250 when the Ayyubid sultan and descendant of Saladin, Al-Salih Ayyub, died, Shajar al-Durr, the widow of Al-Salih Ayyub had proclaimed herself ruler. Sensing her lack of support, however, the Mamluk Atabeg, or supreme commander of the slave troops, overthrew her, founding the first, or Bahri Mamluk dynasty.[79] With the fall of Baghdad in 1258 the strong Bahri Mamluk rulers, most notably Baybars (d. 1277) and Sultan Al-Nasir Muhammad (d. 1341), turned Cairo into the new capital of the Muslim world. They gave a ceremonial position to a descendant of the ʿAbbasid Caliphs, thus shifting symbolic authority over all Muslims to their control. They refined the methods of war and created a disciplined military machine for the maintenance of order and the protection of their realm. In the last decades of the Bahri Mamluks, some twenty years before Ibn Khaldun's arrival in 1382, the Mamluks even began to experiment with rudimentary guns and gunpowder, nominally enhancing their power.[80] In 1382, immediately before Ibn Khaldun set sail for Egypt, a new dynasty of slave-soldiers began with a successful coup led by Barquq, a slave-soldier originally from the Cirassian plateau north of the Causasus. Barquq would be Ibn Khaldun's beneficiary and patron until the sultan's death in 1399, when his son Faraj replaced him. As the Maliki Qadi, or one of the four chief judges of Cairo, Ibn Khaldun would have gained had an intimate knowledge of the workings of the Mamluk system. The fact that he predicted the success of Timurlane and the *ᶜasabiyya* of the Tartars, demonstrated, however, how little faith he had in the ultimate sustainability of government by slave-soldiers. Ibn Khaldun overemphasized the power of hearty tribal warriors even as he underestimated the increasing effectiveness of trained, professional troops such as the Mamluks.

The Fourteenth-Century World: Consolidation and Transition

The fourteenth-century world of Ibn Khaldun was dominated by two broad, con-current trends. First, while it was a century characterized by seemingly irrecon-cilable political divisions, it also saw the maturation and consolidation of Muslim institutions and practices, both in the form of educational institutions controlled by the government, such as madrasas, and the establishment and growth of important religious communities and institutions, the Sufi orders, outside direct government control. Second, it was a century that, much more subtly, and in ways virtually unnoticeable to Ibn Khaldun, set the stage for two world historic developments: the rise of European economic hegemony; and the triumph of the Ottoman Empire. It would be irresponsible to expect Ibn Khaldun to predict the rise of the European Renaissance and the domination of the Ottomans, who, when Ibn Khaldun died in 1406, were still a relatively obscure Turkish dynasty that had been defeated by Timurlane. Ultimately, the Ottomans would prevail with a combined system of slave-soldiers mixed with *ᶜasabiyya*. Janissary sol-diers, slave-soldiers much like the Mamluks, were used to maintain control but the Sultan remained, at least in the beginning, ultimately independent from the Janissaries. Using land grants and conquests, the Ottoman dynasty relied on the *ᶜasabiyya* of sipahis or noble cavalry and well as the solidarity of the original Turkish warriors who brought the Ottomans to power.[81] Ibn Khaldun understood intimately, however, the important impact of *ᶜasabiyya*, of small dedicated bands of tribal warriors, as the early Ottomans were. He also understood how non-human, environmental factors, such as the plague, could be world-changing events. Indeed, it was the plague, and the changed world that it caused both for him personally and for history more generally, that initially inspired him to write his philosophy of history.

NOTES

1 From the interviews with Dr Evans see Richard Evans, *Jung on Elementary Psychology* (London, 1979), 153.

2 In the medieval Islamic period *'ilm*, or 'science,' meant more than science in the technical modern sense, but 'science' in the sense of knowledge and its application, both spiritual and philosophical.

3 On Timurlane's love of history see John Woods, 'The rise of Timurid historiography,' *Journal of Near Eastern Studies*, 46 (2), April 1987, 81–108.

4 For Ibn Khaldun's description of his encounter in the original Arabic see *Al-Ta'rif bi Ibn Khaldun rihlatu gharban wa sharqan*, Muhammad Tawit al-Tanji (ed.) (Cairo, 1951), 366–77. For an authoritative French translation by Ibn Khaldun expert, Abdesselam Cheddadi, see the *Autobiographie*, section of *Le Livre des Examples* (Paris, 2002), 237.

5 It should be noted here that although he meant tribal solidarity in this context, Ibn Khaldun did not always think of *'asabiyya* exclusively as a force of tribal solidarity, but also sometimes the force of social solidarity more generally. Although *'asabiyya* appears in many forms, tribal *'asabiyya* was the most important form of *'asabiyya* since, unlike urban *'asabiyya* which could only really decline, tribal *'asabiyya* preceded the formation of the city and the dynasty. Abdesselam Cheddadi, a prominent Moroccan scholar on Ibn Khaldun discusses these varieties of meaning attached to *'asabiyya* in *Actualité d'Ibn Khaldun* (Casablanca, 2005), 193–4.

6 Although Ibn Khaldun was a significant inspiration, Gellner pointed out Ibn Khaldun's own generalizations, generalizations that led to errors of geography. Ibn Khaldun, according to Gellner, was 'in error when he supposed, as he evidently did, that he was analyzing human society as such anywhere, anytime.' *Muslim Society*, 29, 1991, 88–9.

7 The importance of placing Ibn Khaldun 'in his time' was enunciated as early as 1933 by H. A. R. Gibb with his influential article, 'The Islamic Background of Ibn Khaldun's Political Theory', *Bulletin of the School of Oriental Studies*, 7 (1), 1933, 23–31, in which he argued that Ibn Khaldun should be seen as a Malikite *faqih* who was faithful to Muslim tradition and beliefs, even if he did write about ideas that seemed somewhat revolutionary at the time. Franz Rosenthal, the translator and philologist, similarly believed that Ibn Khaldun was best seen as a product of his time. See 'Ibn Khaldun in his Time', in Bruce Lawrence (ed.), *Ibn Khaldun and Islamic Ideology* (Leiden, 1984), 15–26. Finally, Aziz al-Azmeh insisted that taking Ibn Khaldun out of context inevitably led to orientalist discourse, see *Ibn Khaldun: An Essay in Reinterpretation* (Budapest, 2003).

8 *Al-Ta'rif*, 372–3; *Autobiographie*, 237. On the importance of divination during Ibn Khaldun's time see H. P. J. Renaud, 'Divination et histoire nord-Africaine aux temps d'Ibn Khaldoun,' *Hespéris*, XXX, 1943, 213–21. In his book, *Society, State and Urbanism: Ibn Khaldun's Sociological Thought* (New York, 1988), 6–10, Fuad Baali, however, makes the convincing argument that Ibn Khaldun can be compared with modern historians if not equated with them. While many scholars have insisted on putting Ibn Khaldun into context, few, with the exception of Cheddadi, have actually approached his autobiography as a whole.

9 P. Nwya, *Une Mystique Prédicateur: Ibn 'Abbad de Ronda (1332–1390)*, (Beirut, 1961).

10 Walter Fischel, 'Ibn Khaldun's sources for the history of Jenghis Khan and the Tatars,' *Journal of the American Oriental Society*, 76 (2), April–June 1956, 91–9.

11 H. A. R. Gibb, 'The Islamic Background of Ibn Khaldun's political theory,' *Bulletin of the School of Oriental Studies*, 7 (1), 1933, 30.

12 Patricia Crone described the way Sunni *ulama* assumed religious leadership at the expense of the Caliphate in *God's Caliph* (Cambridge, 2003).

13 M. Hodgson, *The Venture of Islam* (Chicago, IL, 1974), vol. II, 371.

14 Tilman Nagel, *The History of Islamic Theology: from Muhammad to the Present*, (Princeton, 2000).

15 Ibn Khaldun had a surprisingly rich understanding of Mongol and Tartar history and knew about the incursions into China. W. Fischel, 'Ibn Khaldun's sources for the history of Jenghis Khan and the Tatars.'

16 James Boone and Nancy Benco, 'Islamic settlement in North Africa and the Iberian Peninsula,' *Annual Review of Anthropology*, 28, 1999, 58.

17 P. Cressier, M. Naimi, and A. Touri, 'Maroc saharien et Maroc méditerranéan au Moyen Age: le cas des ports de Nul Lamta et de Badis,' *Histoire et Archéologie de l'Afrique du Nord: Acts du Ve Colloque International*, Congrès National des Sociétés Savants, Avignon, Avril 9–13, 1990, 393–407.

18 Felipe Fernandez-Armesto, *Before Columbus: Exploration and Colonisation from the Mediterranean to the Atlantic, 1229–1492* (Philadelphia, PA, 1987), 126–34.

19 *Muqaddimah*, vol. II, 278.

20 *Muqaddimah*, vol. II, 314.

21 *Muqaddimah*, vol. II, 136. See Boone and Benco, 'Islamic settlement,' cited above, for the archaeological evidence of urbanization.

22 Ibn Khaldun has often been compared with Machiavelli. See Barbara Stowasser, *Religion and Political Development: Some Comparative Ideas on Ibn Khaldun and Machiavelli* (Washington, DC, 1983). For a detailed account of the later Middle Ages in North Africa see Mohamed Kably, *Societe, Pouvoir et Religion au Maroc à la fin du 'Moyen-Age'* (Paris, 1986).

23 On the Hafsids and Ibn Khaldun's relationship with them see R. Brunschvig, *La Berbérie Orientale Sous les Hafsids* (Paris, 1940).

24 Evidence for this remarkable Almohad hierarchy is found in a series of manuscripts collected in the volume *Documents Inédits d'histoire Almohade*, É. Lévi-Provençal (ed.) (Paris, 1928). (Includes the *Kitab al Ansab*, letters and sermons by Ibn Tumart and 'Abd al-Mu³min and Ibn Tumart's biography by his personal biographer al-Baydhaq.) See also J. Hopkins, *Medieval Government in Barbary* (London, 1958). My forthcoming book, *The Almohads: The Rise of An Islamic Empire* (London, 2010), describes the origins of Almohad Berber hierarchy in detail.

25 For Ibn Khaldun's description of Hafsid history see *Histoire des Berbères*, vol. II, 281–481, esp. 281 on the origins of the Hafsids, and vol. III, 40–123.

26 On the influence of Christian doctrine on the later Almohad caliphs see Allen Fromherz, 'North Africa and the twelfth century Renaissance: Christian Europe and the Almohad Islamic Empire,' *Islam and Christian–Muslim Relations*, 20 (1), 2009, 43–59. See also, P. Lopes, 'Los Obispos de Marruecos desde siglo XIII,' *Archivo Ibero-American*, 14, 1920, 409–27.

27 *The History of the Maghrib*, 201.

28 For a fairly comprehensive study of the political, administrative and religious organization of the Hafsids see the second volume of Robert Brunschvig, *La Berbérie Orientale Sous les Hafsides*, 2 vols. (Paris, 1947). Most importantly, he revealed the remarkable

heterogeneity of those living under Hafsid rule: Arab tribes that had invaded two centuries before, autochthonous Berbers, Christian traders, mercenaries, Jews, Andalusis who had fled the Christian conquest, African traders, freed slaves, etc. In many ways, Hafsid Tunis became what medieval Al-Andalus was before the Christian reconquest: a remarkable caldron of acculturation, 418–20.

29 Michael Brett, 'The way of the nomad,' *Bulletin of the School of Oriental and African Studies*, 58 (2), 1995, 251.

30 Muhammad Kably, *Societe, Pouvoir et Religion* 2.

31 Ibn Khaldun, *Histoire des Berbères*, vol. III, 308–9.

32 For more discussion of the relationship between the Marinid legitimacy and *jihad* as well as the parallel efforts of the Christians to legitimate their rule through reconquista see Amira Bennison, 'Liminal states: Morocco and the Iberian frontier between the twelfth and nineteenth centuries,' in J. Clancy-Smith (ed.), *North Africa, Islam and the Mediterranean World*, Portland, Oregon, 11–29, 16.

33 *A History of the Maghrib in the Islamic Period*, 111.

34 Ibn Khaldun, *Histoire des Berbères*, vol. IV, 25–488. He goes into great detail about the genealogy of the Marinids and the biographies of even its minor leaders. His history remains an essential reference for any study of the Marinids. Also, see the recent publication by Maya Shatzmiller, *L'Historiographie Mirinide: Ibn Khaldun et ses Contemporains* (Leiden, 2007) and *The Berbers and the Islamic States: The Marinid Experience in Pre-Protectorate Morocco* (Princeton, 2000).

35 For a history of the Zayyanids see Ibn Khaldun, *Historie des Berbères*, vol. II, 326–495. Also see the work of Ibn Khaldun's unlucky brother, Yahya, who worked for the Zayyanids. His history is published in Arabic with French translation as *Histoire des Beni ʿAbd al-Wad, rois de Tlemcen*, Alfred Bel (ed.), 2 vols. (Algiers, 1904–13).

36 F. Broudel, *The Mediterranean and the Mediterranean World in the Age of Philip II* (London and New York, 1972), 277.

37 One should not neglect the Atlantic shore where the Almohads also had an important presence but which was left to the Christians after the division of the Almohad empire into the Marinid, Zayyanid, and Hafsid realms. Ch. Picard, *L'Océan Atlantique musulman de la conquête arabe à l'époque almohade* (Paris, 1997).

38 He called it alternately the Syrian or the Byzantine Sea.

39 And he was certainly not the only Muslim traveler from the fourteenth century whose account we have. See, for example, A. L. Premare, *Maghreb et Andalousie au XIVe siècle: les notes de voyage d'un Andalou au Maroc (1344–1345)* (Lyon, 1981).

40 *Muqaddimah*, vol. II, 41. It should be noted here that in their book, *The Corrupting Sea: A Study of Mediterranean History* (London, 2000), Peregrine Horden and Nicholas Purcell contest what they considered to be Ibn Khaldun's largely hyperbolic assertion of complete Muslim dominance over the early medieval Mediterranean. Ibn Khaldun has often been used to bolster the controversial Henri Pirenne thesis that posited that the Mediterranean was irrevocably divided between Christians and Muslims after the Arab conquest. See Henri Pirenne, *Mohammed and Charlemagne* (New York, 2001).

41 *Muqaddimah*, vol. II, 42.

42 *Muqaddimah*, vol. II, 46.

43 *Muqaddimah*, vol. II, 46.

44 Olivia R. Constable, *Trade and Traders in Muslim Spain* (Cambridge, 2002), 240.

45 I. Abu Lughod, *Before European Hegemony* (Oxford, 1989), 216.

46 For a primer on world systems theory see *World-Systems Analysis: An Introduction* (Durham, NC, 2004), by Immanuel Wallerstein, a founder of world-systems theory. World-systems theory, particularly Janet Abu-Lughod's application of the theory to the medieval world, has not always been accepted uncritically. In 'After world systems theory: concerning Janet Abu-Lughod's before European hegemony,' Donald Neilsen criticized Abu Lughod for understating the importance of civilization, of cultural decisions and particular historical actions. *International Journal of Politics, Culture and Society*, 4 (4), 1991, 481–97.

47 Bernard Doumerc, *Venise et l'émirat hafside de Tunis (1231–1535)* (Paris, 1999), 21.

48 Charles Dufourcq, *L'Espagne catalane et le Maghrib aux XII et XIV siècles* (Paris, 1966), 475.

49 Abu-Lughod, *Before European Hegemony*, 236. On the impact of the black death on trade and economy in Egypt and the Arab world see Michael Dols, *The Black Death in the Middle East* (Princeton, 1977).

50 Abu-Lughod, *Before European Hegemony*, 237.

51 Abu-Lughod, *Before European Hegemony*, 235. On the success of Egyptian merchants in the Red Sea, however, see Subhi Labib, 'Les merchands Karimis en Orient et sur l'Océan Indien,' in *Sociétés et compagnies de commerce en orient et dans l'Océan Indien* (Paris, 1970), 209–14.

52 On difficulties with Venice see R. Brunchvig, *La Berbérie Orientale Sous les Hafsids* (Paris, 1940), vol. 1, 153–5. The Venetians restored their presence in North Africa in a treaty with Tripoli in 1356, 172.

53 Charles E. Dufourcq, *L'Espagne catalane et le Maghrib aux XII et XIV siècles*, 139–44. Also, see David Abulafia, *The Western Mediterranean Kingdoms, 1200–1500* (London, 1997), and his explanation of Aragonese relations with North African amirs. For Italy and the Maghrib see G. Jegel, *l'Italie et le Maghreb au Moyen Age* (Paris, 2001).

54 Jamil Abun-Nasr, *A History of the Maghrib in the Islamic Period* (Cambridge 1987), 139.

55 J. H. Pryor, *Geography, Technology and War: Studies in the Maritime History of the Mediterranean: 1492–1571* (Cambridge, 1988).

56 For an excellent account of the continuing relationship between Mamluk Egypt and its influence on Venice see Deborah Howard, *Venice and the East* (New Haven, 2000), 67–71.

57 *Trade and Traders in Muslim Spain*, 241.

58 See Ibn Khaldun's letter in response to Ibn al-Khatib missives, *Al-Taᶜrif*, 123–8. *Autobiographie*, 118. This refers to the Nasrid Amir of Granada, Muhammad V's victories in 1367. He was so successful that he almost breached the walls of the old Andalusi capital of Cordoba. Hugh Kennedy, *Islamic Spain and Portugal*, 292.

59 Harvey, *Islamic Spain*, 200.

60 Weston Cook, *The Hundred Years War for Morocco: Gunpowder and the Military Revolution in the Early Muslim World* (Boulder, CO, 1994), 63; also see David Ayalon, *Gunpowder and Firearms in the Mamluk kingdom, a Challenge to a Mediaeval Society* (London, 1956).

61 Barbara Tuchman, *A Distant Mirror: The Calamitous 14th Century* (New York, 1978).

62 Jean Froissart, *Chronicles*, trans. Geoffrey Brereton (London, 1978).

63 *Muqaddimah*, vol. III, 117–18.

64 Denys Hay, *Europe in the Fourteenth and Fifteenth Centuries* (London, 1989).

65 Ibn Khaldun's ideas about race had some impact on later thinkers see W. E. Gates, 'The spread of Ibn Khaldun's ideas on climate and culture,' *Journal of the History of Ideas*, 28, 1967, 415–22.

66 According to the *Oxford English Dictionary* (2nd edition) definition, the origin of the word slave is the 'racial name *Sclavus*, the Slavonic population in parts of central Europe having been reduced to a servile condition by conquest; the transferred sense is clearly evidenced in documents of the 9th century.' Also, according to the *Russisches Etymologisches Wörterbuch*, Max Vasmer (ed.) (Heidelberg, 1987), 664–5, the Slavs themselves used the term Slaviani before it was identified with the servile condition.

67 There were differences, however, in the specific laws governing slaves in Islam and Christianity. For the differences between Christian and Muslim slavery in Africa see J. Alexander, 'Islam, archaeology and slavery in Africa,' *World Archaeology*, 33 (1), June 2001, 44–60. It should not be assumed, however, that all writers in Arabic simply accepted the elite view of race and climate posited by Arab scholars such as Ibn Khaldun. Rather, in books such as *The Book of the Glory of the Black Race* they saw the black race as superior to those in other climatic zones. *Al-Jahiz's Kitab Fakhr as-Sudan ʿala al-Bidan*, trans. and ed. Vincent Cornell (Waddington, NY), 1981.

68 Richard Fletcher, *The Cross and the Crescent*, London, 2003, 132.

69 For a comparison of Christian and Muslim responses to the Black Death see Michael Dols, 'The comparative communal responses to the Black Death in Muslim and Christian societies,' *Viator*, 5, 1974, 269–87.

70 In his last published lecture before his death, the famed medievalist, Archibald Lewis, provided a comparative essay summarizing his work on the late medieval Islamic and European worlds in which he emphasized the cycles and risks of the European banking system. The banking system came back to life a few decades after its collapse, once again becoming a generator of European power. One major criticism of Lewis, however, is his downplaying of important interactions between Europe and the Islamic world after the thirteenth century. See 'The Islamic world and the Latin West, 1350–1500,' *Speculum*, 65 (4), October 1990, 833–44. In contrast to Archibald Lewis see Janet Abu-Lughod, *Before European Hegemony*.

71 *A History of the Maghrib in the Islamic Period*, 108.

72 A. Cheddadi, 'À propos d'une ambassade d'Ibn Khaldun auprès de Pierre le Cruel,' 12.

73 *Muqaddimah*, vol. II, 87.

74 *Muqaddimah*, vol. II, 80.

75 Nor could the early *umma*, the Muslim community, survive except as a combination of prophecy and, essentially, the support of the people. S. D. Goitein, *Studies in Islamic History and Institutions* (Leiden, 1968), 31.

76 *Muqaddimah*, vol. II, 74–88.

77 See Ira Lapidus' description of late medieval Cairo in *Muslim Cities in the Later Middle Ages* (Cambridge, MA, 1984).

78 Abu-Lughod noted that the Mamluks had 'no choice but to deal with the Europeans and purchase slaves from Genoese merchants.' Nevertheless, at least the Mamluks were not forced to purchase independent mercenaries outright. *Before European Hegemony*, 213–14. Andrew Ehrenkreutz, 'Strategic implications of the slave trade between Genoa and Mamluk Egypt the second half of the thirteenth century,' in Abraham Udovich (ed.), *The Islamic Middle East: 700–1900: Studies in Economic and Social History* (Princeton, 1981), 335–45.

79 There are several good works on Mamluk history including David Ayalon's *The Mamluks: The Organization and Structure of a Moslem Military Society in the Middle Ages* (Jerusalem: 1961) and his updated *Islam and the Abode of War: Military Slaves and Islamic Adversaries* (Variorum, 1994). See also Robert Irwin, *The Middle East in the Middle Ages: The Early Mamluk Sultanate 1250–1382* (London, 1986).

80 David Ayalon, *Gunpowder and Firearms in the Mamluk Kingdom, a Challenge to a Mediaeval Society* (London, 1956).

81 On the importance of the tribal identity of the early Ottomans see Rudi P. Linder, *Nomads and Ottomans in Medieval Anatolia* (Bloomington, 1983) and Norman Itzkowitz, *Ottoman Empire and Islamic Tradition* (New York, 1973).

2

IBN KHALDUN'S EARLY LIFE

Only when a strong wind was blowing did a faint, sickly odor coming from the East remind them that they were living under a new order.

Albert Camus, *The Plague*

The world seemed to be plunged into primeval silence.

Paul Diaconus (d. *c.* 790)

Some scholars have pronounced it impossible to write an 'interesting' biography of Ibn Khaldun. According to this assessment, Ibn Khaldun did not reveal anything truly personal, anything in the modern sense of what is expected in a proper biography: a psychological analysis of an individual. In the introduction to his monumental translation of the *Muqaddimah*, Franz Rosenthal noted that Ibn Khaldun rarely provided intimate biographical information. He barely mentioned his mother, siblings, and family, except when they were taken away by tragic events. Even pertinent information about Ibn Khaldun's psychological relationship with his contemporaries, was, in Rosenthal's view, extremely lacking. Although Ibn Khaldun's account of his life was 'the most detailed autobiography in Medieval Muslim literature,' a psychologically compelling work for Rosenthal it was not. Rosenthal thus warned against any attempt to write a complete biography of Ibn Khaldun beyond the dry, bare bones translation of his narrative. His warning has stuck. The only existing biographies of Ibn Khaldun are translations of Ibn Khaldun's autobiography or cursory discussions of the outlines of his life.[1] There was a largely descriptive book by the scholar Walter Fischel on Ibn Khaldun's life in Egypt written in 1967, but it starts in 1382 and curiously leaves out the entire, formative first half of Ibn Khaldun's life.[2]

Perhaps it was the time in which Rosenthal was translating, the 1960s, when the ideas of Freud and challenges to Freud were all the rage, but Rosenthal did not seem to recognize that psychological depth could be expressed in ways other than the lurid details of immediate, intimate relations. What Ibn Khaldun did not say in his autobiography was sometimes just as important as what he did say. Regardless, as this chapter will show, Ibn Khaldun did, in fact, provide some brief and fascinating clues about his own psychological make-up and personal disposition, clues that become abundant upon a close reading not only of his narrative but of his poetry as well. Rosenthal himself pointed out the rich source of information on the mind and thinking of Ibn Khaldun found in the *Muqaddimah*. Tensions, contradictions, and conundrums exist in Ibn Khaldun's writings, as they might exist in the writings of any intellectual. It is thus with optimism that this book sets out to examine the life of Ibn Khaldun, the man, as much as it examines Ibn Khaldun, the philosopher of history.

A PSYCHOLOGY OF SOLITUDE

Ibn Khaldun was born in 1332 to a family of some prestige and standing in Tunis. Tunis was the capital of the Hafsid empire, one of the last remnants of the once-vast Almohad power in North Africa. Ibn Khaldun lived a relatively pleasant early childhood, but soon, however, he was thrust into the reality of events after he witnessed the death of his parents and his friends to the plague.

Following the death of much of his family in Tunis, Ibn Khaldun was often alone. Read as a whole, his autobiography and even the tone of the *Muqaddimah* was tinted by a mood or disposition of solitude brought about by loss of family, loss of his own social bonds or ʿasabiyya. He was a self-styled independent thinker. He appreciated the importance of interactions between small closely-knit, personal groups over those of large institutions and governments. Sometimes he chose solitude, such as when he divorced himself from all worldly and political concerns to write his masterpiece, the *Muqaddimah* at the remote tribal fortress of the Banu Salama, a type of intellectual hermitage. More often, however, solitude was forced upon him by plague, by shipwreck, or by the political uncertainty that characterized his times. This loneliness, subtly but potently expressed in his autobiography, seemed remarkable for a man who devoted his work to understanding and explaining the importance of tribal and familial bonds or ʿasabiyya. It was precisely these all-important familial bonds, the bonds that Ibn Khaldun saw as the essential glue of human existence, that Ibn Khaldun lost almost completely, not once but twice in life. First, he lost his family and friends after the plague struck and took away not only his mother and father and most of his extended family but also the vast majority of his intellectual family, the teachers and mentors who had stirred him into pursuing the life of the mind. There were many other plagues and outbreaks that would seem to arbitrarily knock out and kill other relatives and friends he could trust. Later in life, he lost his own wife and a number of his children to a storm at sea. Even those close to him who survived and whom he thought he could trust, such as his mentor, the prolific Andalusi historian, Ibn al-Khatib, betrayed him even as they were cut down by jealousy, intrigue, and circumstance. In a time of political upheaval the smallest of mis-steps could lead to imprisonment and death. For much of his political career, Ibn Khaldun was himself in prison, even as he intrigued to put others there instead of him. It could be argued that Ibn Khaldun lived in an especially brutal age and that his loneliness was no exception. Yet even by the standards of his day, Ibn Khaldun seemed to be repeatedly and unusually struck by tragedy. Nevertheless, it may have been that these experiences were what inspired Ibn Khaldun to deliberately distance himself from the pains, troubles, and seeming randomness of his world, to look at society from a cool, clinical distance, to see the key to the success of human societies in the social bonds that he, in many ways, lacked.

OBSESSION WITH ANCESTRY

Genealogical information fascinated Abu Zayd ᶜAbdu al-Rahman bin Muhammad bin Khaldun al-Hadrami or Ibn Khaldun. The science of ancestry and the importance of lineage was a primary basis for his understanding of society. In the *Muqaddimah* he repeatedly analyzed the use of lineage and ancestry and the importance of ancestral bonds as the natural glue of social organization. Ancestry was the root of ᶜ*asabiyya*, tribal solidarity, the glue of human society. He described the manipulation of ancestry for political and social expediencies. For Ibn Khaldun the power of ancestry lay in the way it was often a convenient fiction viewed as determined fact.

As the substantial portion of the beginning of his autobiography devoted to his own ancestry reveals, his own genealogy was an especially important topic. In this basic sense, Ibn Khaldun was no more remarkable than most of his Arab and Berber contemporaries. Although it may seem a long list of names, a seemingly endless list of 'ibn this' and 'ibn that' to non-Arab readers, the name and the ancestry determined a complex web of relationships, obligations, and expectations. In many respects, ancestry for the well-born determined a person's fate and sense of self, at least as much as his own experiences. It was for this reason that massive, intricate, and complicated compendiums, ancestral charts, and biographical dictionaries were written. Both simple chroniclers and eminent scholars such as Ibn Hazm compiled this massive, biographical who's who of the medieval Islamic world, called *tabaqat*, or literally 'levels' in Arabic. Although only seventy volumes survive, *The History of Damascus* by Ibn ᶜAsakir was said to exceed 16,000 folios in total and to include the links between almost every person living in Damascus.[3] Similar works were compiled in Al-Andalus and the Maghrib.

Ibn Khaldun wrote a long, detailed, and practically unbroken list of his father's illustrious ancestors in Al-Andalus – governors, rebels, aristocrats, warriors, councilmen – almost all of Ibn Khaldun's male ancestors were politicians and men of state. Ibn Khaldun described his family's genealogy from Seville all the way back to the Hadramawt Oasis in southeastern Yemen.

On his maternal side Ibn Khaldun was associated with the Hafsids. The Almohad empire was intact and many of the Hafsids, part of the Atlas Mountain tribal elite that helped govern the Almohad empire, traveled freely between the Almohad capital of Seville and Tunis, the capital of the Almohad province governed by the Hafsids. Ibn Khaldun's maternal ancestor, Ibn al-Muhtasib, gave a Galician (northern Spanish) concubine to Abu Zakariyya of the Hafsid line. This Galician princess bore him three sons. One was the ancestor of the Hafsid ruler of Tunis. Thus, clearly the Banu Khaldun, the Khaldun family or clan, had a close relationship with the Hafsids even while they were in Al-Andalus.[4] Intermarriage between Muslim amirs and Christian women had been common in medieval Al-Andalus ever since the Muslim conquest in 711 AD. The scholar D. F. Ruggles concluded that it was these Spanish wives and mothers of Arab rulers who facilitated acculturation between Spanish Christian and Muslim cultures. Women were in charge of educating and influencing the language and culture of the heir apparent; they were 'mothers of a hybrid dynasty.' The marriage of a Galician into the Hafsid line of Tunis shows that this hybrid intermarriage and acculturation was exported to North Africa, leaving a legacy of Andalusi hybridization hundreds of miles away from Al-Andalus.[5] Although exiles from Al-Andalus, the Khaldun family had little reason to feel alone as Andalusi outsiders in Tunis as the ruler himself could claim Andalusi heritage.[6]

Nevertheless, acculturation, even through blood, did not mean the absence of conflict. As Christians became more organized and as the ideology of crusade spread, much of Muslim Al-Andalus was falling to Christian control. The Banu Khaldun despite their often valiant efforts against the Christians, was forced to flee Seville and move to Ceuta and then to Tunis where they had close ties with the Hafsids. Ibn Khaldun described how his family was intimately involved in the various and complicated dynastic struggles of the petty princes in Spain as well as North African rulers. The sultan of Tunis, Abu Yahya, for example, would leave affairs of state under the administration of Ibn Khaldun's grandfather, who died of old age in 1336 AD.[7]

Most members of Banu Khaldun were embroiled in the tangles, intrigues, and shifting loyalties of Islamic Spain and Hafsid North Africa, where his family was exiled after the conquest of Seville. There was one important break in this chain of statesmen: his father. Ibn Khaldun described how his own father, Muhammad Abu Bakr, unlike any of his previous ancestors, abandoned the life of the statesman and the warrior: 'My father left a career of arms and service to princes and devoted himself to religious sciences and the life of a recluse.'[8] This was an important break, a turning point in Ibn Khaldun's ancestral identity. One of the first indications of Ibn Khaldun's appreciation for solitude comes from his description of his father's ancestry, a man who chose solitude over statesmanship, breaking a long chain of male descendants of the Khaldun family who had served forcefully and openly in public life. This did not mean, however, that Ibn Khaldun would minimize the prestige of his ancient forefathers, who, unlike his father, dove deeply and often willingly into the political fray. Nor did he see his lineage as any less important than others in his society.

In fact, Ibn Khaldun seemed to be victim to his own warnings, laid out so provocatively in the *Muqaddimah*, about the inevitable corrupting of lineage for the sake of prestige. Ibn Khaldun described how tribal lineages became confused; how settled Arabs of Al-Andalus, the very sort of Arabs who were his ancestors, intermingled with other groups and became identified more with their location, their residence, than with their lineage. One would say he was from 'such and such a village' rather than such and 'such a tribe':[9] 'It was clear that a person of a certain descent may become attached to people of another descent . . . When the things which result from (common) descent are there, it is as if (common) descent) itself were there.'[10] The only people who were able to truly maintain their pedigree, in Ibn Khaldun's theory, were the most remote Arab, nomadic tribes, isolated from contact with settled communities. Ibn Khaldun's ancestors, settled as they were in Seville and other major Andalusi cities, certainly did not fit these criteria.

For his own ancestry, nevertheless, Ibn Khaldun seemed to insist on the possession of his own, pure lineage. Ibn Khaldun cites ten generations since the migration of the ancestor Khaldun to Al-Andalus. This could not be true, as there must have many more generations to cover seven centuries. Abu Fadl Ibn Khaldun, an ancestor of Ibn Khaldun from the eleventh century, three centuries before Ibn Khaldun was born, for example, was described in Ibn Hazm's book of biographies as having nine ancestors since the original Khaldun landed in Andalusia.[11] Possibly those who were left out of the lineage included ancestors from diverse backgrounds, such as Berbers, who may have intermarried with the Banu Khaldun over the many centuries they remained in Andalusia and North Africa. It would be difficult to speculate precisely why Ibn Khaldun saw himself as an exception to his own rules, his own observation about the adaptation and change of lineage. This lack of critical analysis was in sharp contrast to the *Muqaddimah* where he demolished what he called myths and fables of pure ancestral blood.

IBN KHALDUN'S TEACHERS

As discussed above, Ibn Khaldun's first and most influential teacher was his father, a man who shaped Ibn Khaldun's appreciation for Sufism and who inspired him to think independently. It was his father who would have encouraged the young and precocious Ibn Khaldun to go out in search of good teachers. As Ibn Khaldun briefly mentioned, 'I was educated under the influence of my father, may God give him mercy, until I reached adulthood . . .'[12]

Besides his father, Ibn Khaldun provided a long list of important mentors who mainly shaped his understanding of Islam and Islamic jurisprudence, history, medicine, literature, mathematics, and philosophical inquiry. Like his description of his ancestors, Ibn Khaldun refrains from analyzing the possible motivations or perspectives of his intellectual mentors. He mainly lists their writings, the books he studied with them, their work for various rulers and their specializations and, most importantly from the point of view of Ibn Khaldun and his contemporaries, the *ijazas*, or the recommendation letters he received from each teacher when he was judged to have successfully learned what he needed to know from a particular mentor.[13] These teachers created, in a sense, his academic ancestry, a line of references who could vouch for Ibn Khaldun's remarkable grasp of Islamic *fiqh* or jurisprudence. Not locked up in any single institution and relying on teachers themselves for his degree, rather than specific schools, Ibn Khaldun's education was remarkably diverse. He had the freedom to choose any teacher who would take him.

The work of several of Ibn Khaldun's mentors, great jurists, intellectuals, mathematicians in their time, has either been lost or relegated to obscure, unknown corners of the history of Islamic law. Many were known only locally, such as Abu al-Abbas Ahmad Ibn Muhammad al-Zawawi: during his time one of the best authorities on the proper recitation of the Qur'an in the Maghrib, but now mainly forgotten. Others, however, had important legacies, such as Muhammad ibn Ibrahim al-Abili, originally from Avila, a town outside Madrid in Al-Andalus. Like Ibn Khaldun, al-Abili was a descendant of a long line of ministers and scholars. His ancestors worked as warrior-scholars in the court of the sultan Yaghmurasan ibn Ziyan in the city of Tilimsan, in modern-day Algeria.[14] Al-Abili sometimes served as a minister for the Zayyanid tyrant, Abu Hammu II. Ibn Khaldun depicted his teacher as a brave 'warrior'-scholar. Like many of the intellectuals of his time, he rarely abstained from joining his patron on the battlefield. Ibn Khaldun would follow his teacher's example and regularly join his patrons in campaigns. Despite the depravations of the fourteenth century, many of these minister warrior-scholars would have been at least as famous as Ibn Khaldun was in his time, even in later years when he reached lofty heights as Maliki Qadi in Cairo.

Al-Abili

In addition to his reputation as Ibn Khaldun's most important teacher, Al-Abili made a significant scholarly impact in his own right. Ibn Khaldun's brother, Abu Zakariya Yahya Ibn Khaldun, himself a historian who shared many of Ibn Khaldun's teachers, wrote about the reputation of Al-Abili in his history of the Banu ʿAbd al-Wad, the kings of the Algerian city of Tilimsan and the surrounding region.[15] According to Yahya, Al-Abili was taught by some of the most brilliant minds of the era, including the eminent Jewish mathematician Khalluf al-Maghili, whose work is unfortunately lost to modern scholarship. In turn, Al-Abili trained an entire generation of teachers and religious scholars. Although none of Al-Abili's writings have survived, he undoubtedly had a significant impact on Ibn Khaldun. In fact, some of Ibn Khaldun's writings as a schoolboy survive. A manuscript discovered in the Escorial library in the early 1950s turned out to be a long essay written by the young Ibn Khaldun when he was a student of Al-Abili. Something of an exam paper or final project for his master, Al-Abili, the *Lubab al-Muhassal fi usul al-din* testified to Ibn Khaldun's early grasp of the philosophical and theological material of the *Takhlis al-Muhassal*, a standard work of *kalam*, or Islamic theology, by the important exegete Umar ibn al-Khatib al-Razi (d. 1209). He also analyzed the work of its commentator, Nasir al-Din al-Tusi (d. 1274). Interestingly, Nasir al-Din was the famed, but also infamous, philosopher from Tus, Persia, who followed the Mongols to the gates of Baghdad and the end of the ʿAbbasid caliphate, the golden era of Islamic history, which was destroyed in 1258.[16]

Most importantly, Al-Abili was a rationalist. Although, like Ibn Khaldun, he had an enormous breadth of encyclopedic, factual, and doctrinal knowledge, he also pursued rational sciences such as logic, mathematics, and metaphysics. He would have been intimately aware of Andalusi and Maghribi rationalists such as the famed Ibn Rushd or Averroes (d. 1198). Al-Abili was also exposed to various rationalist philosophies during his pilgrimage to Mecca and during his seven-year stay in the East. His interest in Nasir al-Din's commentary also demonstrated an exposure to rationalism.[17] Some have even supposed that Al-Abili, having been exposed to Shiite doctrine during his travels, had Shiite sympathies that he had to hide from his almost-uniformly Sunni North African students and patrons.[18]

Madrasas

Ibn Khaldun was one of the last and privileged few whose education did not conform to official norms. His teachers resisted the developing trend toward politically controlled education. Al-Abili displayed a remarkable resistance to the idea of formalized, institutionalized education in the madrasa, or the state-controlled college. Al-Abili's public distain for the madrasa system was known well enough for his views to be recorded by the sixteenth-century historian Al-Maqqari:

> In madrasas, according to Al-Abili, 'students are attracted by the scholarships and material benefits offered there and go to the teachers designated by the government to govern and teach in these madrasas, or to the teachers who have agreed to subject themselves to the authorities. This separates the students from [those other] teachers who represent true science and who have not been appointed to the madrasas, for if they had been appointed they would have refused, an had they accepted it would not be to fulfill the role demanded of the others.'[19]

Privileged by his aristocratic background, Ibn Khaldun was not exposed directly to the indoctrination and controlled knowledge found in the madrasas. Ibn Khaldun's freely formed education and curriculum must at least partially explain Ibn Khaldun's creative output.

Official madrasas were becoming a major social phenomenon in thirteenth- and fourteenth-century medieval North Africa.[20] Every major city had a madrasa by the middle of the fourteenth century. Some major cities, such as Tunis and Fez, had more than two. It was also in this period that large numbers of European educational religious institutions, that is, universities, were popping up in cities and towns across Italy, France, and Spain.

As Al-Abili noted, madrasas were specifically founded to promote particular points of view that supported those who financed them and those in power. In the words of one historian, madrasas were a 'new instrument of power' used to 'educate bureaucrats of all levels and to control the future servants of the realm' and to eliminate so-called Almohad heresies, anti-establishment elements of Sufism, as well as aberrant or independent rulings or opinions.[21] A prolific, conservative Egyptian jurist, Khalil ibn Ishaq al-Jundi (d. *c.* 1378), a contemporary of Ibn Khaldun, was a notorious proponent of arid, rote interpretations of doctrine.[22] He summarized Maliki law into a single abbreviated volume, thus limiting the perspective and latitude of jurists. Ibn Khaldun, in contrast, was able to develop not only his own independent study, but also perhaps even more importantly, an ambiguous relationship with institutions in general. For Ibn

Khaldun it was never simply apparent that the built, the institutionalized, the established curriculum or way of thinking was superior to his freelance education. Far from it. Ibn Khaldun called career teachers, or those who make their only profession teaching, 'weak, indigent and rootless.'[23] Ibn Khaldun, in fact, would face fierce opposition to his constructivist approach later in his career as scholars such as the jealous jurist Ibn ᶜArafa, the grand qadi under Abu al-ᶜAbbas of Tunis who knew and resented Ibn Khaldun as a school boy, frequently condemned Ibn Khaldun's disrespect for simplified legal manuals.

According to Ibn Khaldun, Ibn ᶜArafa and his ilk had turned teaching the law into a mere craft or occupation that was far from the 'pride of ᶜ*asabiyya*' or independent thinking. Teaching in his day, Ibn Khaldun claimed, was a far cry from the way it was practiced during the first years of Islam. Although it could hardly be considered a major reason for his genius, Ibn Khaldun's lack of a typical madrasa education, even as most new and upcoming scholars and intellectuals were following such an institutionalized course, may go some way in explaining why Ibn Khaldun was open to writing so independently and critically in the *Muqaddimah*.

Another reason for Ibn Khaldun's strong critique of the Maliki madrasas was his defense of the Islamic mysticism, or Sufism, practiced by his father, and, although less overtly, by himself. The expert on Moroccan Sufism, Vincent Cornell, argued that often the purpose of the Marinid madrasas was the promotion of a common 'epistemology based on legal reason.' The Marinid emphasis on jurisprudential education was 'a revival of juridical arguments against Sufism.'[24] One of the more effective anti-Sufi polemics was presented by a Hanbali scholar, Ibn Taymiyya, who is most famous today as the primary influence on Muhammad ibn ᶜAbd al-Wahab, founder of Wahhabi Islam in Saudi Arabia. Students of Ibn Taymiyya were prevalent and influential in the fourteenth-century Marinid courts. In contrast to Ibn Khaldun, who was himself a Sufi in many respects and had immense respect for the Sufis of rural Morocco, ᶜAbd al-ᶜAziz al-Qayrawani (d. 1349 or 1350) saw some Sufi leaders or sheikhs of shrines as potential threats to the official religious authorities, or *ulama*, who were more directly dependent on the sultan.[25] In a chapter of the *Muqaddimah* dedicated to the methods of the Sufi saints, Ibn Khaldun called accusations against the Sufis wrongheaded and firmly defended the Sufi way against the narrow-mindedness of jurists trained at official madrasas.[26]

Ibn Khaldun and Education

Yet his defense of Sufism was not the only reason that Ibn Khaldun detested official, standardized judicial education. He also saw it as pedagogically problematic. By the fourteenth century pedagogy had become a well-developed science. Ibn Sahnun (d. 870) was one of the earliest scholars to write a handbook on education, *Rules of Conduct for Teachers*.[27] Like Ibn Khaldun, he came from Tunisia. Ibn Sahnun's work became a standard for teaching students according to the Maliki school of law. Ibn Khaldun would have also been aware of the work of Ibn Sina (Avicenna) and Al-Farabi on child-centered education. Like previous pedagogues, Ibn Khaldun warned against excessive punishment of students and suggested various specific methods for dealing with discipline and curriculum issues in the classroom.[28] For Ibn Khaldun, however, an essential focus of his pedagogy was travel and experience. Staying in one madrasa, or studying only under one scholar, stifled the mind: 'The greater the number of authoritative teachers, the more deeply is the habit one acquired . . . [T]raveling in quest of knowledge is absolutely necessary for the acquisition of useful knowledge and perfection through meeting authoritative teachers and having contact with scholarly personalities.'[29] Clearly, Ibn Khaldun saw in himself, in his intellectual acuity, the benefits of his grueling travels. As a sign of his own educational pedigree, he mentioned almost every scholar he met and spoke with, even into his older years.

Other Early Teachers

There were, indeed, several scholars in addition to Al-Abili who, according to his *Autobiography*, had an important impact on the education of Ibn Khaldun. Ibn Khaldun studied and memorized the Qur'an under a series of esteemed teachers. Since there were small variations between Qur'anic texts he used a specific variation, the Ya'qub recitation, popular in North Africa at that time. Having become a *hafiz*, or one who has memorized the Qur'an, at a very young age he then went on to memorize volumes of poetry, literature, and *hadith*, sayings of the Prophet Muhammad. Compared with the limited reading expected of modern high schools Ibn Khaldun's curriculum was truly vast. He read and memorized large parts of the famous and voluminous *Kitab al-Aghani*, the famed book of often-irreverent but grammatically and poetically superb 'Arab songs' compiled shortly after the rise of Islam and considered a core text for the education of a refined intellectual. He studied the *Burda*, a group of long poems written in praise of the prophet. He learned and memorized the entire repertoire of Muslim bn al-Hajjaj (d. 875 AD), one of the chief authorities on the *hadith*, except his book on hunting. He studied and memorized portions of the commentaries on these epic works as well. His grasp of the legal literature was similarly vast. The precocious Ibn Khaldun studied under a group of teachers, masters of the Maliki law books, or *Mudawana*. Ibn ʿAbd Allah al-Jayyani specifically taught him the entire *Kitab al-Muttawa'*, the basis of the Maliki school (there were four Sunni schools of law) written by the Imam Malik (d. 796). Ibn Khaldun thus studied the original rulings and opinions of Imam Malik, instead of the cropped and strategically edited version taught in most official madrasas. Abu ʿAbd Allah Muhammad ibn ʿAbd al-Salam, the grand Qadi of Tunis, perhaps the most important religious scholar in the city, took an interest in the young Ibn Khaldun, personally showing him how to apply Maliki law to specific cases.

Most of the mentors of the young and eager Ibn Khaldun were killed by the great plague, with few of his teachers and mentors spared by the pestilence.[30] It was the same plague that killed much of his family and his father. It is difficult to speculate what impact this may have had on the young Ibn Khaldun's education, but the devastations of plague did not dim his curiosity. It may have even solidified his desire to improve on the knowledge that had been passed on to him by these scholars and by his father in particular, making his work, in some sense, a eulogy for so many lost teachers for whom he felt a deep sense of respect.

Despite the tragic death of his original mentors, Ibn Khaldun would never stop learning from other scholars. Throughout his life, he gained insights from mentors and colleagues such as Ibn al-Khatib, the wazir in Granada, and Abu Mahdi ʿIsa al-Zayyat, an important Andalusi Sufi master, on a wide variety of disciplines and subjects, especially Islamic mysticism. One of the most important lessons learned by Ibn Khaldun was the limit of knowledge and scholarship in the political realm.

Between Scholarship and Politics

Scholars, especially political scientists, historians, and philosophers, often believe that they know best when it comes to politics. If only scholars could gain power, the world would be run more justly and rationally. Plato famously called for the ideal rule of a philosopher king and attempted to direct the tyrant Diogenes of Sicily according to his mold with disastrous results. There was also a long tradition in Islamic philosophy and in certain forms of Islamic rule of elitism, of the superiority of obscure, elite knowledge. The Ismaili Fatimid rulers of Egypt and North Africa, for example, were famous for tightly guarding their control over 'secret knowledge' about the true nature of the Qurʾan, a control that conferred legitimacy on their rule.[31]

In contrast, Ibn Khaldun, himself a scholar and, by the time he wrote the *Muqaddimah*, a reluctant politician, thought the opposite. Although he obviously had a very high regard for scholarship and the scholars who taught him, he did not see scholarship as necessarily a suitable qualification for ruling. In fact, Ibn Khaldun claimed 'scholars are, of all people, those least familiar with the ways of politics,' and the least capable in ruling.[32] Scholars conceived of things as forms, as abstractions, as ideas, not as particular or practical problems. Scholars liked to generalize and to see the Qur°an and the Sunna, the example of the life of the Prophet, in ideal forms: 'Thus, in all of their intellectual activity, scholars are accustomed to dealing with matters of the mind and with thoughts. They do not know anything else. Politicians, on the other hand, must pay attention to the facts of the outside world and the conditions attaching to and depending on (politics).'[33] Ibn Khaldun even warned against politicians getting too deep into matters. A good politician should not be 'infected' with abstractions and mental speculations.

Ibn Khaldun's position seemed counter-intuitive. Why would Ibn Khaldun decry the usefulness of his own profession? There were several possible explanations for his apparent self-criticism. Ibn Khaldun seemed wary of attempts to impose ideology and ideals, philosophical or otherwise, onto the practical effort of governing. He thus seemed to make his own arguments and his own generalizations; his *Muqaddimah* was after all a book of general observations about societies, less relevant or even unhelpful to any ruler who should try to use these observations as a guidebook. Perhaps, however, Ibn Khaldun's denunciation of the idea of scholars as rulers has its roots not in any particular anti-intellectualism but rather in a notion that was repeated throughout the *Muqaddimah*, the notion that those 'Bedouin' not exposed to the luxuries and standardized education of the urban environment are, in fact, the best suited to rule. By possessing nothing of the complexities and contradictions of settled urban life, those from the outside could enter politics with a clean, practical approach. In many respects, as well, Ibn Khaldun saw himself as something of an exception, as an embodiment of his own contradictions. He may not have seen himself as simply a 'scholar' in the narrow sense of the word. Most scholars, or *ulama* as they were called, were religiously trained clerics or elite philosophers who had little understanding of the daily process of rule. Also, at several junctures Ibn Khaldun did not clamor for positions of political authority. He often pretended to actively avoid these responsibilities, even though he could not fully resist the lure of power.

Ibn Khaldun was not educated in the pressure-cooker of political indoctrination that often characterized the madrasa, but by experience, travel, and encounters with a wide array of teachers. Although he was perhaps a reluctant pragmatist, he learned to be one at many junctures in his future political life. As this description of the rest of Ibn Khaldun's life will show in coming chapters, becoming both a man of science and a man of politics in the fourteenth century was fraught with many potential perils. It was because of his independent education that Ibn Khaldun was able to see beyond the weakness of both pure intellectual speculation and pure political contingency. What his education could not prepare him for, however, was the ravages of the plague.

Orphaned by Plague

One of the most deadly perils of fourteenth-century North Africa was not in everyday politics, it was the plague. The plague, described by Ibn Khaldun, resulted from urban overcrowding and decay. It displayed the perils of settled civilization explicitly. In fact, it may have been the plague, more than any other event, that gave Ibn Khaldun, an urbane man from an aristocratic family, raised in the relatively cosmopolitan and vibrant city of Tunis, ambiguous thoughts about city life. He described the plague in almost apocalyptic terms:

> [I]n the middle of the [fourteenth century], civilization both in the East and the West was visited by a destructive plague which devastated nations and caused populations to vanish. It swallowed up many of the good things of civilization and wiped them out. It overtook the dynasties at the time of their senility, when they had reached the limit of their duration.[34]

Here Ibn Khaldun referred to dynasties as 'senile' since dynasties acted and aged liked human bodies – just as old and weak people were killed by plague, so were the old and the weak dynasties. It was an inevitable part of the cyclical process of history.

> Their situation approached the point of annihilation and dissolution. Civilization decreased with the decrease of mankind. Cities and buildings were laid waste, roads and way signs were obliterated, settlements and mansions became empty, dynasties and tribes grew weak. The entire inhabited world changed . . . *It was as if the voice of existence in the world had called out for oblivion and restriction,* and the world had responded to its call. God inherits the earth and whomever is upon it.[35] (Emphasis added)

It was due to the plague, because it had changed 'the entire creation' and the 'whole world had been altered,' that Ibn Khaldun felt it necessary to write the *Muqaddimah* and a new history of the world. Other contemporary historians, such as the Egyptian Al-Maqrizi, described similar devastation. In Cairo the entire year 1348–9 had to be exempted from the agricultural tax accounts. Thus, '[I]n that year everything died, the year itself included.'[36] The plague did not merely have an impact on population, it even threw the established legal order into chaos. The Hafsid ruler Abu al-Hasan's plans in 1348 to establish a unified

Marinid empire across North Africa, although doomed by other factors such as a lack of tribal ᶜ*asabiyya*, were set back by the plague. He was forced to withdraw from Tunis. The plague even changed Islamic law. David Powers, a Maghrib specialist, described how the sheer numbers of dead and the wholesale wiping out of families caused a crisis in the application of inheritance law, a central tenet of *sharia*.[37]

In Cairo alone, more than 1,000 a day were dying, there were traffic jams of coffins, and dead bodies littered the streets.[38] It was just as bad in North Africa and Al-Andalus, as a number of accounts of the plague attest. Ibn Khaldun was, by no means, the only scholar of the western Mediterranean impacted by the Black Death. In addition to Ibn Khaldun's description of the Black Death of 1348, several accounts survive of the plague. In fact, it seemed to inspire an intense interest in medical knowledge and science in the medieval Mediterranean generally. Ibn Khaldun's friend and colleague in Granada, Ibn al-Khatib, known as much for his medical knowledge as his knowledge as an historian, wrote extensively about the Black Death in his *Manual on Diseases and their Transmission*. Various herbal remedies are suggested.[39] Abu Jaᶜfar Ahmad ibn Khatima (d. 1369) of Almería, who wrote perhaps the most detailed Islamic manual on the plague, denied evidence that the plague was spread by contagious contact. He denied the existence of contagion despite his own observations because of religious restrictions in some *hadith* on the idea of contagion.

The Plague

Most Muslim scholars agreed that plague was an act of God – plague victims were martyrs. Ibn al-Wardi of Aleppo, for instance, compiled a series of sayings and religious traditions about the plague suggesting that 'The plague is for the Muslims a martyrdom and a reward, and for the disbelievers a punishment and a rebuke.' He cited Muhammad the Prophet's famous question about infection and contagion: 'Who infected the first?' How could infection and contagion exist, the reasoning went, if there did not seem to be an explicable origin? The plague was even given a voice. In the writings of Al-Wardi the plague says to the inhabitants of the house: 'I have an order from the *qadi* to arrest all those in the house.' The plague was seen as beneficial as it focused the mind for the final journey and made all hope of material reward fruitless. Only God could save the people from the plague with his mercy.[40] Avoiding the notion of contagion, Al-Khatima spoke of the need to avoid 'luxuries' to change the atmosphere, to be 'as quiet as possible.' As Ibn Khaldun would similarly do in his *Muqaddimah*, Al-Khatima claimed direct correlation between the excessive luxuries of the urban environment and catching the plague.[41] Indeed, the plague would color Ibn

Khaldun's reluctant attitude toward the urban throughout his life. Were it not for the plague's brutal signs, the apparently mortal perils of urban luxury and excess may not have been so evident to Ibn Khaldun.

Ibn al-Khatib, Ibn Khaldun's friend and colleague in Granada, approached the plague in a much more analytical, personally dangerous way. In fact, it was for his boldly rationalist position that the plague was a contagion that he was put on trial and accused of heresy.[42] He boldly suggested that the evidence contradicted established religious tradition, that contagion did exist and that the best way to avoid it was to avoid its spread between infected patients. Disease was not simply a sign from God but the result of contagious transfer between people. Explicitly asserting the primacy of observation and deduction over divine law Ibn al-Khatib remarked:

> If it were asked, how do we submit to the theory of contagion, when already the divine law has refuted the notion of contagion, we will answer: The existence of contagion has been proved by experience, deduction, the senses, observation, and by unanimous reports, and it is not a secret to whoever has looked into this matter . . . that those who come into contact with [plague] patients mostly die, while those who do not come into contact survive . . . even an earring has been known to kill whoever wears it and his whole household.[43]

Ibn Khaldun did not venture into these dangerous theological waters. Ibn Khaldun, unlike Ibn al-Khatib, Al-Khatima, and others who searched desperately for the specific causes and treatments for the plague, avoided the imbroglio and looked at broader historical meanings. Ibn Khaldun knew that a plague of this magnitude had created a need to prescript history, to, in the words of Ibn Khaldun, 'systematically set down the situation of the world among all regions and races, as well as the customs and sectarian beliefs that have changed for their adherents.'[44] The plague may have shaped Ibn Khaldun's personal and intellectual outlook more than any other event in his life.

When Ibn Khaldun said that the situation of the world had changed completely, he was not predicting the birth of a new brilliant era at the end of the plague, or predicting the western Renaissance as some historians have speculated; rather he was laying bare the cold reality of an age besieged by disease, disunity, and instability.[45] Ibn Khaldun did not blame the troubles of his era on God's will; his was an age that demanded forthright, analytical study of the reasons for the rise and demise of dynasties and peoples. While Ibn al-Khatib would focus his rational method on the plague in particular, Ibn Khaldun would use the plague to launch a new method of understanding history as a whole.

In addition to shaping his view of the world, the plague affected Ibn Khaldun personally, killing an overwhelming number of his close contacts, family and friends. Even for his era, the young Ibn Khaldun, 16 when the Black Death struck hardest in 1348, was a precocious and ready learner. Life in his parent's home would have been a quiet, if eerie refuge. For a family of his status, it would have been a large but unostentatious *riyad* or small palace with a courtyard, a fountain, and servants. Since his family was from Al-Andalus, it would have been built in an Andalusi style, colorful stone tiles fitted together in intricate patterns even as the light reflected off the fountain. Probably trees and fragrant plants filled the atrium. Like the riyad-style houses that survive today in the old city or *medina* of Tunis, his house probably had no more than a single, solid door looking out into a small alley. The restless and troubled world outside the walls of his house could be locked out. Inside would have been relatively carefree and relaxed, even as the rumblings of change and rebellion beset the streets of Tunis. He absorbed the teachings not only of grammarians and scholars of the Qurʾan but of the poets, scientists, and mathematicians who regularly visited his home in Tunis. Before the plague, Ibn Khaldun's father, the one who had wisely retreated from political life to concentrate on Sufism and the life of the mind, had created something of an intellectual salon in his home. Ibn Khaldun described how poets such as ʿAbd al-Muhaymin, the court poet of Tunis who had cleverly created a large collection of verses starting with the letter H in honor of the Marinid sultan, Abu al-Hasan, would come and visit regularly, inspiring Ibn Khaldun to write his own verses. ʿAbd al-Muhaymin even took refuge in the house of the Khalduns when the inhabitants of Tunis revolted against the charismatic Sultan Abu al-Hasan, who had come with great ambitions from Fez to unite all of North Africa. Yet Abu al-Hasan and his armies would not remain the primary threat to Tunis for long. The plague and the disastrous Battle of Kairouan where Abu al-Hasan's fighters were routed after his Arab tribal contingents abandoned him ended Marinid hopes for a trans-Maghribi empire. Excessive battles and wars, food prices and other factors had stretched the limits of the state. The house of Ibn Khaldun was a good place for a poet to hide from angry, hungry, or overstretched subjects.

Life before the plague was relatively comfortable and the Khaldun house seemed to be a center of important intellectual activity, a type of medieval salon and even refuge for scholars out of favor with the regime. The refined and educated Ibn Ridwan, the same man who taught Ibn Khaldun in the small school or *kuttab* near Ibn Khaldun's narrow street, regularly visited the house of the Khalduns and described to the young Ibn Khaldun the feats and discussions of the 'great savants' in the palace of the sultan before the siege.[46] Many of these savants poured into the house of the Khalduns to take refuge from political turmoil. In the end they met the same fate that befell Ibn Khaldun's parents:

death by the plague. His elder brother Muhammad, about whom we know little, would have become the head of the family.

The trauma of the plague may explain some of Ibn Khaldun's somewhat ambiguous relationship with urban life. Although he benefited from the intellectual stimulation and culture of the city, Ibn Khaldun blamed the very fact of city life as itself a source of plague and pestilence. The cities were crowded with people and life. This could only lead to the spread of death and disease.[47] Ibn Khaldun linked pestilence to famine and the decay of dynasties and their control over the countryside. Also, the air itself was literally 'corrupted' by too much 'civilization' or population:

> According to Ibn Khaldun, '[plague] results from the putrefaction and the many evil moistures with which (the air) has contact. Now, air nourishes the animal spirit and is constantly with it. When it is corrupted, corruption affects the temper of (the spirit). If the corruption is strong, the lung is afflicted with disease. (Pneumonia: it was likely that Ibn Khaldun witnessed the pneumonic form of the disease) . . . The reason for the growth of putrefaction and evil moisture is invariably a dense and abundant civilization such as exists in the later (years) of a dynasty.'[48]

In fact, survival and protection from the plague could only be afforded by 'waste regions' interspersed between cities: 'This makes circulation of the air possible. It removes the corruption and putrefaction affecting the air.' The rural was the savior of the urban. Indeed, Ibn Khaldun fled, as did many, out of the city. Certainly, during his life as a young man in the house of his gentle and learned father, he would have been exposed to the pleasures and benefits of urban life. The punishment of the plague, however, a reflection of God's will as it was, dashed Ibn Khaldun's youth and thrust him into an uncertain and ambiguous world. Although he wrote about it stoically, the full emotional impact of the plague and the siege of Tunis, two events that overturned his life, could only have been terrible experience for Ibn Khaldun, a young man in the midst of his formative years. The house of Ibn Khaldun had kept almost all the dangers of the world out of its walls, but nothing could protect against the plague.

In many respects Ibn Khaldun's statement that the whole known world was changed by the plague was accurate. The plague was a worldwide phenomenon. Medical treatises and literature from all around Europe and Asia described death by plague in morbid detail. The writer Boccaccio, an Italian contemporary of Ibn Khaldun, indicated in the *Decameron*: 'at the outset of the disease women and men developed swellings in the groin and armpit the size of an apple or egg . . . And in a short time these deadly inflammations covered the whole body.' Chronicles from Spain described the deaths of up to two-thirds of the population.

The plague spared no one. People of all classes and backgrounds, even royalty, the powerful King Alfonso XI of Castile and Leon, for example, were carried away by the disease.[49] It was unclear what could be done to stop the progress of the disease. Cleansing of the streets and clearing of the markets sometimes had some effect, but the coffins still seemed to pile up.

Originating possibly in western China or the central Asian steppe, plague was carried into the Mediterranean by Genoese merchants who were trading at the city of Kaffa on the Black Sea. It was brought to Sicily in 1347 and would have passed easily and quickly into Tunisia, where there were a number of Italian merchants. The Genoese were by this time one of the most prolific of the great Italian trading states. They, like other Italian city-states such as Pisa, had extensive contact with Tunisia. Although Ibn Khaldun did not know it, one of the major consequences of a gradual shift in Mediterranean power, the growth of the Italian fleets and merchant marines, the new focus on Atlantic trade, the voyages of the Genoese to remote ports and destinations, had already turned the tide against the Islamic world. For while Europe quickly entered a period of Renaissance, the affects of the Black Plague in the Near East would sow disunity and division until the eventual conquest and consolidation of the Islamic world by the Ottomans.

In the context of Ibn Khaldun's life, however, the plague was at least as important a teacher of the nature of human civilization and the nature of the world as anything he would have learned from his kind father and doting tutors in the quiet home of his youth. There was some sense in his autobiography of a youthful idyll of learning and parental love that he may have hoped would never end. The death of so many thrust Ibn Khaldun and his brothers, the younger Yahya and the elder Muhammad, into an adulthood where loyalties and fortunes could turn. As Ibn Khaldun's first forays into public service would teach him, prestige and lineage was no defense against the politics of a particularly brutal era characterized by the fatalistic inevitability of decline.

NOTES

1　Abdesselam Cheddadi, a translator of Ibn Khaldun's biography into French, is exceptional in this respect with his interpretive essay and extensive footnotes in *Le Livre des Exemples*.

2　Walter J. Fischel, *Ibn Khaldun in Egypt* (Berkeley, 1967).

3　Chase Robinson, *Islamic Historiography* (Cambridge, 2003, 68–72).

4　*Autobiographie*, 56. For Ibn Khaldun's description of his family in Al-Andalus see *Al-Ta͑rif*, 4–8.

5　D. F. Ruggles, 'Mothers of a hybrid dynasty: race, genealogy, and acculturation in al-Andalus,' *Journal of Medieval and Early Modern Studies*, 34 (1), Winter 2004, 65–94.

6 Franz Rosenthal suggested that Ibn Khaldun may have felt 'marginal' in Tunis as an Andalusi. Although he may have regretted the decline of his ancestral family and their power in Seville, it was difficult to find evidence in the autobiography to suggest this sense of being marginal in any obvious way. F. Rosenthal, 'Ibn Khaldun in His Time,' in Bruce Lawrence (ed.), *Ibn Khaldun and Islamic Ideology* (Cleiden, 1984).

7 *Al-Ta^{c}rif*, 14; *Autobiographie*, 59. F. Rosenthal stated, however, that he may have only been a doorkeeper. Perhaps it was this lack of high official rank that allowed Ibn Khaldun's grandfather a certain flexibility in fulfilling his duties. *Muqaddimah*, vol. I, xxxvii.

8 *Al-Ta^{c}rif*, 14; *Autobiographie*, 59.

9 *Muqaddimah*, vol. I, 266.

10 *Muqaddimah*, vol. I, 265.

11 Ibn Hazm, *Jamhara*, É. Lévi-Provençal (ed.), (Cairo, 1948), 430. Quoted in F. Rosenthal, 'Introduction,' *Muqaddimah*, vol. I, xxxiii, note 11.

12 *Al-Ta^{c}rif*, 15; *Autobiographie*, 59.

13 Much has been said about the transmission of knowledge through the *ijaza* or 'diploma.' For a good recent study of the *ijaza* see Jonathan Berkey's book on medieval transmission of knowledge in Mamluk Cairo (under which Ibn Khaldun would himself work as a Qadi), *The Transmission of Knowledge in Medieval Cairo: A Social History of Islamic Education* (Princeton, 1992) See also Dale Eickelman, 'The art of memory: Islamic education and its social reproduction,' *Comparative Studies in Society and History*, 20 (4), 1978, 485–516.

14 Nassif Nassar, 'Le maitre d'Ibn Khaldun: Al-Abili,' *Studia Islamica*, 20: 1964, 103–14. Muhsin Mahdi refers briefly to Ibn Khaldun's education in *Ibn Khaldun's Philosophy of History* (London, 1957), 34–5.

15 Abu Zakariya Yahya Ibn Khaldun, *Histoire des Beni ^{c}Abd el Wad, rois de Tlemcen*, trans A. Bel (Algiers, 1903), 71–2. The original first and last folios of the manuscript by Yahya Ibn Khaldun are missing. Thus, the exact date when this history was written is unknown. Ibn Khaldun: The Mediterranean in the 14th Century, Exhibition Catalogue, SPAIN, 2006), 47. See Ibn Khaldun's description of Al-Abili's life in *Al-Ta^{c}rif*, 33–3; *Autobiographie*, 67–71.

16 *Muqaddimah*, vol. 1, xlv. Fr. Luciano Rubio published an edited version of the *Muhassal fi usul al-din* (Tetuan, 1952). Ibn Khaldun's text was dated by his own pen to 1351 AD, making Ibn Khaldun only 19 years old at the time of its writing. Although he was trained by Andalusis, such as Al-Abili and claimed Andalusi, Arab ancestry it is apparent from this manuscript that Ibn Khaldun wrote in Maghribi script. *Ibn Khaldun: The Mediterranean in the 14th Century, vol. II, Exhibition Catalogue*, (2006), 66.

17 N. Nassar, 'Le maitse d'Ibn Khaldun,' 108.

18 N. Nassar, 'Le maitse d'Ibn Khaldun,' N. Nassar, 108. *Taqiyya*, or the deliberate hiding of Shiite beliefs from hostile others, was a common practice by this time. There does not seem to be any substantial proof, however, that Al-Abili was Shiite.

19 Al-Maqqari, *Nafh al tib min gusn al-Andalus al-ratib*, Ihsan Abbas (ed.), 8 vols. (Beirut, 1968), vol. V, 275–6. Quoted in Virgilio M. Enamorado, 'Knowledge, power and madrasas at the time of Ibn Khaldun,' *Ibn Khaldun: The Mediterranean in the 14th Century*, 343. As Virgilio Enamorado mentioned, 'To a great extent, from the 12th century, these institutions were to favor the homogenization of legal texts and the hadith. The end of teaching in small mosques or in the residences of learned men brought the curtain down on a certain autonomous culture,' 345.

20 M. Shatzmiller, 'Les premiers Mérinides et le milieu religiuex de Fès: l'Introduction des Médersas,' *Studia Islamica*, 43, 1976, 109–18.

21 L. Govin, 'La Medersa, nouvel "outil" du pouvoir,' *Autrement*, 13, 1992, 94.

22 Jamila Bargach claimed that Khalil died in 1365. See *Orphans of Islam* (Lanham, MD, 2002, 241.

23 In a rather elitist statement he distinguished between teaching as a 'craft' that merely 'serves to make a living' and what he considered the noble act of scholarship. *Muqaddimah*, vol. I, 58–9.

24 Vincent Cornell, *Realm of the Saint: Power and Authority in Moroccan Sufism*, 129.

25 According to ᶜAbd al-ᶜAziz, the corruption of the Sufis 'is quicker than the coursing of poison through the body and is more harmful to religion than sexual promiscuity, theft, or any other transgression or sin.' Quoted. in *Realm of the Saint*, (Austin, TX, 1998), 129.

26 *Muqaddimah*, vol. III, 80–90.

27 Sebastian Gunther, 'Be masters in that you teach and continue to learn: medieval Muslim thinkers on educational theory,' *Comparative Education Review*, 50(3), August 2006, 369.

28 'Severity to students does them harm . . . It makes them feel oppressed and causes them to lose their energy.' *Muqaddimah*, vol. III, 305.

29 *Muqaddimah*, vol. III, 308.

30 *Autobiographie*, 61. See *Al-Taᶜrif*, 15–22 for Ibn Khaldun's descriptions of his first teachers killed in the plague. Ibn Khaldun so esteemed his teachers that he included panegyric poetry dedicated to their accomplishments. Often left out of the A. Cheddadi edition and translation of the *Autobiographie*, probably because of their digression from the main narrative, Ibn Khaldun's many lengthy poetic interludes can only be fully appreciated in *Al-Taᶜrif*. See, for example, 23–6.

31 On the Fatimids and their devotion to obscure knowledge see Heinz Halm, *The Empire of the Mahdi: The Rise of the Fatimids* (Leiden, 1996).

32 *Muqaddimah*, vol. III, 308.

33 *Muqaddimah*, vol. III, 309.

34 *Muqaddimah*, vol. I, 64.

35 *Muqaddimah*, I, 64.

36 Al-Maqrizi, *Kitab al-Suluk li-Maᵓrifat duwal al Muluk*, M. Mustafa Zyada (ed.), vol. 2, (Cairo, 787).

37 David Powers, *Law, Society and Culture in the Medieval Maghrib, 1300–1500* (Cambridge, 2002) 141.

38 David Powers, *Law, Society and Culture*, 778–86.

39 Abu ᶜAbd Allah al-Shaquri likewise wrote about the Black Death, speculating on some of its possible causes. His and other manuscripts on the plague are kept in the Library of the Royal Monastery of the Escorial. See *Ibn Khaldun and the Fourteenth Century, Exhibition Catalogue*, 170–1.

40 Michael W. Dols, 'Ibn al-Wardi's Risalah al-nabaᵓᶜan al-waba', a translation of a Major Source for the History of the Black Death in the Middle East,' in *Near Eastern Numismatics Iconography, Epigraphy and History: Studies in Honor of George C. Miles*, Diecran K Kouymjian (ed.) (Beirut, 1974) 454–5.

41 Abu Jaᶜfar Ahmad Ibn Khatima, *Tahsil al-gharad al-qasid fi tafsil al-marad al-wafid*, German translation in *Archiv fur Geschichte der Medizin*, 19, 1927.

42 See Justin Stearns, 'Contagion in theology and law: ethical considerations in the writings

of two 14th century scholars of Nasrid Granada,' *Islamic Law and Society*, 14(1), 2007. Stearns compared Ibn al-Khatib's rationalism with that of his more dogmatic teacher, Ibn Lubb. On the trial of Ibn al-Khatib see M. Isabel Calero Secall, 'El Proceso de Ibn al-Jatib,' *Al-Qantara*, 22, 2001, 421–61.

43 M. J. Muller, 'Ibnulkhatib's Bericht uber die Pest,' *Sitzungsberichte der Konigl. Bayerischen Akademie der Wissenchaften*, 2, 1863, 2–12. For the English translation see John Aberth, *The Black Death: The Great Mortality of 1348–1350* (Boston and New York, 2005), 114–16.

44 *Muqaddimah*, vol. I, 65.

45 Husam al-Abbadi speculated that Ibn Khaldun was predicting the renaissance. See 'Bubonic plague in the Orient,' in *The Mediterranean in the 14th Century*, 254–8.

46 *Al-Taᶜrif*, 68–9; *Autobiographie*, 64.

47 *Muqaddimah*, vol. II, 135–6.

48 *Muqaddimah*, vol. II, 136–7.

49 Julio V. Baruque, 'The Black Death in the universe of the 14th century,' in *The Mediterranean in the 14th Century*, 248–53.

IBN KHALDUN THE STATESMAN

Happiness and profit are achieved mostly by people who are obsequious and use flattery. Such character disposition is one of the reasons for happiness.

Ibn Khaldun, *Muqaddimah*, II, 328

Moving mountains from their places is easier for me than to influence people . . .
Popular Arabic phrase quoted in Ibn Khaldun, *Muqaddimah*, II, 3.

Like many with gifted minds, Ibn Khaldun did not conform to bureaucratic expectations. His first job was not particularly inspiring. With more than a touch of sarcasm he wrote: 'I filled this office [of calligrapher] . . . which consisted of writing in big characters the formulaic text at the end of letters and orders of the Sultan [of Tunis]: "Praise and Thanksgiving to God." '[1] He had studied with the finest minds of North Africa. He had spent three years steeping himself in philosophy under the supervision of his master Al-Abili. Compared with his rich intellectual training, Ibn Khaldun found the job of calligrapher particularly boring. The devastations of the plague in Tunis did not help and must have made the city less and less inviting. For Ibn Khaldun, it was time to leave. The capital of the Hafsids was simply not the same after the death of Ibn Khaldun's parents and teachers.

Fired by what he termed the 'ambitions of youth,' Ibn Khaldun resolved to escape the dull confines of his birthplace. Little did he know that in the future, having become exhausted with political intrigue and adventure, he would look back upon that birthplace with a longing to return to the simple expectations of home. Although it was a vibrant center of learning under more powerful Hafsid sultans, Tunis had quickly become a boring backwater with the rise of the Marinids in Fez. Scholars were itinerant and quite fickle. Those savants and teachers who had survived the plague had joined the Marinids and left Tunis, headed for success and patronage at the Marinid capital in Fez. Before describing his departure for the Marinid court, however, Ibn Khaldun revealed some intimate information about his relationship with his older brother, Muhammad. Muhammad was Ibn Khaldun's only surviving elder relative. He thus had a special duty to protect and guide his younger sibling. Muhammad, perhaps afraid of being left alone in an abandoned house and a decimated city, or fearing for the safety of his headstrong younger brother, prevented Ibn Khaldun from leaving. Ibn Khaldun did not give many details of their conversation except to suggest that he confronted his brother, asked him to change his mind, and impressed upon him his need to leave. One can only imagine their conversations as both brothers, traumatized by the death of their parents and friends, chose different paths: Muhammad staying home to tend to the family property and his duties as eldest man in the household; Ibn Khaldun venturing off in search of something more exciting than writing 'thanks be to God' at the end of a weak sultan's documents.[2]

Almost immediately after leaving Tunis, Ibn Khaldun's thirst for excitement was quenched. He was thrust into the whirlwind of conflict stirring incessantly between the sultans, tribes, and dynasts of the fourteenth-century Maghrib. After leaving the walls of Tunis, Ibn Khaldun and the army of his patron, Ibn Tafragin (the one who employed him as official calligrapher), entered the lands of the Huwara tribe, where Ibn Tafragin's troops were defeated decisively. In one of many lucky escapes, Ibn Khaldun avoided capture. Intriguingly, it is unclear here how loyal Ibn Khaldun would have been to Ibn Tafragin. Judging from his previous comments about wanting to leave for the Marinid court, Ibn Khaldun was, at best, a tepid supporter of Ibn Tafragin and may have even desired the defeat of Ibn Tafragin's forces. This frequent attitude of ambivalence, especially toward rulers who did not meet Ibn Khaldun's expectations, would continue throughout most of his career. In the constantly changing political brew of the region, however, one should not mistake Ibn Khaldun's pragmatic ambivalence with modern notions of treason or lack of 'patriotism.' Treason requires a true power or nation against which to be treasonous – the situation in medieval North Africa was much more complex.

Leaving the battlefield as soon as the results were obvious, Ibn Khaldun managed to flee to the house of the Sufi sheikh and hermit, ʿAbd al-Rahman al-Washtani, and used the hermit's secluded abode to wait for calm, to recover, and to return to the road. Often residing deep in the mountains in modest caves, hermits and troglodytes such as ʿAbd al-Rahman al-Washtani were increasingly common in the Maghrib. Attempting to concentrate on a mystical path to God, hermit caves and lodges such as Al-Washtani's also probably served as a place of arbitrage and a sanctified refuge from inter-tribal conflict.[3] It is interesting to note here that Ibn Khaldun already knew Al-Washtani whom he called 'eminent.' He may have learned about the hermit from his late father who, as mentioned previously, had also chosen the mystical path despite so many invitations to work as a functionary in the Hafsid court in Tunis.

IBN KHALDUN AND ABU ʿINAN: THE FALL OF IMPERIAL AMBITIONS

Continuing his journey to Fez, Ibn Khaldun went west to Tebessa, an ancient town on the border of what is now Algeria and Tunisia, and stayed with the governor there. The governor generously provided Ibn Khaldun with an Arab escort – necessary to protect him during his travels. Ibn Khaldun's plans, however, were sidetracked by rebellions in the region of Algeria against the Marinid sultan, Abu ʿInan, who had just conquered the key Algerian city of Tilimsan. Instead of meeting the Marinids in Fez, he would only need to meet them in Algeria. Encountering the Marinid armies on the road, Ibn Khaldun met with Al-Batha ibn Abi Amr, a wazir and commander for powerful Sultan Abu ʿInan, whose ambition, like so many sultans, was to reunite the lands of the Almohads and the greater Maghrib. Al-Batha, obviously impressed by Ibn Khaldun's erudition and intelligence, greeted him with honors he 'could hardy expect.' Ibn Khaldun then accompanied Al-Batha to Bijaya where helped the army of Abu ʿInan conquer the city for the Marinids. It is unclear from the text how much Ibn Khaldun personally engaged in combat; he did, however, 'assist with the conquest of the city.'[4] He was met by Sultan Abu ʿInan who endowed with yet more honors and made him a high-ranking member of his court. Describing himself as only a 'beardless boy' Ibn Khaldun seemed overwhelmed.[5] He had taken a short-cut from calligrapher to minister and was still only an ambitious youth. Swept up with the thrill of victory, Ibn Khaldun seemed intoxicated by the rise of the powerful Abu ʿInan, seemingly the best hope for political stability and unity in the region. As Ibn Khaldun, would describe it, however, his hopes would soon be dashed against the hard ground of political and dynastic incoherence – an incoherence that characterized the end-stages of a dynasty, the downward spiral in Ibn Khaldun's cycles of history. It was Ibn Khaldun's vivid experiences, his inside observations of the upwelling and decline of dynastic ambitions that would form the basis of his philosophy of history.

At first, all seemed to be going well in Fez. In fact, Ibn Khaldun's honeymoon period at Abu ʿInan's court would last for a while. After returning triumphantly to Fez, Abu ʿInan immediately resolved to 'reunite' all the men of learning in the Maghrib, to revive Fez as a center of learning. Just as he had reunited much of the Maghrib politically he now sought to organize, and control, the learned scholars who would both interpret the law and provide him with the legitimacy of the *sharia*, interpreted by scholars under his control. Abu ᶜInan consciously attempted to unite governmental control of Islamic learning in the madrasa with everyday worship in the mosque, limiting and circumscribing the role of independent-minded *ulama* and scholars such as Ibn Khaldun, much as the ᶜAbbasid caliphs had tried to do centuries earlier. Unlike Egyptian madrasas built mainly by private endowments, Abu ᶜInan made the madrasa an extension of dynastic power. He erected magnificent madrasas with shops, a mosque, and rooms for resident students, the most famous being his namesake the Bou ᶜInaniyya in the center of Fez.[6] Ibn Khaldun would have visited or used this madrasa, even though he criticized the way it was established deliberately by Abu ᶜInan as way of concentrating his power over intellectual production and the interpretation of the law. Instead of using original sources, abbreviations and abridgements were often memorized. Ibn Khaldun would later decry this shift from education to indoctrination in his *Muqaddimah*.[7]

Abu ᶜInan was not the first North African sultan to concentrate the major scholars at court. Ibn Khaldun, his teachers, and colleagues should not be viewed in the way academics are viewed today. Abu ᶜInan's gathering of scholars was almost certainly a political act, not a personal whim or a result of his interest in learning. In fact, sultans such as Abu ᶜInan valued their scholars and counselors so heavily that they were willing to fight over them. Writing about the ruler's dependence on his court Ibn Khaldun remarked, 'It should be known that, by himself, the ruler is weak, and he carries a heavy load. He must look for help from his fellow men.'[8] As Ibn Khaldun would experience multiple times in his life, it was not uncommon for one sultan to use almost any means to steal and entice a learned scholar to join him from another court. This led to a tug-and-pull game that was, more often than not, dangerous for the life and health of the scholar. The sultan would often resolve that if he could not have the best scholar, wazir, doctor, or secretary nobody could. Consolidating the theological and political support of Islamic scholars was the first step to launching an empire.

Abu ᶜInan, in particular, was widely known for his brutal ambition and the way he jealously tested the loyalty of his councilors. He came to power in a brutal fashion, killing and deposing his father, Abu al-Hasan al-Marini, who had recently, if fleetingly, conquered territory from Fez to Tunis. While the youthful Ibn Khaldun and his colleagues supported him in the beginning of his reign, Abu ᶜInan always had influential detractors. The reclusive Sufi and patron saint of the Moroccan town of Salé, Ahmad ibn ᶜAshir al-Ansari, who commanded a wide following throughout the Maghribi countryside, famously criticized Abu ᶜInan and questioned the legitimacy of his rule. Decrying the sultan's lack of social justice Ibn ᶜAshir commented in a letter to Abu ᶜInan, 'The commander of the Faithful [Abu ᶜInan] must remember that neither his servants nor his bodyguard will save him. Instead, they will flee from him on the Day of Judgment as he will flee from them.' In reply, Abu ᶜInan recognized his faults but commented rather skeptically and unapologetically that 'all who hold power are unjust and despotic, are deceived by their confidants, and allow their intimates to carry them away with their passions.'[9] Indeed, this frank realpolitik, this lack of specific religious legitimacy, or even a vague sense of idealism such as the idealism preached by the Almohads centuries before, was, in Ibn Khaldun's view, one of the reasons for the transience of Abu ᶜInan's project to reunify the Maghrib. He could not rely on the deep wellspring of support from the countryside when influential religious leaders such as Ibn ᶜAshir denied his legitimacy. Indeed, beset by paranoia, perhaps stemming from the assassination of his father, he even saw his closest confidants, such as Ibn Khaldun, as shadowy enemies, conspiring constantly for power and influence and his eventual overthrow. His fear of an overthrow came true, but it was not at the hands of his councilors. A group of tribal Marinid sheikhs who guarded their independence resisted Abu ᶜInan's attempts at creating a centralized state across North Africa. Had Abu ᶜInan secured the loyalty of religious leaders such as Ibn ᶜAshir the results of his project may have been different. Writing on this very topic, the important role of religious inspiration in the founding of dynasties, Ibn Khaldun commented, 'anything [done by royal authority] that is dictated [merely] by considerations of policy or political decisions without supervision of the religious law, is also reprehensible, because it is vision lacking the divine light . . . Political laws consider only worldly interests.'[10] As Ibn Khaldun would soon experience first hand, pragmatic rulers such as Abu ᶜInan may have appeared powerful and may have temporarily held together a loose collection of tribes and loyalties, but true and sustainable power, especially the sort of power necessary to unite an empire, came from a combination of religious legitimacy and ᶜ*asabiyya*. According to Ibn Khaldun, 'dynasties of wide power and large royal authority have their origin in religion based either on prophecy or on truthful propaganda.'[11]

IMPRISONMENT

Abu ᶜInan feared that Ibn Khaldun was supporting a rival. Ibn Khaldun had developed a friendship with Muhammad, the Hafsid prince of Bijaya, an important city in what is now Algeria. Ibn Khaldun knew Muhammad because of his family's close ancestral relationship with the Hafsids. Apparently, however, Ibn Khaldun did not use the proper amount of discretion. His friendship with the prince of Bijaya, a rival of the Marinids, made Abu ᶜInan jealous. He erupted into a 'great fury' and imprisoned Ibn Khaldun before leaving Fez to lead a siege against the Algerian city of Tilimsan.[12] After the exuberant experience of achieving his first major position, Ibn Khaldun now felt the blunt arbitrary hand of political injustice. Determined to get himself out of prison and return home, the young Ibn Khaldun wrote poetry that praised Abu ᶜInan and spoke of his loneliness in prison. He expressed his ardent desire to see the simple things of the world again. He hoped that the following verses might soften the ruler:

> Only the memory of places consoles me
> These witnesses of past nights
> The breath of wind rekindles my desire to see them again . . .[13]

The poem, one hundred lines long according to Ibn Khaldun, had an effect. Abu ᶜInan decided to let him go, but only after his return to Fez. Clearly, Abu ᶜInan knew he needed to watch Ibn Khaldun closely. If he released him before his return, Ibn Khaldun would probably attempt to flee or even support a rival while the sultan was away. Yet only five days after arriving in Fez in November of 1358 Abu ᶜInan, the ruler of the Marinids, the hope of a unified Marinid empire across the Maghrib, grew violently ill and died.

IBN KHALDUN: KINGMAKER AND MINISTER OF THE TRIBES

Ibn Khaldun was not let out of prison until his friend, the minister Al-Hasan ibn ᶜAmar, had taken over the affairs of government as regent to Al-Saᶜid ibn Abu ᶜInan the son of Abu ᶜInan.[14] The regent released him along with a large group of prisoners, as was customary on the death of a ruler. He gave him an expensive robe of honor and a ceremonial jacket and restored Ibn Khaldun to his previous position.

This conferring of robes, clothes, and jackets onto statesmen should not be seen as a simple gift, as it may be seen today. The historian S. D. Goitein described textiles as 'more durable and more expensive than they are nowadays . . . Fantastic prices were paid for single selected pieces . . . Clothing formed part – sometimes a considerable part – of a family's investment . . .'[15] These robes of honor were also of great monetary value. Ibn Khaldun protested, however, that what he wanted at this point was not a new position, but the chance to return to Tunis.[16] Although he claimed disinterest in politics and a desire to simply return home to Tunis, the future intrigues of Ibn Khaldun against his minister and friend, Al-Hasan, proved that he still had great political motivations.

Al-Hasan tried to keep Ibn Khaldun under tight watch. Although he had released him and showered him with honors, he suspected that this astute young

scholar might be dangerous. Suddenly, however, the minister, lacking any significant support for his regency, was deposed by a group of rebellious Banu Marin,
members of the original Marinid tribe. Ibn Khaldun, in fact, admitted to being
intimately involved in this revolt against the hapless, if generous, Al-Hasan who
had freed him from prison just months earlier.

It was years before he began writing the *Muqaddimah*. Nevertheless, Ibn
Khaldun, the political actor, not the scholar, was already implementing key
ideas he would later examine in his great text. As his rallying of the Banu Marin
against the regent minister demonstrated, he knew the importance of maintaining
the *ᶜasabiyya* of those who had brought a dynasty into power. Despite the apparent legitimacy of Al-Saᶜid and his regent's claims to power, without the Banu
Marin their claims were easily disputed. A rival, Sultan Abu Salim, had crossed
over the straits of Gibraltar to claim the Marinid capital as his own. This rival
called upon Ibn Khaldun to aid him in his overthrow of the child-prince. Instead
of refusing out of some sense of loyalty to Al-Hasan, Ibn Khaldun readily
agreed. Ibn Khaldun was well placed for this betrayal as one of his duties was
as secretary to the minister in charge of the Marinid chiefs and Marinid tribes.
Using his special access to the Marinid chiefs, Ibn Khaldun went out and rallied
the chiefs of the Marinids against the child-prince and in favor of Abu Salim: 'I
took the affair into my own hands, went out on my own accord, and met with
the great chiefs of the Banu Marin confederation. I pushed them to favor the
side of Abu Salim.'[17] One can imagine Ibn Khaldun audaciously leaving the city
walls in the dead of night, just as he would leave Damascus to meet Timurlane,
and riding perhaps hundreds of miles to meet with the Marinid chiefs. With his
knowledge of Berber society and vast interest in Berber history, Ibn Khaldun
was able to maintain good relations with the Marinid chiefs, a position that provided him with a great deal of clout: a position as negotiator between rural tribes
and urban rulers, be they Arab or Berber, that he would exploit throughout his
career in the Maghrib.

Although he credited his co-conspirator, Ibn Marzuq, who had been secretly
working for Abu Salim in Fez all along agitating for the overthrow of Al-Hasan,
Ibn Khaldun claimed that it was his work in securing the Banu Marin tribes
that was the most decisive factor leading to the overthrow of the child-prince.
Ibn Marzuq led the revolt from within the city walls and it was he who gained
prestigious positions under Abu Salim, but Ibn Khaldun knew that the real credit
belonged to him: the budding tribal negotiator.

In 1359 Ibn Khaldun entered the city of Fez along with the triumphant entourage of the new sultan, Abu Salim. Abu al-Hasan waited for them at the gates
of the city in submission. In recognition of Ibn Khaldun's services, Abu Salim
made him private secretary in charge of secret correspondence. Predictably,

Ibn Marzuq, who had secured support for Abu Salim within the city walls from merchants, jurists, and courtiers, as opposed to Ibn Khaldun who went out to the tribes to secure support, became jealous of Ibn Khaldun, and his archrival for the attentions of the new sultan they had recently put in power. Although Ibn Khaldun claimed that he buried himself in his work, and 'kept his distance from [Ibn Marzuq]' he really had attempted, but failed, to surpass Ibn Marzuq in his ascent up the ladder of the sultan's favor.[18] Unlike the court and the bazaar that Ibn Marzuq knew so well, the Banu Marin were not immediately close at hand to help Ibn Khaldun, especially once they had their choice of leader in power. In fact, Ibn Khaldun, keen and willing to draw support for his schemes from the fickle *ᶜasabiyya* of nomadic tribes, would consistently underestimate and miscalculate the importance of urban institutions of power.

Ibn Marzuq became especially wary of Ibn Khaldun after the young upstart managed to be named *mazalim*, or appellate judge. Originating with the ᶜAbbasid caliphate, the *mazalim* would hear cases of abuse, bribery, or corruption committed by governmental officials.[19] According to Ibn Khaldun, Ibn Marzuq descended into a furious tirade of envy, not only against him but also against 'other dignitaries at court.' The intrigues of Ibn Marzuq gave Ibn Khaldun a very good excuse to explain the fall of Abu Salim, the man he had helped put in power. 'He [Ibn Marzuq] did not cease to intrigue against me and other dignitaries at court, even unto the day the Sultan lost his power because of him.'[20]

With his connections to the Banu Marin and his skills as a writer and judge, Ibn Khaldun had little to fear from the overthrow of Abu Salim in 1360. His prestige and position only increased when the minister ᶜAmar ibn ᶜAbd Allah revolted against Abu Salim and took power. Ibn Khaldun had been ᶜAmar's dear friend years before: ᶜAmar and Ibn Khaldun formed an intellectual coterie and a group of friends, and likely conspirators, around the exiled amir of Bijaya, Abu ᶜAbd Allah – the same friendship that had caused Abu ᶜInan to grow jealous and throw Ibn Khaldun into prison years before. Nevertheless, ᶜAmar would 'turn against' Ibn Khaldun and give him the 'cold shoulder,' much as Ibn Khaldun had conspired against some of his older friends. It was at this point that Ibn Khaldun, as mentioned previously, decried the follies of youthful trust and hopefulness: 'Ah, how youth brings about excess . . .'[21] Ibn Khaldun asked yet again to be allowed to return to this brother in Tunis, but ᶜAmar refused, afraid Ibn Khaldun might go to work for Abu Hammu II, the despotic Zayyanid ruler of Tilimsan in modern Algeria. Ibn Khaldun wanted, 'at any price' to return. He turned to one of his closest friends, Ibn Masay, who still had ᶜAmar's favor and eventually persuaded ᶜAmar to release Ibn Khaldun on one condition: he would never work for Abu Hammu II.

Although he complained about wanting to go home to Tunis, Ibn Khaldun chose instead to go to Granada, where he justifiably thought that he had solid friends. In the early part of 1362 he sent his wife and children to their uncles in Constantine and set sail for the small, wealthy Nasrid principality of Granada, that remnant of Muslim Al-Andalus so enticingly visible from the North African shore.

THE ALHAMBRA PALACE

Ibn Khaldun was a personal friend of the great Muhammad V (d. 1391), Nasrid amir of Granada, resident of the resplendent Alhambra, the man credited with the restoration of Muslim hopes for Al-Andalus when he was not so powerful.[22] Ibn Khaldun met Muhammad when the prince was a relatively poor and powerless dynast in exile in Fez, dependent on the generosity of the powerful Marinid sultan, Abu ʿInan, for his survival. Before he even set sail for Al-Andalus, Ibn Khaldun already had a foothold there. It was a foothold established both through personal ties to Muhammad, ties that he established as a precocious, young minister, and through ancestral ties to his once illustrious ruling family of Seville before the Christian conquest in the middle of the thirteenth century.

Nevertheless, Ibn Khaldun's attachment to Al-Andalus should not be overemphasized. Some scholars such as Franz Rosenthal have identified Ibn Khaldun's Andalusi heritage as being the most important influence on Ibn Khaldun's identity and character: 'It would seem that not his Arab descent, but his Spanish origin was the crucial factor in his intellectual development and outlook . . .'[23] Rosenthal believed 'his basic loyalty to Spain and its civilization had a much more far-reaching effect on Ibn Khaldun's personality and work than these transient ties [to various North African rulers].'[24] Although Ibn Khaldun certainly had a strong ancestral affiliation with the memory of Al-Andalus, Rosenthal overstated his case. Ibn Khaldun did praise Al-Andalus and did list the detailed accomplishments of his illustrious ancestors in Seville, but it had been more than two centuries since his family had crossed over to North Africa. He had a much more obvious affinity for Tunis, which he called his homeland and place where his ancestors were buried.[25] Ibn Khaldun was no more loyal or attached to Spain and the memory of Al-Andalus than to the North African teachers who had taught him as a child. Nor did he see the division between Spain and North Africa as anything more than a thin geographical barrier. Al-Andalus and North Africa were one, politically and culturally. In fact, North African claims on Islamic Spain were still alive during Ibn Khaldun's tenure at the Marinid court.

The Marinids had a great interest in expanding the amirate of Granada, the last outpost of Muslim rule in Iberia and last hope for a prestigious Muslim resurgence against Christian Spain; a resurgence that would have rallied support for Abu al-Hasan's and Abu ʿInan's project to reunify North Africa.[26] In 1340, in fact, the powerful Abu al-Hasan had allied with Yusuf I, Nasrid amir of Granada, to fight against the Castilians. Although the Muslims won the naval battle, King Alfonso XI defeated the combined Marinid and Nasrid forces on the Rio Salado.[27] Only the plague and civil war prevented the Castilians from taking Gibraltar in 1349. In 1354 Yusuf I, the experienced Nasrid amir of Granada who is often credited with the flourishing of the golden age of Nasrid culture, was murdered in the mosque by a mentally unstable slave. Muhammad V, Ibn Khaldun's friend, was the son and heir of Yusuf I and only 16 years old when he assumed the throne. After only five years, however, Ismail, Muhammad's half brother, along with about a hundred conspirators, climbed the walls of the Alhambra and took the palace. Slipping away, Prince Muhammad narrowly escaped. He eventually fled to Fez, capital of Marinid Morocco. Muhammad would spend years in exile in Morocco under the reign of Abu Salim. This was the same ruler for whom Ibn Khaldun rode out to chiefs of the Banu Marin to secure their support. Ibn Khaldun was introduced to Muhammad by his new chief wazir, Ibn al-Khatib, who had followed his sovereign into exile. Ibn Khaldun seemed to get to know Muhammad quite well: 'I had friendly relations with him and helped serve his interests.'[28] Soon, however, due to alliances established by Ibn al-Khatib, Ibn Khaldun's friend, the situation for Muhammad of Granada would vastly improve.

Before the young Muhammad fled to Fez in 1359 the ambitious Ibn al-Khatib, friend of Ibn Khaldun, was effective ruler and regent of Granada. Ibn al-Khatib initiated reconciliation and even an alliance between Granada and their old enemy, Castile. The fleet of Castile used Nasrid ships. Pedro, known as 'the Cruel' or 'the Just,' according to which side the chronicle was on, the new king of Castile since 1350, adopted a similar attitude of reconciliation with Granada, even using *morisco*, that is, Nasrid styles in the building of his *alcázar*, his palace in Seville. Soon enough, Pedro realized that it would be better to have his ally Muhammad as Nasrid amir and Ibn al-Khatib as the amir's first minister. It was Pedro of Castile who in 1362 pledged support to Muhammad, urging him to return secretly to Granada to overthrow his rivals.[29]

Since the Nasrid amir was embarking on a risky venture, however, he decided to leave his family, his wives, concubines, and children in Fez under the protection of none other than his trusted friend Ibn Khaldun. From the way Ibn Khaldun described it, one could imagine a young man busily tending to their every need, effectively becoming *in loco parentis* of the Nasrid royal house. As Ibn Khaldun breathlessly put it: 'I was [so] occupied with their affairs. I gave their children provisions . . . even provided for their domestic chores.'[30]

Eventually Muhammad, with the help of Pedro the Cruel of Seville, was able to successfully regain his throne. Soon, however, he would need to call upon the young Ibn Khaldun yet again. Muhammad's relations with Pedro of Seville had deteriorated soon after regaining his position. Muhammad had agreed with Pedro that, as a condition for his help, he would cede certain strategic fortresses to the Christians. This caused an uproar among more strident, or opportunistic, Muslims who did not want to agree to such conditions. Ibn Khaldun was called upon to mediate a solution for Muhammad. He claimed to successfully arrange for the city of Ronda to be established as a Muslim base for *jihad*. For these services to Muhammad and his family in Fez, Ibn Khaldun received 'extraordinary gifts' from the Granadine amir.[31] It was thus with an expectation of great welcome that Ibn Khaldun set out for Granada and his ancestral homeland.

After leaving Fez and the intrigues of Abu Salim's minister, Ahmar, Ibn Khaldun made his way to the port city of Ceuta. In Ceuta an independent governor, patron of poetry and science Al-Sharif Abu al-Abbas Ahmad ruled only under the consent of the unusually powerful city council.[32] Al-Sharif of Ceuta outfitted Ibn Khaldun for the journey across the straits and even provided him with a ship. Soon, Ibn Khaldun saw the rock of Gibraltar on the horizon and disembarked, sending a letter to Ibn al-Khatib and the amir of Granada to announce his arrival. Setting out on the road to Granada, the amir's postal service intercepted him and gave him a letter from Ibn al-Khatib, welcoming Ibn Khaldun to the amir's service. It contained the following poem:

> Your coming is like a beneficent rain which, in a dried out land, comes and encourages the bird, the vast countryside and the plains . . .[33]

In flowery prose he continued that if he had 'a choice between the return of youth and your [Ibn Khaldun's] coming' he would choose his coming. Ibn al-Khatib then admits to feeling lonely and longing for the companionship of Ibn Khaldun.

Assured of this welcome from the amir and his chief minister, Ibn Khaldun entered the walls of Granada in December 1362. The amir had reserved one of his guest palaces for the young scholar, bedecked with the finest carpets and equipments. He sent out noble steeds to meet the scholar on his way into the city and gave him an expensive robe of honor. Soon, Ibn Khaldun became Muhammad's companion during his hunting expeditions. He ate with him at the amir's table, and enjoyed all the pleasures and diversions of his company and the magnificent garden palace of Alhambra.

EMBASSY TO PEDRO OF SEVILLE

In 1363, only shortly after his arrival, Muhammad sent his trusted new minister on a vital mission as ambassador to the Christian king and ally, Pedro of

Seville, in order to revive a treaty of peace between himself and Pedro. With Ibn Khaldun he sent a resplendent gift for the king of Castile: a great entourage of fine racehorses 'weighed heavy with tackle made completely of gold.' Ibn Khaldun met Pedro in Seville, where, as he wrote in somber prose: 'I saw with mine own eyes the vestiges of my family.'[34] The king treated Ibn Khaldun generously and with great honors, 'rejoicing in my presence.' He knew that Ibn Khaldun's family had been the *de facto* rulers of the city before the Christian conquest. He introduced Ibn Khaldun to his old friend from the Marinid court of Abu ʿInan, Ibn Zarzar, the Jewish physician and astronomer. Famous throughout the western Mediterranean and aware of the most advanced medical methods of the time, Ibn Zarzar had left the Marinids, and then the Nasrids, to work for Pedro as his personal physician. Doctors at the time, especially doctors who used effective methods, were in great demand. The fact that he was Jewish was irrelevant to rulers hoping to extend their lives and their reigns as long as possible. He had fled to Pedro of Castile after the Marinids tried to force him to return to Fez.[35]

Pedro asked Ibn Khaldun to rest in his new palace, to stay with him for a while and, possibly with the persuasive word of his friend, Ibn Zarzar, agree to stay permanently. Pedro, knowing how valuable this young Muslim scholar, so keenly aware of the inner workings and alliances of North African politics, would be to have at court, gave Ibn Khaldun an extremely generous offer: the return of all of his ancestral lands and goods if he agreed to stay. This was no idle offer, the Banu Khaldun had great holdings in Seville and Ibn Khaldun could have enjoyed a life of great luxury under the generous Christian king. Yet he refused. As Ibn Khaldun must have sensed, the political situation for Pedro, the last king of the 'three religions' was not particularly stable.

Enrique de Trastámara, the rabid critic, half brother and eventual murderer of King Pedro of Castile (r. 1350–69), listed promoting and enriching of Moors and Jews and 'ennobling them' as a most serious grievance against Pedro of Castile.[36] This grievance, with others, justified labeling Pedro with 'the Cruel,' a sobriquet that has stuck to this day, defaming the name of the monarch for posterity. Although most of Enrique's diatribes have since been disproved, Pedro was, at the very least, not openly hostile to Muslims. According to a recent study of Pedro the Cruel, the Muslim community in Seville was generally tolerated during his reign if not necessarily 'ennobled.'[37]

One example of Pedro's interest in Muslim culture was architectural. In 1353 Pedro rebuilt the *alcázar*, the Almohad castle in Seville. Instead of using a triumphalist, obviously Christian style, he used Muslim *mudejar* architects, who laid out lush gardens, groves, fountains, and rooms plastered with geometric arabesques and *muqarnas* that had more in common with the subtle forms of the Alhambra in Muslim Granada than the Romanesque or Gothic Christian architecture of the Christian North. The *mudejars*, from the word meaning 'permitted to remain,' were those Muslims living under Christian rule. It was into this newly built *alcázar*, a monument of *mudejar* art, that Ibn Khaldun entered as an emissary from the amir of Granada. As Ibn Khaldun would have certainly noticed, the architecture in the *alcazar* of Seville and the Alhambra of Granada was almost the same. Even though Pedro was a Christian he appreciated the refinement of Muslim culture. Yet not all rulers were as tolerant as Pedro and Pedro's relatively open nature and tolerant policies towards Jews and Muslims had not always been the norm.

In fact, when the Christians first conquered Seville in 1248 there were no *mudejars*. Nobody was allowed to stay behind.[38] Ferdinand III ordered all Muslims to evacuate the city within a certain number of days. Soon, however, the Castilians realized that they needed Muslims and Jews to cultivate the land and to populate the city's markets and streets. Seville had become something of a ghost town after the expelling of the Moors. Muslims and Jews were invited back into the city and settled in designated religious communities, *morerías* for Muslims and *juderías* for Jews. In the 1260s however, there were major Muslim *mudejar* revolts against their Christian overlords. This led to the expelling, again, of a significant proportion of the Muslim community in Spain. By the 1350s, a decade before Ibn Khaldun's arrival, the number of Muslims had increased since the time of revolts but there were still probably many fewer Muslims than Jews. They were also less visible or prosperous.[39] L. P. Harvey, the scholar of medieval Iberia, claimed that the Castilian *mudejars* deliberately adopted a less visible position, seeking 'survival at the price of accepting a limited role and a secondary status in society.'[40] It was even more remarkable then that Pedro the Cruel offered Ibn Khaldun not only a prominent position in his court but the return of all of Ibn Khaldun's ancestral lands if Ibn Khaldun would agree to work for him. Although we do not know all the reasons why he refused Pedro's astounding offer, the subordinate state of the *mudejar* community in Seville was likely part of what convinced him to politely decline.[41] Ibn Khaldun was by this time astute enough to know how quickly the political tides could change against his favor. Indeed, Pedro would be the last king to proclaim himself the king of the three religions: Christianity, Judaism, and Islam. It was also possible that Ibn Khaldun was simply opposed to working for a Christian ruler out of principle. During his voyage to Jerusalem decades later, Ibn Khaldun refused to enter the Christian church of the Holy Sepulcher: 'I abstained from entering the church . . . I refused to set my feet in that place.'[42] Ibn Khaldun saw himself as a good Muslim, so just as the holiest shrine of the Christians repulsed his otherwise insatiable curiosity, he would have been uncomfortable working under a Christian, if tolerant, king. Despite its present state of Christian domination, Seville would still have reminded Ibn Khaldun of his ancestral roots.

Ibn Khaldun's ancestors had held prominent positions in Seville since the Muslim conquests 550 years earlier when, in Ibn Khaldun's proud statement, 'Khaldun were the first to enter Al-Andalus.'[43] The Banu Khaldun were so well known, in fact, that poetry was written protesting against their powers:

> You overbearing poet whose ancestor is Khaldun:
> You are not satisfied with being vinegar,
> But also want to be mean.[44]

Ibn Khaldun's family had the means to leave when they saw the inevitability of Christian conquest. Many Muslims would have left even if they were not so ordered. Leaving Christian lands to avoid the humiliation of Christian rule was encouraged by prominent Muslim jurists such as Ibn Rushd (Averroes) who said: 'The obligation to emigrate from the lands of unbelief will continue right up to the Day of Judgment.'[45] Perhaps this obligation was in Ibn Khaldun's mind when he refused the king's offer. Although he seemed to promise much, Pedro's offer could have been no more than a generous symbolic gesture that Ibn Khaldun was really meant to decline. Ibn Zarzar, as a Jew, could move and work openly for a Christian king, as could the laborers and craftsmen who made up most of the *mudejars*. The elite minister and scholar, Ibn Khaldun, however, had a palace and riches waiting for him back in Granada where, though his luck would be brief, he was still in favor with the amir and his minister, Ibn al-Khatib. Pedro outfitted Ibn Khaldun with provisions and a sturdy mount, a mule with bridle of gold that he presented as Pedro's gift to the amir.[46]

ALHAMBRA INTRIGUE

Returning from his successful embassy to Pedro, Ibn Khaldun settled into a comfortable routine at the Alhambra. He was named a master of ceremonies for the celebration of the birth of the Prophet Muhammad and for the circumcision of the son of the amir. He wrote long, elaborate poems for both occasions. The amir insisted that Ibn Khaldun send for his family – the admiral of Almería personally escorted them to Al-Andalus. Ibn Khaldun went down to meet his family at the port, anxious to bring them back to his residence where he had proudly prepared everything for them: the garden; the house; and 'all the necessities of daily life.'[47] Ibn Khaldun seemed profoundly content with his life in Granada.

It was not long, however, before whispers of court intrigue became increasingly audible, and swept away this false sense of repose. Again, Ibn Khaldun portrayed the situation as the result of jealousy. Ibn Khaldun claimed that his enemies did not cease to portray him as an upstart, as a threat to Ibn al-Khatib, the chief minister. After all, was not Ibn Khaldun spending almost too much time with the amir, Muhammad V, unduly influencing his policies and decisions with his new ideas and reflections on human society? Should not Ibn al-Khatib, the chief minister, the great and experienced intellectual and scientist, be the chief influence on the amir? Ibn al-Khatib changed his attitude toward Ibn Khaldun, adopting a 'certain reserve.' As he became more and more paranoid, Ibn al-Khatib attempted to gain more and more control over the government.[48] In many respects, Ibn al-Khatib had reason to fear for his safety. He clearly sensed the rivalry of another court poet, the upstart and less aristocratic Ibn Zamrak, who in 1371 would successfully depose him as chief minister and exile him to Marinid Fez.[49] It was the poetry of Ibn Zamrak the new chief minister that was carved into arabesque patterns in stucco to decorate the Court of the Lions, the crown jewel of the new Alhambra palace constructed under Muhammad V.[50]

Ibn Khaldun's experience in the Marinid court had taught him to read the signs of intrigue. After observing little more than the reserved facial expressions of Ibn al-Khatib, he saw his plans for a comfortable life in Granada disintegrate. He knew almost immediately that he must leave Granada as soon as possible. For his own safety and the safety of his family he asked Muhammad V for an authorization to work for Abu ᶜAbd Allah, the ruler of Bijaya in Algeria. Wisely wanting to preserve his friendship, Ibn Khaldun kept quiet about his falling out with Ibn al-Khatib. Muhammad V was reluctant to let Ibn Khaldun go but he eventually gave his consent after Ibn Khaldun provided some skillfully constructed excuse. Ibn al-Khatib graciously provided Ibn Khaldun and his family with a letter of protection for their journey back to North Africa.[51]

BIJAYA CHAMBERLAIN

Abu ᶜAbd Allah of Bijaya had every reason to trust Ibn Khaldun and desire his services. As mentioned previously, Abu ᶜAbd Allah was a Hafsid, an indirect relative of Ibn Khaldun. After all, Ibn Khaldun had been imprisoned by the late Marinid sultan, Abu ᶜInan for his friendship with Abu ᶜAbd Allah. Ibn Khaldun had been accused of conspiring with Abu ᶜAbd Allah to flee back to Bijaya and take back control of the city from Abu ᶜInan. According to their secret pact, Ibn Khaldun was to be his chamberlain. This was an important post, often second only to the sultan or the prime minister. As Ibn Khaldun explained: 'the chamberlain was the sole and unique intermediary between the Sultan and the people.'[52]

After the death of Abu ᶜInan, Abu ᶜAbd Allah was installed as governor of Bijaya by Abu Salim, the Marinid leader in Fez. His cousin, Abu al-ᶜAbbas, was made governor of the Algerian city of Constantine. As governors, these Hafsid relatives, nominally under Marinid authority, ruled their cities independently and with the consent of the urban population. They were eventually able to release themselves from Marinid control completely. Now an independent ruler, Abu ᶜAbd Allah asked Ibn Khaldun if he wished to join him. He had made a pact with Ibn Khaldun to make him chamberlain should he gain power. Embroiled in the intrigues resulting from the weakening hold of Abu Salim's authority in Fez, Ibn Khaldun refused Abu ᶜAbd Allah's offer to become chamberlain in Bijaya. To fulfill his pact to serve his old friend, Ibn Khaldun sent his younger brother Yahya in his stead. Nevertheless, even as Ibn Khaldun worked for the amir of Granada, Abu ᶜAbd Allah would maintain a correspondence with his old conspirator. In 1364 Abu ᶜAbd Allah sent a letter to Ibn Khaldun inviting him to come to Bijaya. Ibn Khaldun received the letter just at the moment when he was becoming aware of the intrigues against him, but it would not be until 1365 that he could obtain all of the permissions necessary to travel safely to the Mediterranean port of Bijaya with his family.

Abu ᶜAbd Allah gave Ibn Khaldun a ceremonial welcome, sending all of the ministers of state on mounts to receive him. People from all parts of the realm came to embrace him and 'touch his garments.' Ibn Khaldun was given the most important robe of honor and asked to give the sermon in the main mosque of the city. After sunset and a long day of attending to the affairs of the state, Ibn Khaldun described how he would retire to the mosque to write and contemplate. Yet despite his strong support in Bijaya, Abu ᶜAbd Allah's claims were constantly contested by his cousin, Abu al-ᶜAbbas, governor of Constantine. Constantine was a slightly inland city built on a dramatic, strategic plateau about 80 kilometers from the Mediterranean coast and more than 100 kilometers from Bijaya. There were constant quarrels between the brothers about the frontiers between their two realms. There were also frequent attempts to steal away important functionaries, such as Ibn Khaldun and tribal chiefs from either side. Ibn Khaldun would play an instrumental role as a representative to, and of, the powerful Dawawida tribe who switched their allegiance between the brothers according to which side paid them the most. Attempting to shore up his position and gain an important ally, Abu ᶜAbd Allah sent his daughter to marry the amir of Tilimsan. He was not aware how much his popular support, his popular ᶜasabiyya, was disintegrating around him. Ibn Khaldun's direct witnessing of the power of the Dawawida and their obvious ability to hold the future of the central Maghrib in their hands had an impact on Ibn Khaldun's description of the various types of tribal ᶜasabiyya. In the *Muqaddimah*, Ibn Khaldun distinguished between 'meek and docile' tribes who submitted to payment of imposts, and proud tribes destined for 'royal authority' that refused to pay any taxes but, instead, demanded monies from rulers. 'When one sees a tribe humiliated by the payment of imposts, one cannot hope that it will ever achieve royal authority.' He even cited sayings of the Prophet Muhammad who said, 'A man who has to pay imposts talks – and lies. He promises – and breaks his promise.'[53] Indeed, later in his journey Ibn Khaldun would actively attempt to engage in such humiliation of tribes, taking hostages from the Berbers of the mountains to raise money to give to the Dawawida.

Abu al-ᶜAbbas, sensing the weakness of his cousin, sent spies throughout the realm of his rival to sow dissent. Eventually, through secret correspondence, he was able to gain the support of the most important councilors and functionaries in the city of Bijaya. They agreed to revolt against Abu ᶜAbd Allah and accept Abu al-ᶜAbbas as their amir. Abu ᶜAbd Allah, Ibn Khaldun's longtime friend and confidant, made desperate flight to the mountains of Lizu where he found refuge. After chasing him through the mountains, Abu al-ᶜAbbas eventually captured and killed his rival.

All of this occurred while Ibn Khaldun was in the citadel. Many loyalists to Abu ᶜAbd Allah pressed Ibn Khaldun to name his successor but he wisely abstained from making any decisions until the return of Abu al-ᶜAbbas. When Abu al-ᶜAbbas returned triumphant to the city with the head of Abu ᶜAbd Allah he restored Ibn Khaldun to his previous position. Quickly, however, Ibn Khaldun found his position yet again under threat from a wave of intrigue as Abu al-ᶜAbbas established his control over the city. After much pleading Ibn Khaldun eventually gained permission to leave the service of Abu al-ᶜAbbas. Having no place to go, he found protection under Yaᶜqub Ibn ᶜAli, an Arab tribal chief. After granting his leave, however, Abu al-ᶜAbbas quickly changed his mind and decided he wanted the services of the wily Ibn Khaldun after all. When Ibn Khaldun refused, he threw Yahya, Ibn Khaldun's younger brother, into prison and confiscated the property, houses and money Ibn Khaldun had left behind in the city. Resigned to his fate, Ibn Khaldun retreated to the protection of friends in the small, oasis Berber city of Biskra a few hundred miles inside what is now the Algerian–Tunisian border.[54]

Meanwhile, Abu Hammu, the powerful Zayyanid amir of Tilimsan west of Bijaya, who had just married the daughter of the lately killed Abu ᶜAbd Allah, used the death of his son-in-law as an excuse to attack Abu al-ᶜAbbas and claim the city of Bijaya as his own. Before leaving Tilimsan and heading to Bijaya, however, Abu Hammu II amassed the support of the powerful tribes of Zughba who lived near Tilimsan. He also gained the support of their women, indicating, perhaps, the importance of women in the tribe.[55] The entire tribe, including the women, would participate and move as an encampment rather than as a mere expeditionary contingent among Abu Hammu II's forces. Surprised by Abu Hammu's bold attack, Abu al-ᶜAbbas had left only few forces in Bijaya. Immediately, Abu al-ᶜAbbas imprisoned all the relatives of Abu Hammu II. He knew that he would need to depend on the surrounding Berber tribes. Abu Hammu, meanwhile, in a move that did not shore up much ᶜ*asabiyya*, threatened the Zughba with imprisonment if they did not successfully capture Bijaya. Abu al-ᶜAbbas sent out a small expeditionary force that was able to secure a strategic plateau. Little by little, like the peeling of an onion, the Zughba were forced to flee. At night Berbers loyal to Abu al-ᶜAbbas streamed down from the surrounding mountains and began to attack. Abu Hammu was left virtually alone with his personal guard and was forced to flee to the coast and sail back to Tilimsan.[56]

Before the battle, Abu Hammu had learned that Abu al-ᶜAbbas had detained Ibn Khaldun's brother, Yahya, and had confiscated all the property and wealth of the Khaldun brothers. In an attempt to gain Ibn Khaldun's support and service, he wrote asking him to join his court and fight for the return of his property. Wisely, however, Ibn Khaldun declined Abu Hammu's offer. According to Ibn Khaldun 'the situation was rather ambiguous.' Obviously, Ibn Khaldun knew that it would be best to wait in Biskra under the protection of its amir, Ahmad ibn Muzni, who had helped Ibn Khaldun in the past. Abu Hammu was most interested in gaining Ibn Khaldun's support in rallying the Arab tribes of the Riyah, which included the most powerful Dawawida clan. Ibn Khaldun had not only negotiated with them but had 'commanded' these tribes and 'they had submitted to my authority.'[57] Obviously, Ibn Khaldun knew how to take advantage of the ᶜ*asabiyya* of this Arab confederation. Pleading for Ibn Khaldun's support, Abu Hammu wrote a personal letter that made Ibn Khaldun seem indispensable, asking him to become the chamberlain of his Sublime Portal, the phrase used to indicate the court of rulers. Abu Hammu even sent a delegation of ministers to plead with Ibn Khaldun for his support. Instead, however, he sent his younger brother, Yahya, who had just been released from prison and had come to Biskra to see his older brother. It was unclear if Yahya wanted to go or if he was simply following the directives of his older brother. Ibn Khaldun himself 'abstained from exposing myself to the perils inherent in this position.' He had 'renounced the mirage of title and rank and had suffered from neglecting my scientific studies for so long. I no longer wished to be involved in the affairs of kings and I put all of my efforts into teaching and studying.'[58]

It was unclear why he did not advise his younger brother Yahya against taking up the inherently risky position. Perhaps he felt that Yahya could benefit from the experience, despite its perils. One could imagine Yahya wanting to follow in the footsteps of his now illustrious brother. After all, he began writing his own history of the Zayyanids just as his brother wrote the history of the Berbers and Arabs of North Africa. He had even experienced political imprisonment, just like his brother. Perhaps even this experience had not made him jaded about political service, or possibly he was especially keen to work for a rival of Abu al-ᶜAbbas. Yahya was murdered in Tilimsan before he could complete his work.

IBN AL-KHATIB AND IBN KHALDUN: A CORRESPONDENCE OF GREAT MINDS

During his stay in Biskra and his retreat from political affairs, Ibn Khaldun received several letters from Ibn al-Khatib, the grand wazir of Granada. The letters were delivered secretly by Granada's ambassadors in Tilimsan, as were Ibn Khaldun's responses. This remarkable, secret correspondence, preserved by Ibn Khaldun, provides a window onto the international exchange and interchange between men of elite position. Even political chaos and upheaval, even the betrayals and political intrigues of the past, did not stop the interactions between these great minds. Ibn Khaldun had fallen out with Ibn al-Khatib and lost his political support when he was working in Granada. Nevertheless, they reached out to each other as scientific colleagues.

Although the letters were intended to be personal in nature, the prose style used by Ibn al-Khatib in his letters was still, to a modern ear, incredibly ornamented and florid. Indeed, it was a style of writing reserved for the highest ministerial class that required years of training and practice as well as artistic talent.[59] Even Ibn Khaldun, with his profound learning, had not completely mastered the form. In his responses to Ibn al-Khatib, Ibn Khaldun humbly admitted to being inferior to his senior colleague in the art of prose and letter writing: 'Responding to Ibn al-Khatib's missives, I could only aspire to respond in [comparatively] stilted prose. I could never equal him in this art [of writing]. Indeed, nobody could measure up to him!'[60]

The content of the letters mainly reflected the political developments in Al-Andalus. They also alluded to the increasingly tenuous political situation for Ibn al-Khatib under Muhammad V as his rival, the less aristocratic, but still remarkably ambitious minister, Ibn Zamrak, pushed him aside. Instead of simply informing Ibn Khaldun of these developments, however, Ibn al-Khatib book-ended the meat of his letter with flattery and treatises on the virtues of friendship. Behind all this flattery and florid prose, however, were indications of his loneliness, his sincere desire to escape his disintegrating political situation and to revive a sincere friendship with Ibn Khaldun: '. . . My desire to see you is more vast than the oceans.' Although Ibn al-Khatib had essentially conspired for Ibn Khaldun's departure from Al-Andalus he proclaimed that his departure led to the 'gnashing of teeth.' He 'sought remedy [for loneliness] by frequenting solitary places . . . [He] found the traces of my sadness in morning visits to abandoned ruins.'[61] He wrote with envy about Ibn Khaldun's protection and refuge in remote Biskra, where Ibn Muzni, the chief of Biskra, provided 'hospitality without parallel.' At times, these letters might strike a modern reader as professions of love. Indeed, he expressed his profound platonic love for Ibn Khaldun and wished for a happy reunion.[62]

In response to these letters Ibn Khaldun wrote: 'My glorious and noble sir, you who are my unique treasure that I wish to keep, you who I venerate and have affection for as if you were my father . . . I greet you like the desert greets the rain, like the appearance of light to a nighttime traveler who had been marching throughout the eve.'[63] Then, rather revealingly, Ibn Khaldun evoked the Sufi saints, as he would when he addressed Timurlane decades later. Clearly, here was another instance indicating Ibn Khaldun's mystical Sufi tendencies. Praising Ibn al-Khatib for some of Granada's recent, but ephemeral military victories he proclaimed, 'It is by the dignified grace of the Saints . . .'[64] After describing the general political situation in the Maghrib, the fall of Bijaya to Abu al-ʿAbbas, the flight of Abu Hammu, he signed off and revealed how he hoped the letter would be delivered. He used the network of pilgrims crossing through the Maghrib on their way back and forth from Mecca to take his messages. He first gave his letter to a man returning from pilgrimage to the west. The pilgrim would give the letter to Ibn Khaldun's brother, Yahya. Yahya would then transmit the letter through Granada's envoys in Tilimsan.[65]

In a final, touching letter, Ibn al-Khatib revealed how illness had struck him in Granada, how his situation had disintegrated with the amir, and how he wished to 'live a life of asceticism and learning' just like Ibn Khaldun's in Biskra. Ultimately, Ibn al-Khatib's fate was far less placid. Escaping Granada and the ire of Muhammad V and his new minister, Ibn Zamrak, Ibn al-Khatib found refuge in the Marinid court of Fez in 1371. In 1374 the great minister, thinker, scientist, and master political hack, but also accused heretic for his rationalist stance on the plague, finally ended up without friends or protection. He was attacked by rivals and murdered.[66] Although he never stated it explicitly, Ibn Khaldun likely saw the death of Ibn al-Khatib as a lesson in the importance of humility and obsequiousness. In the *Muqaddimah* he stated:

it should be known that such haughtiness and pride are blameworthy qualities. They result from the assumption (by the individual) that he is perfect, and that people need the scientific or technical skill that he offers. Such an individual, for instance, is a scholar who is deeply versed in his science, or a scribe who writes well, or a poet who makes good poetry. . .He develops a feeling of superiority. . .They belittle all others, because they believe they are better than other people. One of them may even disdain to be obsequious to a ruler and consider such obsequiousness humiliating, abasing, and stupid. . .[67]

Although he did not dare to state it, Ibn Khaldun must have seen the ups and downs of Ibn al-Khatib's life and his gruesome end as yet another example of the dangers of haughtiness and scientific, intellectual pride in an era that valued power and protection over ability, finesse, and reason. Despite his vast accomplishments, his deft expansion of Muslim power in Al-Andalus, his desire to stop the plague through an appeal to human reason, not to God, Ibn al-Khatib was still considered a heretic. Had he been more secretive about his rationalist tendencies, had he, like Ibn Khaldun, deftly couched his arguments with appeals to the saints and openly condemned rational philosophy even as he used it, he may have survived both calumny and murder.[68]

Yet even as he remained safe studying in Biskra, Ibn Khaldun continued to receive requests from Abu Hammu to help rally the Riyah and the Dawawida yet again against his hated rival Abu al-ᶜAbbas. Abu al-ᶜAbbas had released Abu Hammu's hated cousin, Abu Zayyan, who engaged in a long tribal war against Abu Hammu until his eventual capture of Algiers from Abu Zayyan in 1378.[69] In 1370, however, most of the Arab tribes, perhaps remembering Abu Hammu's cruel threat to throw them in prison if they did not capture Bijaya, had allied with Abu Zayyan and, consequently, Abu al-ᶜAbbas. Eventually, after repeated appeals, Abu Hammu was able to secure Ibn Khaldun's help only by demanding the assistance of his protector in Biskra, the amir, Ibn Muzni. Thus, with some reluctance, Ibn Khaldun joined his generous host and protector, Ibn Muzni, and marched down from Biskra to join Abu Hammu's army.

This time, however, Abu Hammu would not have the advantage of a surprise attack as Abu al-ᶜAbbas had already been appraised of the arrival of Abu Hammu's army. Instead, he had already established the support of the Dawawida against Abu Hammu, who eventually had to retreat yet again to Tilimsan. Ibn Khaldun, now pressed into the service of Abu Hammu, continued to attempt to repair the Zayyanid sultan's ties with the Riyah and to turn them against Abu al-ᶜAbbas. Ibn Khaldun personally gained the support of a large number of Arabs; he even led them in prayer on a plain outside Algiers. He recited a poem to the assembled Arab tribes, rallying them to war against Abu Zayyan and Abu al-ᶜAbbas. Ultimately, however, Ibn Khaldun had to admit to his inability to rally the Riyah Arab confederation into a coherent fighting force for Abu Hammu. At least, that was the excuse he used when he asked Abu Hammu for permission to return to Al-Andalus. Ultimately, however, another major turn of events would prevent Ibn Khaldun from returning immediately to Granada.

Even as Abu Hammu, Abu Zayyan, and Abu al-ʿAbbas continued to fight against one another, a more powerful threat was emerging in the mountains near Marrakech. ʿAbd al-ʿAziz, the new and headstrong ruler of the Marinids, was outraged at some of the skirmishes in the borderlands between the Marinid and Zayyanid realms. Aware that Abu Hammu was occupied in Algiers, ʿAbd al-ʿAziz quickly headed toward Tilimsan, the Zayyanid capital. As ʿAbd al-ʿAziz moved his army through the mountain pass of Taza in Morocco, Ibn Khaldun was stuck waiting for a ship in the port of Hunayn (the port city of Tilimsan), just to the northeast of the Marinid's army. Ibn Khaldun seemed desperate to go, he 'felt powerless,' especially after ʿAbd al-ʿAziz learned of his location from an informant.[70] Desperate to secure the services of this famed tribal emissary, and knowing that Ibn Khaldun could rally the Arabs to the Marinid side, ʿAbd al-ʿAziz sent a detachment of troops to Hunayn to force Ibn Khaldun into his service. He and the detachment eventually met the Marinid sultan near Tilimsan. ʿAbd al-ʿAziz immediately reproached Ibn Khaldun for leaving the Marinid court so many years ago. Ibn Khaldun protested that he was forced to flee because of the intrigue of the minister ʿAmar. To verify this account, he called for the testimony one of the old counselors of the sultan, Wanazmar Ibn ʿArif, who had witnessed the intrigues of ʿAmar. The sultan continued to integrate Ibn Khaldun, asking him about his support for the ruler of Bijaya. The sultan kept Ibn Khaldun locked up in prison for the night but released him soon enough, aware of how valuable this experienced minister would be for his court. After his release Ibn Khaldun immediately fled to the shrine of the Sufi saint, Abu Madyan, for refuge. He went there, as he had gone to Biskra, with the object of 'renouncing this world and dedicating myself to scientific study.'[71]

Search for solitude: from the Sufi shrine of Abu Madyan to Qalʾat Ibn Salama

Abu Madyan Shu'ayb was born in 1126 AD in Cantillana, northeast of Seville. Although he was a humble weaver, his independent search for mystical knowledge inspired him to travel thousands of miles to Baghdad. He returned not to Al-Andalus but to Bijaya, Algeria where his knowledge and interpretation of the law made several Almohads rulers envious. Both intrigued and concerned about his popularity, the Almohad ruler summoned him to the capital Marrakech. Abu Madyan died en route (d. 1198), however, at ʿUbbad near Tilimsan. His followers were fairly hard-core Sufis, known for their rigorous practices of abstention from food, including a 'fast of intimate union' based on the model of the Prophet's fast in the cave of Hiraʾ before receiving the Qurʾanic revelations.[72] The pupils of Abu Madyan, including ʿAbd al-Salam bin Mashish and his disciple, Abu al-Hasan al-Shadhili, founded the Shadhiliyya order, considered one of the most important Sufi orders in North Africa.

According to the rituals and way of life established by Abu Madyan, the Sufi should go into seclusion for forty days, drinking only water. He should constantly repeat the phrase 'there is no God but God' without a break. Although Ibn Khaldun did not explicitly mention that he engaged in this ritual, it was almost certain he did participate in some version of the practice. Many aspects of Abu Madyan's practice would have appealed to Ibn Khaldun as, like Ibn Khaldun, the followers of Abu Madyan were not completely withdrawn from society. According to the scholar of medieval Sufism, Vincent Cornell, 'the [Abu Madyan] mystic was a full participant in social life, who used discipline and detachment from the world to maintain a constant vigilance over oneself and one's neighbors.'[73] Indeed, this aspect of Abu Madyan's Sufism may have been what attracted Ibn Khaldun, a man who had certainly been engaged in society during his past, to the shrine. Indeed, during his short time at the shrine, he had only begun to follow their way and was 'resolved to cut myself from the world.'[74]

In addition to spiritual growth, another reason for Ibn Khaldun's choosing the shrine of Abu Madyan may have been refuge: the order could provide some political protection. Abu Madyan's shrine was situated on the border between the Marinid and Zayyanid realms. Control over the shrine and the legitimacy conferred by the head sheikh of the Abu Madyan shrine thus frequently passed from the Marinids to the Zayyanids and back again. Placed in this neutral zone between rival powers, the mosque and tomb complex of Sidi bu Madyan was constructed next to the tomb at Rabitat al-ʿUbbad by the Marinid sultan, Abu al-Hasan, the illustrious grandfather of ʿAbd al-ʿAziz in 1338 as 'one of the finest examples of Hispano-Maghribi architecture in North Africa.'[75] Augustin Berque, the eminent French anthropologist, described the contours of this shrine as: 'Emblazoned with the octagonal star, symbol of the cosmos, repeated five times and ordered into four bands . . .'[76] Sheila Blair, an expert on Islamic architecture, has explained the significance of the inscriptions on the tomb, including inscriptions asking God to assist in triumph and victory. The Marinid sultan thus used the shrine as a conduit for his prayers, as a conduit for military success.[77] Yet even this cosmic shrine, established by the Marinid sultan to ensure his ultimate victory, could not protect Ibn Khaldun from the demands of ʿAbd al-ʿAziz. ʿAbd al-ʿAziz did not abstain from his demands even though he was the successor of Abu al-Hasan, the sultan who had built the shrine where Ibn Khaldun found refuge.

Ibn Khaldun was able to remain at the shrine of Abu Madyan in ʿUbbad only a few months before ʿAbd al-ʿAziz insisted once again on obtaining Ibn

Khaldun's support in rallying the Arab tribes of the Riyah. The sultan personally approached and consoled Ibn Khaldun, asking for his support in a heartfelt way. Ibn Khaldun could do 'nothing but acquiesce' to the sultan's demands,[78] and he changed out of his simple hermit's clothes and back into an illustrious robe of honor. The sultan provided him with a well-appointed mount and, in the year 1371, Ibn Khaldun went out to the tribes, this time in support of yet another patron, the Marinid ʿAbd al-ʿAziz. The situation remained complex, however, and Ibn Khaldun returned to Biskra. In the meantime, Ibn al-Khatib had just landed at Tilimsan where he joined the main forces of ʿAbd al-ʿAziz. The two great ministers were once again working for the same ruler and their correspondence revived. Nevertheless, various disorders, tribal rebellions and disturbances conveniently prevented Ibn Khaldun from traveling to Tilimsan.

Eventually, after making a large monetary payment to the Dawawida, the type of payment likely facilitated by Ibn Khaldun during his many negotiations with the nomadic tribesmen, ʿAbd al-ʿAziz was able to secure the loyalty of these fierce, aristocratic camel herders. He sent a letter to Ibn Khaldun asking him to lead the Dawawida in battle. After besieging him successfully in the mountains, Ibn Khaldun and the Dawawida camel army pursued Abu Zayyan to the mountains of Ghammara. However, Abu Zayyan had escaped, fleeing all the way to the remote Saharan oasis of Ouragla, 200 miles directly south of Biskra.

Meanwhile, in Biskra Ibn Khaldun's wife gave birth to a son named Al-Fadl al-Rida. Ibn al-Khatib congratulated Ibn Khaldun in a letter evoking the honor of the Yemeni 'house of Hadramawt' the Arab ancestors of the Khaldun family.[79] Unfortunately, however, Ibn Khaldun and his family's long stay at Biskra were about to come to an end. Ibn Muzni, Ibn Khaldun's old protector, who had paid so much of his revenue to the Arab tribes of the Riyah, was growing concerned about Ibn Khaldun's extensive influence over the Riyah and Dawawida, an influence that was even greater than that of Ibn Muzni. He sent a letter to Tilimsan condemning Ibn Khaldun. By the time Ibn Khaldun had left Biskra with his family, however, he learned that ʿAbd al-ʿAziz had grown ill and died. Almost immediately, Abu Hammu returned from the Saharan castle where he had been hiding from ʿAbd al-ʿAziz and recaptured Tilimsan from the Marinids. Abu Hammu, on learning about Ibn Khaldun's flight from Biskra, asked the Yaghmur clan to secretly attack the Awlad ʿArif tribe with whom Ibn Khaldun and his family had found refuge.

Around the spring waters of the river Zab, deep in the desert some 200 miles southwest of Biskra, the Yaghmur clan pounced on the unsuspecting caravan. Ibn Khaldun and his family only barely managed to flee into the mountains of Debdou. However, everything, all the possessions they had brought with them, had been pillaged and several riders, including Ibn Khaldun, were forced to eat their horses. As Ibn Khaldun dramatically put it, 'I spent several days in the desert, naked and without shelter.'[80] Eventually he was able to find his way back to the main encampment at Debdou. Throughout these travails, Ibn Khaldun recalled many miraculous 'interventions from God' that protected him. Eventually, Ibn Khaldun and his retinue made it to Fez, only to find the Marinid court divided between different successors and embroiled in a dispute with the amir of Granada, who had taken advantage of these dynastic disputes to take control of Gibraltar, which had been in the possession of the Marinids. Wanting to support his authority, ᶜAbd al-Rahman, a claimant to the Marinid sultanate, made a pact with the Hafsid, Abu al-ᶜAbbas who now claimed authority over Fez. ᶜAbd al-Rahman would move the Marinid court to Marrakech. Ibn Khaldun, however, asked permission to leave North Africa yet again and make his way to Al-Andalus.

From 1374 to 1375, Ibn Khaldun worked for Ibn Zamrak, the old rival of Ibn al-Khatib. During a trip to congratulate Abu al-ᶜAbbas, Ibn Zamrak soon discovered, however, that Ibn Khaldun had attempted to save the life of Ibn al-Khatib without success. He booted Ibn Khaldun off of his ship at the port of Hunayn, leaving him at the mercy of Abu Hammu, the same sultan who had ordered that Ibn Khaldun's caravan be attacked. Once again, Ibn Khaldun sought the protection of the Sufis at Abu Madyan. Abu Hammu pressured Ibn Khaldun to join him and secure the support of the Dawawida. Pretending to follow his orders, Ibn Khaldun instead furtively left his escort behind and quickly retreated with his family to the mountain of Guzul and the Qalᵓat ibn Salama under the protection of the Awlad ᶜArif, the same tribe who had so graciously helped him survive the attacks of Abu Hammu. They welcomed Ibn Khaldun 'with open arms' and even arranged several good excuses for Ibn Khaldun's family to be released from the clutches of Abu Hammu at Tilimsan. Ibn Khaldun and his family were finally safe under the protection of the fiercely independent Awlad ᶜArif. Ibn Khaldun would remain at the Qalᵓat Ibn Salama[81] for some four years. It was in this year, 1375, that he started his first draft of the *Muqaddimah*. Fortunately for Ibn Khaldun no major events distracted from his writing during this most productive sabbatical. Only a 'torrent of words and ideas' were produced.[82]

RETURN TO TUNIS

Ibn Khaldun's retreat from politics was coming to an end. He completed a first draft of the *Muqaddimah* in the Qalᵓat Ibn Salama in November 1377. Soon, however, he came down with a fever. He had written with almost no books or references, only his memory. In fact, the highly generalized and philosophical nature of the *Muqaddimah* betrayed a free form of thinking. Sweeping ideas about the cycles of history and the power of tribal lineage did not come out of the cold mud brick of the Qalʿat. They had been germinating in Ibn Khaldun's mind during his studies with the great intellectual masters and mixed with intimate and vivid experience both at court and in the remotest corners of North Africa. It was these experiences, in addition to this scholarship and learning, that allowed him to consider the problems of the creation of dynasties, the stages through which they change, and the various ways in which a dynasty, or a state, declines.[83]

He would have remained longer in the remote fortress had he not fallen ill, with a fever consuming him. The exact nature of his sudden illness was unclear but considering that he was 'only saved by divine favor,' it may have been as serious as the plague.[84] He certainly did not willingly leave his retreat from the hustle and bustle of political intrigue in the cities, but out of medical necessity and the need to research his finds. It was clear that the 'most magnificent and solid castle' of Abu Bakr, the chief of the ʿArif tribe who hosted him, appealed to Ibn Khaldun. The silence of the countryside, and the lifestyle of the nomadic ʿArif, inspired him. Several years in this hermitage were sufficient to detoxify years of political disappointment and callousness. There was a sense from his words that the act of writing itself calmed him: writing came from his 'spirit.'[85] Writing and categorizing history was one act that seemed free from the active, personal complexities, compromises, and relationships required of a wazir. Again, the contrast with Ibn Khaldun's Sufi father was striking. Whereas his father used solitude and retreat to approach a closer union with God, Ibn Khaldun used solitude in the service of ambition – an ambition not only to practice power in this world but also to understand it.

Sickness was not the only reason Ibn Khaldun came down from mountainous and remote Qalʿat Ibn Salama. He had left Tunis, his older brother Muhammad, his ancestral home, and his 'boring' job as a calligrapher decades ago. He seemed relieved to return to Tunis, 'Fatherland of my fathers, where they built their houses, where the traces of their tombs still remain.'[86] The scholar of the medieval Mediterranean S. D. Goitein pointed out that this sense of belonging, of loyalty to a 'homeland' was quite common in the medieval Mediterranean: 'Yearning after one's home' was a well-known theme of ancient Arabic poetry. The traveler Ibn Jubayr noted how Muslims returned to their homeland city of Tyre even after Christian crusaders had captured the city.[87]

It was only natural for Ibn Khaldun to feel this sense of yearning for his homeland. He had left in search of adventure and challenge and had found it all, all too easily. He rose to the heights of power, even as he was torn down, exiled, banished, imprisoned, and threatened with death, by envy, disease, political intrigue inflicted because of malice and also, perhaps, due to his own stubbornness and pride. Although there was still a great deal of adventure and travel ahead of him; there was a clear sense in his autobiography that on his return to Tunis he felt done, finished with the itinerant life and perils of a traveler. He put it most vividly saying: 'I had thrown away my walking stick, my traveler's staff [for good]!'[88]

After so many close encounters with death and danger both to himself and to his family while in political service, Ibn Khaldun seemed to experience a sense of profound disillusionment with his own initial ambitions in life. In some respects, it was this midlife disillusionment that must, at least partially, be blamed for the creative brilliance of the *Muqaddimah*, but it was a disillusionment that would be quickly snuffed by the demands of political service. Moreover, in the period that Ibn Khaldun had been in his retreat, Abu al-ᶜAbbas had consolidated his power as pre-eminent ruler in the Maghrib, allowing for a modicum of political stability and predictability. In fact, Abu al-ᶜAbbas was finally able to restore control over the tribes of the hinterland not by buying their tribal ᶜasabiyya as Ibn Khaldun might have suggested, but by encouraging the urban populations to rebel against the domination of the tribes and join him in the establishment of a more truly centralized power.[89]

Ibn Khaldun entered Tunis in the late autumn of 1378 and quickly enough became an official and functionary, caught up again in the very webs of deceit and jealousy that had inspired him to retreat into the Qalᵓat ibn Salama. The now immensely powerful Hafsid caliph, Abu al-ᶜAbbas, the very same man who had taken Ibn Khaldun's family's wealth and properties in Bijaya and imprisoned his brother only years before, immediately give Ibn Khaldun a pension, a new residence, and designated pasturage outside the city for his 'animals to forage.' Ibn Khaldun and men of his class were not simply dependent on the caliph's salary or monetary compensation spent while living in the city. Animals and land provided a consistent wealth and security, a sustainable pension that money alone could not necessary afford. Yet just as the sultan could provide an entire livelihood, he could also take it away at a whim, making Ibn Khaldun and others in his position almost completely dependent on the sultan's largess. He could not take the ruler's pension or land with him.

For those envious of his learning and his easy access to the powerful, Ibn Khaldun seemed impossible to like. At the same time, there is the impression that Ibn Khaldun was a somewhat intractable character; he seemed unwilling to soothe his colleagues with flattery and white lies about their intellectual abilities, even if such flattery could potentially go far. Perhaps his colleagues saw Ibn Khaldun as someone who was almost too smart, and too aware of his intelligence. This was especially true when he arrived in a new sultan's court, literally out of the wilderness, often escorted between cities by groups of powerful Arab tribes whom he had befriended, and automatically demoted many of the caliph's advisors when he assumed what he called the 'closest position' to the caliph. Almost immediately after returning to the court of Abu al-ᶜAbbas in Tunis, Ibn Khaldun was accused by the sultan's jealous courtiers of not being sufficiently loyal to him, for not writing the typical panegyric praise poetry that was the often sickeningly rich, if occasionally eloquent tradition of Muslim courts as far back as the earliest caliphs. As Susan Stetkevych, expert in the history of Arabic poetry, has explained, panegyric poetry formed a myth of legitimate Islamic rule, tying leaders in the present with the great rulers of Islamic and Arab tradition.[90] There was also, however, a clear element of pure flattery. At least according to his own version of events Ibn Khaldun was initially too proud to kow-tow, but he was now put on the spot.

With these panegyric poems, both power and the corruption of power were expressed in excess. They were also, however, emblematic of Ibn Khaldun's realization that he did, in fact, need to please the ruler, a man who was often his own defense against a largely hostile court. Although Ibn Khaldun often professed a lack of ability in poetry and prose, he was proud enough to include several of them in his autobiography. A few lines will suffice to express the formulaic niceties of this poetic style. He begins the panegyric with the customary evocation of the sultan's hospitality to strangers – hospitality had been considered to be the highest duty of a man of honor since pre-Islamic times:

> Would the stranger hope to knock on any other door than yours
> and have it opened?
> Your great ambition sharpens your willpower
> Just as the sharpener of swords polishes the length of the blade
> You are the matrix of the world, the place where desires are realized
> You are abundant rain . . .

After placing Abu al-ᶜAbbas at the center of an imagined cosmic scheme, he then goes on to the specific bases of Hafsid legitimacy, praising the 'partisans of the Mahdi' Ibn Tumart, the founder of the Almohad doctrine that the Hafsids still professed.

Although Ibn Khaldun's panegyric was written in the same style as panegyrics used in classical Arabic poetry, the source of legitimacy had changed. Instead of relying only on classic references to the original Arab foundations of Islam, Ibn Khaldun described the doctrine of Mahdi and the Berber Almohads as the 'edifice of piety' on which the Hafsid ruler established himself. He evoked both Abu Hafs, the Berber founder of the Hafsid dynasty, and the great Arab caliph, ᶜUmar ibn al-Khattab, and thus equated them.[91] As a source of legitimacy, Almohad doctrine was just as important as the original Islamic doctrine of Muhammad the Prophet and the first caliphs. Ibn Khaldun's praise for the Almohads may at first seem odd considering his training as a Maliki judge; the Maliki school of law being the preferred school of the enemies of the Almohads. By this time, however, many aspects of Almohad doctrine, expect perhaps the doctrine of the Mahdi, had been adapted into a Maliki framework. Ibn Khaldun then implies that Abu al-ᶜAbbas was the only true Caliph, the predominant ruler of the western Mediterranean world. He rhetorically implores the listener to 'Ask Tilimsan and the Zanata tribe and the Marinid tribe . . . Ask Al-Andalus and the cities of their kings . . . Ask even Marrakech . . .' He then described Abu al-ᶜAbbas as a column of stability in a chaotic time: 'You have come in a difficult time, an austere and turbulent time . . . People turn toward you.'[92] He then turns from the figure of the caliph to the sources of his power: the tribes.

In a long passage that subtly reinforced his own position, his own theory of the importance of tribal solidarity, he evoked those powerful tribes who gave Abu al-ᶜAbbas obedience and loyalty. These tribes were the specific sources of group feeling, of ᶜ*asabiyya* available to the caliph: 'The Salwa available with their great force . . . the Duwayb and the Maᵓqil who organize attacks.' He described, in vivid detail, those important tribes and allies who followed the caliph's commands. It was as if Ibn Khaldun was demonstrating, in poetic form, the power and importance of tribal support, the type of tribal support he could confer not only as an expert but also as an ambassador and emissary to the tribes:

> Amazing men, always in motion . . .
> Demigods, they have nothing but the desert mirage for drinking,
> And for their subsistence, a lance that they manipulate skillfully . . .
> But you have given them your favors,
> Thus they have given in to your power.[93]

In these last two lines, a reciprocal relationship, give and take, not a relationship of absolute authority, was clearly admitted. Thus, even in a panegyric poem allegedly written to enforce the power of the caliph, Abu al-ᶜAbbas was portrayed as submitting deals with the tribes, deals that were often conveniently brokered by Ibn Khaldun. Even in a panegyric universe, the caliph could not demand the complete and unconditional submission of the tribes. The implication was obvious: Ibn Khaldun the tribal diplomat was needed as a bridge between the tribes and the caliph. In fact, Ibn Khaldun's unique political position and abilities vis-à-vis the tribes and the caliph may help to contextualize, if not explain, the *Muqaddimah* as a political text, not simply a historiographical one.

While the Berbers were pre-eminent in the Atlas Mountains of Morocco and the highlands of Algeria, the most powerful tribes in the Tunisian countryside, the 'demigod' tribes Ibn Khaldun referred to in his poetry that could determine the fate and ambitions of caliphs, were Arab descendants of the Banu Hilal migrations. Most of the Maghrib was Berber before the Banu Hilal, a large confederation of Bedouin, Arab tribes migrated into North Africa in the tenth and eleventh centuries.[94] Of the Banu Hilal, the Riyah were a major branch who occupied the central Maghrib, and of the Riyah were the Dawawida, the most powerful of the Riyah and the largest section of the Arab tribes with whom Ibn Khaldun could negotiate.[95] Ibn Khaldun explained the essential importance of the Dawawida in his autobiography. They favored war and conflict between the sultan Abu al-ᶜAbbas and his brother, ᶜAbd Allah, because this conflict increased their profits as each side attempted to purchase the loyalty, or at least neutrality, of the Dawawida: 'The fire of their [the brothers'] rivalry was stoked by the Dawawida . . . who sought to favor war, source of their profits. Every year the two sovereigns would gather their troops and prepare for war.' As noted earlier, it was not until 1365, after years of warfare that brought large payments into the coffers of the Dawawida, that ᶜAbd Allah was finally defeated. Ibn Khaldun noted that he was the personal intermediary between ᶜAbd Allah and the Dawawida, bringing them 'massive amounts of money' from ᶜAbd Allah. According to Ibn Khaldun, 'not even a penny was left in his coffers.' In search of money for ᶜAbd Allah Ibn Khaldun led an expedition into the mountainous Berber regions of Kabylie in search of unpaid revenue. He even took Berbers hostage until their taxes were paid. Ibn Khaldun noted that a considerable amount of revenue was extracted using this method. Yet even this Berber money did not buy enough protection from the Dawawida: ᶜAbd Allah was still defeated by his cousin Abu al-ᶜAbbas.[96] When ᶜAbd Allah lost power Ibn Khaldun found refuge among the Dawawida and the Arabs.[97] Ibn Khaldun was sent to negotiate with the Dawawida by his next employer, the Zayyanid ruler, Abu Hammu, in Algeria.[98] The Marinid ruler of Fez, ᶜAbd al-ᶜAziz, who had captured Ibn Khaldun and forced him into his service, similarly sent Ibn Khaldun on a mission to secure the loyalty of the Dawawida.[99] Clearly, Ibn Khaldun was valued by these rulers not simply for his mastery of Islamic law, but for his connections and ties to the Arabs, particularly this most powerful of Arab clans: the Dawawida. Ibn Khaldun's relationship with the Dawawida was mutually beneficial. While the Dawawida could count on Ibn Khaldun to secure payment from various sultans, Ibn Khaldun could count on the Dawawida when he needed safe land passage between cities and when he felt the tide turn against his employers. It was little wonder that Ibn Khaldun spoke in the *Muqaddimah* of the Bedouin people as more inclined toward virtue, and as sources of new civilizations and dynasties, even as they were capable of destroying that civilization. Ibn Khaldun made no mention in his panegyric, however, of the need for Abu al-ᶜAbbas to gain the support of the

urban population against restless tribal demands for tribute. Although politics
should not be seen as the primary inspiration for Ibn Khaldun's writing, this
anti-centralized theory of human society and the idea that all attempts at settled
society were ultimately futile in the face of tribal invasion and power, greatly
supported, in many respects, his own political position in the Maghrib. The more
powerfully he portrayed the Bedouin and the rural tribes in the *Muqaddimah*, a
text specifically dedicated to Abu al-ᶜAbbas, the more powerful his position as
negotiator between tribe and city would seem.

Considering his ties with the fickle Dawawida, Ibn Khaldun's envious rivals
at the Hafsid court had a point in questioning his loyalty and true ambitions.
After all, Ibn Khaldun was a fickle minister; he worked for Abu ᶜAbd Allah, the
old rival of Abu al-ᶜAbbas, as well as for the Marinids and the Zayyanids, historically bitter enemies of the Hafsids. There may have been sufficient reason to
wonder, as well, whether Ibn Khaldun really was working for Abu al-ᶜAbbas or
whether he would defect or simply change his loyalties, especially considering
his powerful position as an effective negotiator with the Arabs. He had defected,
when times were rough, to the Arab and Berber tribal chiefs who protected him
during his journeys. Although he wrote about his employment by sultans, Ibn
Khaldun made clear throughout the autobiography, and more directly in his
Muqaddimah, that tribes such as the Dawawida held the keys to true power in the
countryside, even if it was the Dawawida who constantly pestered the sultan and
had abrogated any concerted attempt to unify the fractured lands of the Maghrib.
They prevented effective tax collection or stable, long-term, centralized control
by the Berber, Hafsid caliph.[100] Concerned with the still-tenuous foundations of
their sovereign's reign, it was little wonder that several suspected Ibn Khaldun
of disloyalty.

JEALOUSY

Muhammad ibn ᶜArafa, the imam of the great mosque of Tunis, one of the most
important religious positions in the realm, was Ibn Khaldun's most strident
and envious enemy. Like Ibn Khaldun, Muhammad ibn ᶜArafa had grown up
in Tunis. He had attended the same lessons as Ibn Khaldun and had the same
masters at the small Qurʾan school or *kuttab*.[101] But Muhammad ibn ᶜArafa
seemed, to put it charitably, both intellectually and politically less adventureous
than Ibn Khaldun. From Muhammad's perspective, he had remained in Tunis,
loyal to the Hafsids, even as Ibn Khaldun traipsed around the Mediterranean in
the service of a range of courts, rulers, and tribes. Of course, Ibn Khaldun did not
acknowledge this perspective.

Rather, according to a snide passage in his autobiography, Ibn Khaldun explained Muhammad's jealousy and rancor as simply the result of so many of their mutual teachers' identification of Ibn Khaldun as intellectually superior to him, 'even though he [Muhammad] was much older . . .'[102] Ibn Khaldun described how this childish jealousy had 'encrusted around his heart.' Furthermore, in a hazardous situation for untenured academics of any age, Ibn Khaldun had become too popular among the students of Tunis. Muhammad ibn ᶜArafa's suspicious jealousy only increased when he saw most of his once-loyal students listening intently to the opinions of the well-traveled Ibn Khaldun. Although he could not turn the students against Ibn Khaldun, Muhammad ibn ᶜArafa did, however, manage to convince the court of Abu al-ᶜAbbas to suspect Ibn Khaldun's intentions. In this respect, Muhammad ibn ᶜArafa may deserve some indirect credit for the publication of the *Muqaddimah*, for it was because of Muhammad ibn ᶜArafa's accusations that Ibn Khaldun decided to dedicate his *Muqaddimah* to Abu al-ᶜAbbas. He hoped the *Muqaddimah* would finally prove his value at court.[103]

In the end neither the dedication of the *Muqaddimah*, nor the panegyric poetry, nor Ibn Khaldun's ties with the powerful Arab tribes could protect him from the calumnies spread by Muhammad ibn ᶜArafa and his associates. Sensing the sword of intrigue falling closer to his neck, Ibn Khaldun decided to develop a plan to flee the court of 'Abu al-ᶜAbbas. He went to the caliph not to ask for permission to leave his position but to go on the pilgrimage, although his intention was, of course, to leave permanently. Abu al-ᶜAbbas probably sensed this when he forced Ibn Khaldun to leave his family back home in Tunis as unofficial hostages who would assure his return. As Ibn Khaldun himself admitted in the *Muqaddimah*, the excuse of pilgrimage to Mecca, or the *hajj*, one of the five pillars of Islam, and a religious necessity for every well-to-do or prominent Muslim, had been used as a means of escape from what he called the 'slavery' of service for centuries: '[R]ulers consider their people and entourage and, indeed, all their subjects as slaves familiar to their thoughts and sentiments. Therefore, they are not disposed to loosen the bonds of servitude binding the person.'[104]

In fact, the practice of using the pilgrimage to escape the virtual 'enslavement' of governmental service and to defect to a more powerful rival court was so common and such a problem that, in extraordinary circumstances, pilgrimage was completely prohibited. A pilgrimage prohibition occurred under the powerful Umayyad dynasty of Cordoba, for example, to prevent ministers from defecting to the more wealthy and powerful ᶜAbbasid court in Baghdad.[105] A similar fear of ministerial brain drain existed in Hafsid Tunis. The most wealthy and powerful dynasty in the fourteenth century was the Mamluks. With their superior system of military organization and their lack of dependence on mercenaries or tribes, the Mamluks had become the dominant power in the Middle East. Abu al-ᶜAbbas had every reason to believe that Ibn Khaldun would defect to the powerful Mamluk ruler of Egypt, Al-Zahir Barquq. Indeed, his fears turned out to be justified. Yet, as Ibn Khaldun put it, even when a ruler was kind enough to loosen the chains of service, the property of their ministers was another matter: 'their kindness would not extend to leaving [the minister's] property alone. They consider it part of their own wealth.'[106] Leaving one court for another was invariably a risky financial proposition and every time Ibn Khaldun left he had to turn over his wealth to the ruler and risk his property being turned over to his successor. Also, even if the minister did get away with his property and moved elsewhere, the new ruler often seized it. Even rulers themselves were subject to deprivations when they traveled or left their realms. Ibn Khaldun provided the example of the Hafsid caliph Abu Yahya Zakariya bin Ahmad al-Lihyani (r. 1311–17) who had grown tired of ruling his realm. He was also concerned about Marinid incursions and invasions from the west, and decided to defect to Egypt. He pretended to go to Tripoli on an official visit, but instead embarked for Alexandria, Egypt. He sold all the treasures of the Hafsid court, jewelry, and furniture and, as Ibn Khaldun noted with some dismay, invaluable books. Quickly after taking up residence in Alexandria, however, his wealth was seized by the Mamluk ruler, Al-Malik al-Nasir.[107]

Power and money were variable and fickle in the fourteenth century. Wealth could not be secured and pensions in any modern sense were worthless. Even royal heritage was no protection. Ibn Khaldun had been shrewd enough, however, to avoid being cleaned out. He had convinced the Hafsid ruler that he was only going on a temporary pilgrimage only; he would thus have still had some money from his service to Abu al-ᶜAbbas. Even so, when he entered a new court in a new land Ibn Khaldun had to rely primarily on his reputation, his pluck, and his intelligence. It was with these invaluable talents that Ibn Khaldun would enter the port of Alexandria in 1383.

NOTES

1 *Al-Taᶜrif*, 55; *Autobiographie*, 83.
2 *Al-Taᶜrif*, 55; *Autobiographie*, 83.
3 For the role of Sufi saints and rural religious figures in arbitrating conflicts see Ernest Gellner, *Muslim Society* (Cambridge, 1983). Written to explain the remarkable success of Islam over communism in the 1980s, Gellner's account, however, must be used with caution. He tends to overemphasize the divisions between rural 'folk' traditions and the intellectual traditions of the urban literary class. Clearly, as this and innumerable other encounters between figures such as Ibn Khaldun, an elite urban scholar, and the charismatic rural religious figures demonstrate, this urban-rural division was often quite illusory. The rural tradition was often also deeply intellectual and even 'literary,' just

less studied and known by scholars. In *Realm of the Saint* (Austin: TX, 1998), 123–54, Vincent Cornell made a convincing argument about the powerful influence of rural Sufi sheikhs in the Marinid period.

4 *Al-Ta{}^crif*, 58; *Autobiographie*, 85.

5 *Al-Ta{}^crif*, 58; *Autobiographie*, 85.

6 On the layout of the Bou ^cInaniyaa which still stands today in the old city of Fez with much of its original splendor see Robert Hillenbrand, *Islamic Architecture* (New York, 1994) 240–51.

7 *Muqaddimah*, vol. I, 58–9.

8 *Muqaddimah*, vol. II, 3.

9 See Mohamed Bencheroun, *La Vie intellectuelle marocaine sous les Mérinides et les Wattasides* (Rabat, 1974), 262–3. Passages translated and quoted in Vincent Cornell, *Realm of the Saint*, 143.

10 *Muqaddimah*, vol. I, 387.

11 *Muqaddimah*, vol. I, 319.

12 *Autobiographie*, 91. For a description of the incident along with Ibn Khaldun's entire poem from prison see *Al-Ta{}^crif*, 66–8.

13 Ibn Khaldun did not remember all of the lines of his poem. *Autobiographie*, 91–2. *Al-Ta{}^crif*, 67.

14 Not only was Ibn Khaldun released but all those Abu ^cInan had held in Fez during his attempted conquest of North Africa, including the elite of Constantine and Bijaya. As Ibn Khaldun described the release of Abu al-^cAbbas, the future patron of the *Muqaddimah* in Tunis, 'When he was released from prison in Ceuta our master [Abu al-^cAbbas] left untarnished *as a piece of gold*' (emphasis added). *Histoire des Berbères*, IV, 326.

15 Solomon Goitein, *A Mediterranean Society: The Jewish Communities of the Arab World as Portrayaed in the Documents of the Cairo Geniza*, vol. I (Berkeley, CA, 1967), 101.

16 'I sought permission to leave for my home country . . .' *Al-Ta{}^crif*, 28; *Autobiographie*, 92.

17 *Al-Ta{}^crif*, 28, *Autobiographie*, 93.

18 *Al-Ta{}^crif*, 77; *Autobiographie*, 94.

19 See *Autobiographie*, 94, note 3.

20 See *Autobiographie*, 94, note 3. For a more complete history of the decline of Abu Salim and his battles against Abu Hammu of Tilimsan see *Histoire des Berbères*, III, 442–3.

21 *Al-Ta{}^crif*, 77; *Autobiographie*, 95.

22 For the life of Muhammad V see L. P. Harvey, *Islamic Spain, 1250–1500*, (Chicago, IL, 1992), 206–19.

23 Introduction, *Muqaddimah*, vol. I, xxxiv.

24 Introduction, *Muqaddimah*, vol. I, xxxvi.

25 *Al-Ta{}^crif*, 230; *Autobiographie*, 153.

26 For the history of the Marinid intervention in Al-Andalus see A. Huici Miranda, *Las Grandes Batallas de la Reconquista durante las Invasiones Almoravides, Almohades, y Benimerines* (Madrid, 1956), 329–87.

27 Hugh Kennedy, *Muslim Spain and Portugal* (New York, 1996), 288.

28 *Al-Ta{}^crif*, 77; *Autobiographie*, 95.

29 He also depended on Muslim support and had the backing of the powerful Berber sheikh ^cUthman bin Yahya Rahhu, Kennedy, *Muslim Spain and Portugal*, 290.

30 *Al-Ta{}^crif*, 79; *Autobiographie*, 96.

31 *Al-Ta^crif*, 79; *Autobiographie*, 96.

32 *Al-Ta^crif*, 80; *Autobiographie*, 97. The existence of this magisterial council at Ceuta seemed to indicate another exception to what was once the conventional wisdom of scholars of the pre-modern Islamic city, that 'Islamic cities, did not and could not claim formal recognition as autonomous units of the still larger *umma*, or community of Islam . . . There were no urban republics as in northern Italy.' S. D. Goitein, *A Mediterranean Society: An Abridgement in One Volume* Jacob Lassner (ed.), (Berkeley and Los Angeles, CA, 1999), 40. See also Xavier de Planhol, 'Geographical setting,' in *The Cambridge History of Islam*, 2 vols., Peter M. Holt *et al.*(eds.) (Cambridge, 1970), vol. 2, 456–68.

33 For the entire poem see *Al-Ta^crif*, 82; *Autobiographie*, 98.

34 For Ibn Khaldun's too brief description of his embassy to Pedro see *Al-Ta^crif*, 84–5; *Autobiographie*, 99. There have been some studies of this embassy to Pedro the Cruel, see Sánchez-Albornoz and Claudio Meduiña, 'Ben Jaldun ante Pedro el Cruel,' in *La España musulmana según los autores islamitas y cristianos medievales* (Buenos Aires, 1946), vol. II, 422–3.

35 A. Cheddadi, 'À propos d'une ambassade d'Ibn Khaldun auprès de Pierre le Cruel,' *Hespéris-Tamuda*, 1982–3, 15.

36 Luciano Serrano, *Cartulario del Infantado de Covarrubias* (Madrid, 1907), 217–19.

37 'The *morerías* or Muslim communities, unlike the seemingly parallel *juderías*, escaped major physical and ideological assault during Pedro's reign.' Clara Estow, *Pedro the Cruel of Castille: 1350–1369* (New York, 1995), 175.

38 'The Castilian conquerors of Seville in 1248 expelled every Muslim from the city in an act of what would later be called ethnic cleansing designed to render it exclusively Christian,' Richard Fletcher, *The Cross and the Crescent* (London, 2003), 112.

39 *Pedro the Cruel*, 177.

40 Harvey, *Islamic Spain: 1250–1500*, 1990, 54.

41 A. Cheddadi, *Hespéris-Tamuda*, vols. 20–1, 1982–3, 5–23.

42 *Al-Ta^crif*, 350; *Autobiographie*, 222.

43 *Al-Ta^crif*, 1; *Autobiographie*, 51.

44 Ibn Kisra al-Malaqi (d. *c.* 1206). *Cf.* Rosenthal, *Muqaddimah*, vol. I, xxxiv.

45 Ibn Rushd, quoted in Harvey, *Islamic Spain: 1250–1500*, 1990, 56.

46 *Al-Ta^crif*, 85; *Autobiographie*, 99.

47 'The Sultan regularly mentioned his satisfaction with my work and provided me with generous favors,' *Al-Ta^crif*, 100; *Autobiographie*, 100.

48 *Al-Ta^crif*, 90; *Autobiographie*, 101.

49 Kennedy, *Islamic Spain and Portugal*, 291.

50 Oleg Grabar, *The Alhambra*, (London, 1978), 144–7.

51 *Al-Ta^crif*, 90–1; *Autobiographie*, 101.

52 *Al-Ta^crif*, 94; *Autobiographie*, 104.

53 *Muqaddimah*, vol. 1, 289–90.

54 *Al-Ta^crif*, 99; *Autobiographie*, 106. For Ibn Khaldun's views on the rulers of Biskra see M. Brett, 'Ibn Khaldun and a dynastic approach to local history: the case of Biskra,' in *al-Qantara*, 12, 1991, 157–70.

55 *Al-Ta^crif*, 101; *Autobiographie*, 107.

56 Ibn Khaldun provided a much more detailed history of Abu Hammu II and his plans to expand the Zayyanid realm in the Kitab al-^cIbar. See *Histoire des Berbères*, vol. II, 436–95.

57 *Al-Ta^{c}rif*, 102; *Autobiographie*, 108.

58 *Al-Ta^{c}rif*, 103; *Autobiographie*, 110.

59 On the necessity of advanced poetry and prose for royal secretaries and ministers see Ibn Khaldun, *Muqaddimah*, vol. II, 30 and vol. III, 341.

60 *Al-Ta^{c}rif*, 123; *Autobiographie*, 117.

61 *Autobiographie*, 111. See Ibn al-Khatib's entire letters and poems *Al-Ta^{c}rif*, 103–15.

62 *Autobiographie*, 112

63 *Autobiographie*, 118. See Ibn Khaldun's complete and poetic response in *Al-Ta^{c}rif*, 123–8.

64 *Autobiographie*, 118.

65 *Al-Ta^{c}rif*, 128; *Autobiographie*, 121.

66 See Kennedy, *Islamic Spain and Portugal*, 291. See also Justin Stearns, 'Contagion in theology and law: ethical considerations in the writings of two 14th century scholars of Nasrid Granada,' *Islamic Law and Society*, 1(14), 2007, 110. For more detailed biographical information on Ibn al-Khatib see Emilio M. Lopéz, *Ibn al-Jatib* (Granada, 2001).

67 *Muqaddimah*, vol. II, 331–2.

68 Ibn al-Khatib did not, by any means, reject Sufism. He wrote a book on Sufi notions of holy love: *al-Rawdhat Ta^{c}rif bi al-Hubb al-Sharif*. Aziz al-Azmeh mentioned that 'Direct borrowing by Ibn Khaldun in his book of mysticism from Ibn al-Khatib's [book] is extensive and very clear.' *Ibn Khaldun: An Essay in Reinterpretation* (Budapest, 2003), 6, note 8.

69 Abun-Nasr, *A History of the Maghrib in the Islamic Period*, 141. Abu Hammu would eventually be forced to abdicate and escape ignominiously in a Catalan ship after a court rebellion instigated by his son in 1387.

70 *Al-Ta^{c}rif*, 134; *Autobiographie*, 126.

71 'I headed for the monastery [*ribat*] of the sheikh and saint [*wali*] Abu Madyan with the object of renouncing the world and dedicating myself to knowledge . . .,' *Al-Ta^{c}rif*, 134; *Autobiographie*, 126.

72 An enlightening account of Abu Madyan and his followers is found in Cornell, *Realm of the Saint*, 131–8. Also see the works of Abu Madyan, *The Way of Abu Madyan: Doctrinal and Poetic Works of Abu Madyan Shu'ayb ibn al-Husayn al-Ansari*, trans. and ed. Vincent Cornell (Cambridge, 1996).

73 Cornell, *Realm of the Saint*, 138.

74 *Al-Ta^{c}rif*, 135; *Autobiographie*, 127.

75 Cornell, *Realm of the Saint*, 134. See Anthony Hutt, *Islamic Architecture: North Africa* (London, 1977), 43–5, 122–5.

76 Augustin Berque, *L'Agérie, terre d'art et d'histoire* (Algiers, 1937), 190.

77 Sheila Blair, 'Sufi saints and shrine architecture,' in *Muqarnas*, 7, 1990, 42.

78 *Al-Ta^{c}rif*, 135; *Autobiographie*, 127.

79 See Ibn al-Khatib's letter and the long poem at the end dedicated to Ibn Khaldun's new son in *Al-Ta^{c}rif*, 140–55; *Autobiographie*, 143.

80 *Autobiographie*, 144.

81 Ibn Khaldun described the fortress as 'built by Abu Bakr Ibn ^{c}Arif.' It was among the 'most solid and most magnificent fortresses.' *Al-Ta^{c}rif*, 230; *Autobiographie*, 152. According to M. Tawit al-Tanji, the Qal$^{\circ}$at ibn Salama is also called the Qal$^{\circ}$at Taoughzout in Berber and is located south of Oran near the small city of Frenda. He gives the coordinates 35° 6′ North and 1°, 25′ East. *Al-Ta^{c}rif*, 228, note 4.

82 *Al-Ta°rif*, 228–9; *Autobiographie*, 151.
83 *Dawla*, the word Ibn Khaldun used here, can mean both dynasty and/or state.
84 He also needed to 'consult his sources in Tunis.' *Al-Ta°rif*, 230; *Autobiographie*, 152.
85 *Al-Ta°rif*, 229; *Autobiographie*, 151.
86 *Al-Ta°rif*, 230; *Autobiographie*, 152.
87 Goitein, *A Mediterranean Society*, 66.
88 *Al-Ta°rif*, 231; *Autobiographie*, 153.
89 Abun-Nasr, *A History of the Maghrib in the Islamic Period*, 130. These urban rebellions only really gained momentum after 1380.
90 Suson Stetkevych, *The Poetics of Islamic Legitimacy: Myth, Gender and Ceremony in the Classical Arabic Ode* (Bloomington, IN, 2002).
91 Ibn Khaldun used °Umar's nickname 'Al-Faruq.' *Autobiographie*, 155; For the entire series of panegyric poems, totaling more than 150 lines, see *Al-Ta°rif*, 233–44.
92 *Autobiographie*, 156.
93 *Autobiographie*, 157.
94 On the Banu Hilal and their impact on Berber history see Michael Brett and Elizabeth Fentress, *The Berbers* (Oxford, 1997).
95 On the 'hegemony' of the aristocratic Dawawida Arabs in this period see R. Bruschvig, *La Berbérie Orientale Sous les Hafsids* (Paris, 1940), vol. 1, 293–4. The Dawawida were camel-herding Bedouin who dominated their Berber neighbors and regularly migrated between north and south in search of pasture.
96 *Al-Ta°rif*, 98–9; *Autobiographie*, 105.
97 *Al-Ta°rif*, 99; *Autobiographie*, 106.
98 *Al-Ta°rif*, 132–3; *Autobiographie*, 124.
99 *Al-Ta°rif*, 135–7; *Autobiographie*, 127–9. Ibn Khaldun went on another expedition to pay off the Dawawida in the years 1372–3 AD. In 1375 AD he was again asked by Abu Hammu to secure their support.
100 Abu al-°Abbas was, however, somewhat more successful than many of his Hafsid predecessors. He defeated Arab chiefs south of Tunis and secured the submission of the Arab chieftain at Tozeur, an important desert port city to the southwest, as well as Gafsa and the Jerid region of central Tunisia. *Autobiographie*, 153.
101 Qur°anic schools or *kuttab* for teaching young scholars the basics of the Qur°an and the *hadith* and usally financed by private donations should be distingushed from official madrasas used for indoctrination. A plaque identifies a small mosque near the Rue de la Riche in the madina of Tunis as Ibn Khaldun's Qur°an school.
102 *Al-Ta°rif*, 233; *Autobiographie*, 153.
103 *Al-Ta°rif*, 234; *Autobiographie*, 154.
104 *Muqaddimah*, vol. II, 100.
105 In fact, the situation became so bad that all pilgrimage was forbidden. 'The Spanish Umayyads thus prevented their people from going abroad to fulfill the duty of pilgrimage. They were afraid they might fall into the hands of the °Abbasids.' *Muqaddimah*, vol. II, 100.
106 *Muqaddimah*, vol. II, 100.
107 *Muqaddimah*, vol. II, 101.

EGYPT

All, except God, is vanity.

Saying of the Prophet Muhammad

When he entered Cairo for the first time in January 1382, Ibn Khaldun was overwhelmed.[1] As he traveled down the Nile from Alexandria he saw Cairo and the Pyramids emerging on the horizon. He got off the boat and started walking through the streets. The variety and richness of the city was dizzying. He encountered a seemingly endless number of madrasas, colleges, mosques; this was a true metropolis, a city substantially greater in size than Tunis, Fez, or Granada. There may have been above 500,000 inhabitants under the reign of Sultan al-Nasir Muhammad (d. 1340), although the population suffered greatly from the plague and was probably significantly below that number when Ibn Khaldun arrived.[2] Nevertheless, Cairo still outshone every city west of China. He wrote down his first impressions of Cairo:

> Capital of the world, garden of the universe, forum for the gathering of peoples . . . palace of Islam, throne of power, a city embellished with palaces and mansions, ornamented with colleges and schools, its scholars are like shining stars. The city lays across the Nile, river of paradise, receptacle of heavenly water . . . One could not stop speaking of this city, of its high degree of civilization, of its prosperity.[3]

Ibn Khaldun knew about the splendors of Cairo when he was still living in the Maghrib. He asked the scholar and pilgrim, Al-Maqqari, 'How is Cairo?' Al-Maqqari responded to Ibn Khaldun saying, 'One who has not seen [Cairo]

knows not the power of Islam.' Similarly, he asked a wise man in Bijaya about
Cairo who responded, 'Its inhabitants overflow [the city], as if returning from the
last judgment!' Finally, there was the account of the minister of military affairs
in Marinid Fez, Abu al-Qasim al-Barji, who returning from a voyage to Cairo
stated, 'that which humans can imagine surpasses reality, because imagination is
more vast than all sensible things. There is, however, one exception: Cairo. This
city surpasses all that one could imagine.' Even the powerful sultan, Abu 'Inan,
attempted ruler of all the Maghrib, was stunned to hear this.[4]

The fact that Ibn Khaldun was impressed by Egypt and eventually settled
down there for the rest of his life did not mean that he abandoned his Maghribi
identity or his clear affiliation with the North African Maliki school of Islam.
According to one surviving source, Ibn Khaldun had a 'love of being contrary
in everything.' Unlike other immigrants from North Africa who changed their
dress, Ibn Khaldun continued wearing the judicial robes of a North African, not
an Egyptian.[5] Perhaps Ibn Khaldun knew that standing out was one of the best
means of being noticed and promoted. While his skills as a negotiator between
tribe and city served him in the past, his identity as a Maghribi would make him
a valuable member of the Mamluk court and judicial system.

TEACHER AND JUDGE

Almost immediately, Ibn Khaldun caused a stir in the academic and religious
community of Cairo. He claimed it was only a few days after arriving in the
city that students came to him in droves, demanding lessons and accepting no
excuses. He quickly found a place to teach in the Al-Azhar mosque. The Al-
Azhar was much more than simply a hall of worship; it was a university more
than simply a mosque, a great center of learning considered to be the most important in Sunni Islam to this day. Ibn Khaldun established himself as a leading
Maliki scholar. His teaching method contrasted with the standard lectures on
religious law taught by his contemporaries. His student, Muhammad bin Ammar,
mentioned, in fact, that Ibn Khaldun not only taught jurisprudence but the
Muqaddimah and historical method in the madrasas of Cairo. History or historical criticism as a subject was not officially recognized but Ibn Khaldun taught it
anyway.[6]

With his fame as a uniquely gifted, if somewhat eccentric, scholar from the
Maghrib, Ibn Khaldun soon secured the patronage of the Mamluk ruler of Egypt
with the help of friends such as the Mamluk minister of war.[7] Famous before
his arrival, Ibn Khaldun was soon in the position to ask Sultan Barquq to write
a letter Abu al-ᶜAbbas, ruler of Tunis, requesting the release of Ibn Khaldun's
family so that they could join him in Cairo. Ibn Khaldun included the letter

in his autobiography as proof of the esteem in which the sultan held him. The fact that Ibn Khaldun had to ask for the personal intervention of the Mamluk sultan, Barquq, also demonstrated how much Abu al-ᶜAbbas desired to keep Ibn Khaldun in his service and why he had wished to hold Ibn Khaldun's family in Tunis in the first place. This letter is also historically important. It not only demonstrates how rulers in the medieval Islamic world corresponded with each other, it claimes explicitly that the Mamluks, having established important financial ties with Mecca and Madina, were, in fact, the legitimate stewards of the holy pilgrimage to Mecca. Sultan Barquq called himself not only protector of the pilgrimage and the two holy cities of Mecca and Madina but *Shahanshah*, Persian for King of Kings, and 'Alexander of our times.' In contrast, Abu al-ᶜAbbas was referred to more vaguely and with fewer epithets as 'Treasure of Islam' and 'One who triumphs.'[8] Nevertheless, the letter worked and Ibn Khaldun's family was allowed to leave Tunis and meet him in Cairo.

In the meantime, Ibn Khaldun was appointed as the head of the Qamhiyya College, founded as an endowment, or a *waqf*, by the famous Saladin who had recaptured Jerusalem from the crusaders in 1187 AD. These endowments proliferated throughout Cairo, and were a common way to assure positions for the descendants of powerful Mamluks who technically could not inherent the governmental positions of their fathers but could be placed in charge as caretakers of endowments. Yet even higher posts would soon become available. Unlike North Africa where the Maliki legal school, founded by Malik ibn Anas (d. 795 AD) dominated legal opinion almost exclusively, in Mamluk Cairo there were adherents of all four of the major Sunni legal schools of Islam. The sultan appointed the chief judge or Qadi for each of these schools.[9] In 1384 the old Maliki Qadi had fallen into disgrace and the powerful position was open. After much pomp and ceremony, Ibn Khaldun was installed as Maliki Qadi.

Although the Qadi of the Shafiᵓi school, the most widely followed school at the time, was predominant, the Maliki Qadi was also immensely powerful and was somewhat similar to a Supreme Court judge in that he heard appeals of sentences from lower Maliki judges. Another important function of the grand Qadi was rooting out corruption in the lower ranks of the judiciary. Corruption in the office of Qadi had been widespread ever since the interpretation of Islamic law and the teaching of Islamic law to students in madrasas had been co-opted by the government. The Qadi was surrounded by the pomp and grandeur of government power. Indeed, a common proverb said, 'Of three judges, two are in hell.'[10] Ibn Khaldun, of course, saw himself as that one judge out of a typical three who could rise above the temptations of government corruption.

Ibn Khaldun claimed to execute the office of Qadi with utmost probity and effort. He was scandalized that lower court judges under his purview did not vigorously root out and sentence influential Mamluk 'libertines' and those addicted to luxury. It was precisely luxury and libertine behavior that was, for Ibn Khaldun, at the root of social decay: 'The judges abstained from criticizing their comportment and closed their eyes to misdeeds . . . in order to be certain they were protected by the powerful.'[11] In fact, Ibn Khaldun claimed that most of the judges were not even properly trained. They were mere novices in the *sharia*, the Qur'an, and the sayings of the prophet, with many judges being simply the lackeys of important Mamluk princes. Ibn Khaldun seemed perplexed and astounded by the subtle patronage network that, according to the scholar Ira Lapidus, characterized late medieval Mamluk Egypt.[12] Yet without this 'corrupt' patronage system, the Mamluks, a small foreign-born elite, could not have controlled and managed society so effectively. It was little wonder that Ibn Khaldun's calls for reform went unheeded.

Corruption was rampant because of the deliberately confusing nature of the legal system, the 'jungle' caused by contradictions between the four different legal schools in Cairo, and the power of court secretaries who received bribes to alter contracts and wills. Moreover, muftis, those qualified to issue *fatwas*, or legal opinions, often from their own house, were, according to Ibn Khaldun, too numerous. Everyone rich enough could find for himself a mufti who would agree to his position, causing a plethora of fatwas that contradicted one anther. Some lawyers and muftis were so ignorant, according to Ibn Khaldun, that they had 'no experience studying with known scholars'; they simply 'used technical terminology' to appear qualified when, in reality, they found inspiration only 'in Satan.'[13] Many used and corrupted Sufi shrines and the endowments for these shrines as cover and turned these once esteemed places of worship and mystical practice into dens of superstition. These ignorant and corrupt judges and muftis ganged up on Ibn Khaldun, made false accusation, and complained to Sultan Barquq; who shut his ears to most of their gossip.

Ibn Khaldun claimed to turn from the ignorant, to respect the equal application of the law, and to apply the law with severity. He was encouraged by his peers, the Qadis of other schools, to 'satisfy to the great, have regard for notables, find superficial loopholes to judge in favor of the powerful . . .' Ibn Khaldun stubbornly resisted this advice. He ruled against several powerful and high-ranking Mamluks and proclaimed that his judgment was final, that it should not be transferred to another, more amenable judge from a different school for a second look. This caused uproar in the legal system. Sultan Barquq called a council of judges and muftis. However, despite their attempts to sideline Ibn Khaldun, the sultan supported his judgments against the powerful notables. These notables and their contacts, sensing Ibn Khaldun's influence as an affront to their position, and perhaps even an overstepping of judicial power, wore down the sultan with constant, false accusations against the upstart Maliki Qadi. It was in the midst of this interminable fracas that Ibn Khaldun learned of the death of his family, his wife, and children, and the loss of his belongings in a shipwreck. The ship that was bringing them from Tunis had encountered a great tempest and all was lost. Only two of his sons would survive, arriving on a later ship.[14]

TRAGEDY, LONELINESS AND PILGRIMAGE

Like the plague, which took away his parents and his teachers, the loss of his wife and family hit Ibn Khaldun's psyche. He suddenly realized the futility of his efforts as Qadi, the impossibility of finding justice: 'The thought of renouncing the world came back to my spirit anew.' He resolved to resign from his post. At first the sultan refused. Yet Ibn Khaldun was saved by the grace of God. Having pity for Ibn Khaldun's situation and seeing how depressed he had become, he released Ibn Khaldun from 'his chains.' Ibn Khaldun wrote how his sadness made him unable to function, unable to express the sorrow he had for the loss of his family. He spent three years dedicated to teaching, reading, writing 'with the hope that God would allow me to spend the rest of my life in his devotion and to vanquish the obstacles in the way of happiness.'[15] Clearly, Ibn Khaldun was not a soulless bureaucrat or abstract thinker unattached to the pains of the world. He had saved his family so well from the perils of politics but not from the hand of God at sea. Especially after this tragedy, he did reveal his personal side, his vulnerability to depression when he was debilitated by depression and despair. Searching for the help of God and a way out of his destitution, he resolved to go on the *hajj*, the pilgrimage to Mecca, obligatory for all Muslims with the means or opportunity.

Having secured the assistance of the sultan, who gave him provisions, he left Cairo in September 1387. He followed the ancient Red Sea route to the port of Tur on the Sinai and then to Yanbu al-Bahr, 'Spring by the Sea,' the Red Sea port full of incense and spices that was, like Jeddah today, a gateway to the land route to Medina and Mecca. He finally arrived in the holy city of Mecca in December 1387, only some three months after his departure from Cairo. On his way back to Cairo his ship was waylaid by the weather in Yanbu for several days. He used this time in Yanbu to acquaint himself with the important scholars of the city. Extraordinarily, one of the scholars had received a letter addressed to Ibn Khaldun from Ibn Zamrak, the head Qadi of Granada who had ousted Ibn al-Khatib from power and who had forced Ibn Khaldun off his ship when he learned of Ibn Khaldun's efforts to save his friend. The survival of this letter was evidence of a still vibrant, if somewhat informal, postal system linking the disparate political entities of the Muslim world from Al-Andalus all the way to Arabia. The letter would have first gone to Cairo and then been forwarded to Yanbu on a subsequent merchant or transport ship on its way through the Red Sea.

Ibn Zamrak conveniently did not mention Ibn al-Khatib or the incident where he had forced Ibn Khaldun off the boat. Instead, he was typically full of praise for Ibn Khaldun, even commiserating over the loss of his family. Although buried in deep in the letter, Ibn Zamrak admitted he was really after specific, potentially reconnaissance information on the Mamluks. He asked Ibn Khaldun for any information he might have about the Mamluk Turks. Ibn Zamrak knew that Ibn Khaldun remained an important source of information. After informing Ibn Khaldun of the news of a new rebellion in North Africa, he asked him for books from Egypt, desiring the writings of the 'superior' luminaries of Cairo.[16]

After responding to Ibn Zamrak, Ibn Khaldun eventually made his way back to Cairo in June 1388. He went directly to the sultan and recounted the prayers he performed in the sultan's name at Medina and Mecca, the holiest cities of Islam. Quickly realizing that Ibn Khaldun seemed to have recovered from much of his melancholy at the death of his family, the sultan put Ibn Khaldun back to work as head of an important Sufi center. Soon, however, the comfortable routine would be broken by another incident that would try Ibn Khaldun. Within a few months the situation in Cairo became increasingly dangerous for the sultan. In 1389 a rebellion was hatched against him by a Mamluk noble named Al-Nasiri in response to Barquq's attempts to consolidate his power at the expense of the notables; attempts at consolidation that Ibn Khaldun supported and benefited from when he was chief Maliki judge. As Al-Nasiri gained power, Ibn Khaldun acted quickly, too quickly. Perhaps remembering the importance of swiftly shifting loyalties in North Africa, he rashly decided that Barquq's days were finished, that his ῾*asabiyya* had run dry. Less versed in the dynamics of dynastic change in Mamluk Egypt, he did not realize that Barquq still held onto several instruments of power unknown to Ibn Khaldun. He decided to sign a fatwa against his former loyal patron and protector Barquq, a decision that would lead to his demotion and isolation from court.

A SULTAN BETRAYED

Immediately after his pilgrimage and before the revolt of Al-Nasiri, Ibn Khaldun was blessed with lucrative opportunities that reflected his good standing with the sultan. With his depth of understanding of Sufi practice, Ibn Khaldun seemed a natural candidate for the prominent position as head of the Baybarsiyya Sufi center or *khanqa*. As head of the Baybarsiyya, Ibn Khaldun had access to a tremendous *waqf*, or charitable endowment provided by pious and wealthy Sufi brothers and by the Mamluk sultan, Baybars, the 'masher of crusaders,' who founded the *khanqa* at the gate of victory in the center of the city. Unlike Ibn Khaldun's venerable predecessor, Sharaf al-Ashqar, who remained at the Baybarsiyya until his death, Ibn Khaldun would enjoy his tenure for but a few fleeting months. The revolt of Al-Nasiri threw him yet again from quiet certitude into the jaws of political turmoil.

Even as Al-Nasiri gained more and more support from the elite of Cairo, Ibn Khaldun felt compelled to act, to write a legal opinion condemning the exiled Barquq. However, instead of admitting this mistake, Ibn Khaldun said he was forced to sign a fatwa against Barquq. He explained his decision as a simple calculated response to the laws of history. In a long and unwieldy treatise on Mamluk history inserted directly into his autobiography, Ibn Khaldun explained how Barquq was simply the leader of a Mamluk clan, a clan that like any natural, tribal clan happened to gain authority through the forceful eradication of rivals. The Banu Qala°un, that is, the Mamluk 'tribe' of the towers, or the Burjis, supported him. As Ibn Khaldun explained, it was the waning °*asabiyya* of this clan that caused him to shift his loyalties toward Al-Nasiri. Of course, the Mamluks were not tribes at all but groups of slave soldiers trained at different military camps. For Ibn Khaldun, however, the association was the same. A different 'clan,' the Yulbugha, who had lost positions of power under Barquq, supported Al-Nasiri, the rebel. From his base in Aleppo, Syria, Al-Nasiri assembled an army of Turkmen, Arabs, and local rulers who yearned for independence from Barquq. He took Damascus and marched quickly toward Cairo. He took the city and quickly threw the important advisors of Barquq into prison, such as Al-Jubani, the minister for military affairs who had introduced Ibn Khaldun to the sultan Barquq years earlier. Avoiding a seemingly inevitable fate, Barquq himself had somehow managed to escape, almost without notice. In fact, most of those who advised Al-Nasiri as he began consolidating his conquests suggested that Barquq had died. In fact, Barquq had been alive the whole time, waiting for a good time to strike. When he did appear at the gates of Cairo, Al-Nasiri was unprepared and even his most loyal supporters abandoned him.

When they finally regained power, Barquq and his ministers systematically started the process of purging disloyal subjects from the government. Neither Barquq nor his new lieutenant, Sudun, accepted Ibn Khaldun's excuses. The sultan reprimanded all of the judges who had written fatwas against him and, according to Ibn Khaldun, the sultan was especially disappointed in him: 'The Sultan would not accept our excuses . . . especially mine.'[17] Ibn Khaldun even wrote a contrite poem begging for forgiveness:

Sire, it is in you that I place all of my faith . . .
Do not abandon your good opinion of me,
For I would not be able to live without it . . .
Do not abandon me: I never committed treason.

Instead of admitting to his betrayal, although seemingly quite calculated as he admitted earlier when speaking of the ʿasabiyya of the Mamluk clans, Ibn Khaldun blamed not his own judgment but his enemies and conspiracies against him: 'They have circulated the strangest of falsehoods.' He claimed, 'We were forced to write these fatwas . . .;' that they 'brandished their arms against us' and that 'we signed it only in expectation of your magnanimity.' [18] Not surprisingly, Barquq maintained his skepticism. It was remarkable, in fact, that he did not take more decisive action and imprison Ibn Khaldun and the disloyal jurists. Instead, Ibn Khaldun was merely stripped of his prominent position at the Baybarsiyya and allowed to retreat to teach and write. The sultan still occasionally called on him to consult with him on the exchange of presents with the sultans of North Africa. He also consulted Ibn Khaldun on some of the more significant diplomatic matters arising between the Mamluks and the Marinids and Hafsids to the west.

It would not be until 1399, however, when he was finally re-nominated as grand Maliki Qadi that the sultan would really forgive him. Although he claimed to be enjoying his solitude and his opportunity to write and teach, Ibn Khaldun seemed hurt and dismayed by his long exile from significant government service: 'Every time the position became open . . . the Sultan nominated those men he thought would be the most competent. Even as he knew I was the most appropriate for the position, certain Mamluk Amirs and noblemen conspired against me.' Ibn Khaldun was reluctant to admit that his relationship with the sultan had been permanently damaged by his betrayal.

To explain the situation to himself, Ibn Khaldun had to use the same formula he had used more convincingly when he claimed to be the stern uncorrupt judge of years past: it was not the real opinion of the sultan, but conspiracy theories spread by enemies that threatened his position as judge.[19] Ibn Khaldun was restored to the sultan's favor only a few months before his death in 1399. The sultan had laid out clear instructions for the succession of his son Faraj and the Atabeg Aytamash as tutorial regent to the new young sultan. Almost immediately, however, Aytamash attempted to claim complete control, instigating a division between the partisans of Faraj and those of the Atabeg. Although Faraj successfully suppressed his tutor, he was strangled in Damascus; a looming threat from the east would prove an even greater existential threat not only to his reign but also to the very existence of the Mamluk empire.

ENCOUNTER WITH TIMURLANE

Although he was far away in India, crushing remnants of resistance in south Asia, Timurlane had been preparing for the conquest of the Mamluk realm for some time. The death of Sultan Barquq and the ascent of his son Faraj gave Timurlane his chance. As Ibn Khaldun himself put it, Timurlane, 'having heard of the death of the Sultan Al-Barquq of Egypt, changed course and made his way [from India] through Iraq, Armenia . . . and eventually made his way to Aleppo.'[20] Timurlane knew enough about Mamluk politics to realize he had only a short window of opportunity. He needed to strike at the Mamluks and Faraj when they were in the midst of a messy dynastic succession. Sultan Barquq had even sent troops to the Euphrates in anticipation of Timurlane's attack, pushing Timurlane into India. Barquq had been bold enough to execute a rowdy group of Tartar ambassadors Timurlane had sent to Cairo in 1397. Hearing of the death of the powerful Barquq, Timurlane smelled the opportunity for fresh conquest. From India he swiftly moved his army across central Asia and turned toward Syria, capturing Siwas and Aleppo and surrounding Damascus by the fall of 1400. The sheer swiftness with which the shrewd, if illiterate, Timurlane abandoned India and headed for the vulnerable Mamluk realms indicated how much he appreciated, as great conquerors such as Alexander had realized before him, that Egypt was the key to world conquest. The capture of Egypt would allow Timurlane to control the Red Sea and eastern Mediterranean as well as the Indian Ocean, seamlessly linking his conquests in India with the west. The Mamluks were in the way of Timurlane's ambition for world domination and now they were weakly led by a vulnerable sultan.

Timurlane was correct in his assumption that seditious plots and schemes against the new sultan, Faraj, would imperil Egypt. Almost immediately, on January 6, 1401, soon after his arrival at the head of an expeditionary force to hold Damascus against Timurlane, Faraj was forced to speed back to Cairo after hearing of yet another rebellious plot by a rival Mamluk notable named Sheikh al-Jarkasi. Up until that point, the Mamluks had successfully held back Timurlane's armies. It was in this troubling and highly mutable military and political environment that Ibn Khaldun met with Timurlane and skillfully argued for his life and safety, even as he offered his services should the conqueror manage to defeat the green, new sultan, Faraj. Ibn Khaldun had at least as much reason to predict that Faraj would fail and the Mamluks would crumble as he had reason to believe that they would somehow stem the fierce Tartar advance.

Ibn Khaldun did not initially plan to meet with Timurlane. In fact, he headed toward the besieged city of Damascus only after visiting the Muslim holy city of

Jerusalem. According to Ibn Khaldun's citation of al-Bukhari, 'the most excellent places on earth are the three mosques of Mecca, Medina and Jerusalem.' Like many good Muslims who had already completed the major pilgrimage to Mecca and Medina, Ibn Khaldun went to Jerusalem to pray at the Al-Aqsa mosque where Muhammad the Prophet had begun his Night Journey. He also visited the Dome of the Rock, rebuilt by Byzantine artisans working for the Umayyad caliph ᶜAbd al-Malik. While in Jerusalem, Ibn Khaldun encountered the holy places of the Jews and Christians. Although he wrote about the history of the Church of the Holy Sepulcher, the legends of Helena, mother of Constantine who secured the 'true cross' he refused to enter the churches of Jerusalem, despite his curiosity. He claimed that Helena's true cross was found in a pile of excrement, leading her to erect a 'Church of the Excrements' or *qumamah* in Arabic. Ibn Khaldun had obviously misread the name of the church, which was 'Church of the Resurrection,' or *qiyama* in Arabic.[21] Yet Ibn Khaldun did not necessarily see the Christian church as any more unclean than the Dome of the Rock, which was, according to his own account, originally built by the caliph ᶜUmar on a place piled high with dung and dirt.[22] He soon headed to Bethlehem, 'birthplace of the Christian Messiah,' and admired the monuments constructed by the Romans at that site. However, the time for admiring ancient monuments had passed. The sultan's army had already begun its march to Syria, and Ibn Khaldun joined them in Gaza as they made their way to Damascus.[23]

Ibn Khaldun's extraordinary encounter with Timurlane outside Damascus in early 1401, discussed at the opening of this book, did not go unnoticed by his contemporaries. According to a contemporary Egyptian chronicler Ibn Qadi Shuhbah's account, Ibn Khaldun said to Timurlane, 'I have also written your biography and I wish to read it before you so that you can correct the inaccuracies.' Ibn Khaldun had heard of Timurlane not simply from the predictions of Sufi saints but from 'trustworthy merchants' who had traveled from central Asia into Cairo.[24] In fact, an account of the encounter between Ibn Khaldun and Timurlane made its way to Baghdad. Ahmad ibn ᶜArabshah, a secretary for the Sultan of Baghdad, wrote a chronicle of the life of Timurlane shortly after his death in 1405.[25] In this chronicle he gave an account of what Ibn Khaldun said to Timurlane that varies in certain important ways from Ibn Khaldun's own version of events. According to Ibn ᶜArabshah:

Waliuddin ᶜAbd al-Rahman, son of Khaldun, supreme judge of Egypt, who was author of a wonderful chronicle, in which he used a new method, as I was told by a wise doctor and true man of learning, who saw it and marked its diction and substance . . . This Ibn Khaldun had come with the armies of the Muslims into Syria and when they had turned their backs, fate seized them in the claws of

Timur . . . Ibn Khaldun said to Timur and his entourage, having become familiar and pleased with him, 'By Allah! O Lord and Amir, give me your hand, which is the key to conquer the world, that I may glory in the honor of kissing it.'

Although Ibn Khaldun admitted to praising Timurlane in his autobiography, in Ibn ᶜArabshah's account Ibn Khaldun was even more explicit in his panegyrics, his praise for the conqueror, his willingness to work for him, and in his predictions for his success:

> He also said to him . . . 'Oh Lord and Amir! Egypt refuses to be ruled by any ruler but yourself or to admit any empire but yours. But I for your sake have left my wealth, ancestral and new, my family, children, fatherland, country, friends, kindred, relatives, intimates and the kings of mankind and every helper and leader, nay, all men . . . I have no regret or grief except for the time which has passed of my life and my age which has gone, because it has been passed in a service other than yours . . . I will now begin another life in your protection, will consider wicked the time of absence from your side . . .'

Then, according to Ibn ᶜArabshah's account, Ibn Khaldun discussed the importance of his work and how valuable he would be to Timurlane. He made an excuse, saying, that the only way he could possibly serve his new great sultan was to 'return to Cairo' and 'recover them.' Timurlane was 'marvelously pleased thereby and his desire for books of annals and customs roused . . . he did not mark that he was deceived and carried away by the magic of this [Ibn Khaldun's] wonderful eloquence.'[26] Thus, with spectacular wit, Ibn Khaldun avoided becoming a hostage of Timurlane, which could have easily happened. While Ibn Khaldun was allowed to go free to go collect his books, Timurlane forced his hapless colleague, one of the four grand Qadis, the grand Qadi of the Shafiᵓi school of Islam in Cairo, Sadr al-Din al-Munawi, to stay with him until receiving the captured Mongol official Atlmish back from the Mamluks.[27] Crucially, Ibn Khaldun maintained the appearance of loyalty to the conqueror should he manage to actually defeat the Mamluks completely.

The most striking contrast between Ibn ᶜArabshah and Ibn Khaldun was not their different descriptions of the various material details of Ibn Khaldun's encounter with Timurlane. Rather, while Ibn Khaldun made almost no judgment concerning Timurlane's method of rule or the basis of his authority in Islamic law, Ibn ᶜArabshah, who otherwise was rather positive toward Timurlane, accused the conqueror of not following Islamic law but the tribal law of the Tartars. For Ibn ᶜArabshah, who only saw narrowly through a tight historical lens, Islamic law was the only way to maintain a successful empire or government: 'He clung to the laws of Genghis Khan, on whom be the curse of Allah, rather than the laws of Islam.' Ibn Khaldun, in contrast, was fully aware that there were viable nations and civilizations that could thrive on laws other than those set forth in orthodox Islam. While religion was important, the basis of social interaction and the success of various regimes depended fundamentally on *ᶜasabiyya*, something Timurlane seemed to have in abundance as his armies spread across Asia. In his 'general discussion of human civilization,' the first of his famous prefatory theses, Ibn Khaldun boldly stated that religious law was not necessary. Unlike Ibn Khaldun, Ibn ᶜArabshah, as most of his contemporaries, believed that the only restraining influence that keeps society together was 'religious law that has been ordained by God and revealed to mankind by a human being.' Ibn Khaldun knew, however, that this reliance on Islamic law, or any religious law, as the sole and only explanation of human history and human society was 'not logical.' For, 'human [social] life can materialize without [prophecy] through injunctions a person in authority may devise on his own or with the help of a group feeling (*ᶜasabiyya*) that enables him to force the others to follow him wherever he wants to go . . . The latter [those without revealed prophetic law] constitute the majority of the world's inhabitants.'[28] Although Timurlane was ostensibly a Muslim, the law he followed and enforced among his followers was the law of conquest and rule established both by prophetic revelation but also by the particular manifestation of *ᶜasabiyya* that made Timurlane and his army so powerful. Ibn Khaldun had worked for unscrupulous, tyrannical rulers before; Abu Hammu II, Abu ᶜInan and others were just a few examples of ruthless rulers who saw the expansion of personal power, not Islamic law, as their main objective. He most likely would have worked for Timurlane as well.

As he left Timurlane's tent he hurriedly arranged presents for the ruler who now resided in the throne room of the 'stripped palace.' This gift giving was 'an obligation for all visitors to kings.' All of his important gifts were religious. He choose a beautifully bound Qur°an from the book market, a prayer rug, and a copy of the *Burda*, the celebrated poem in praise of the Prophet Muhammad. Timurlane especially appreciated the last gift, the *Burda*, since he had never before heard of the poem, despite its fame in religious circles. To finish off his coup de grâce, Ibn Khaldun presented Timurlane with a specially ornamented box of sweets. As a protection against poisoning Ibn Khaldun was asked to taste the sweets before they were readily distributed.

Having pleased Timurlane with his gifts, Ibn Khaldun used this opportunity to interview the great sultan:

'Sire, may God help you! I would like to submit to you a few questions.'
Timurlane replied, 'Go ahead.'

'I am a double stranger in this land: both as a person of the Maghrib, my
homeland and the place I was born, and as one of the [more traditional]
generation in Egypt. I find myself under your protection and I ask you to say and
do what you can about my situation.'[29]

Although obviously meant to illicit sympathy, Ibn Khaldun's description of
himself as a 'double stranger' not only in Egypt but in 'his generation' was apt.
Ibn Khaldun's sense of exile from the world, his sense of existing on the margins
of both time and geography, was precisely what made him so capable of explaining his age.

Having cracked the outer armor of the conqueror, Ibn Khaldun proceeded to
ask Timurlane for amnesty for the intellectuals, readers of the Qurʾan and muftis,
ministers, the friends and colleagues of Ibn Khaldun under the mercy of the conqueror. Timurlane quickly asked his secretary to write a letter of safety. He even
provided Ibn Khaldun with a mule for his journey back to Egypt. Even as Ibn
Khaldun left, Timurlane revealed the inherently nomadic nature of his conquests.
Although he had just attacked and captured Damascus, one of the most magnificent and wealthy cities in the world, his immediate priority was sending his son
with his animals to the spring pastures on the plains of Shaqhab. Timurlane even
suggested that Ibn Khaldun join his son on the seasonal journey to Shaqhab. Ibn
Khaldun refused only because the itinerary did not match his own.[30]

In a letter written to the Sultan of Tunis describing Timurlane, Ibn Khaldun
gave a sympathetic portrait of the conqueror as human. In some respects, especially his description of the conqueror's unquenchable intelligence, Ibn Khaldun
saw some part of himself in the terrible, if incredible man:

Timurlane is one of the greatest kings and one of the most illustrious rulers.
Some attribute true [Islamic] knowledge to him. Others call him a *rafidi* [a defec-
tor from Islam] . . . Others call him a magician. In fact, he is none of these. He
is simply a man very vigorous with an extreme intelligence, who questions everything, known and unknown, and is opinionated. Aged around sixty or seventy
years, he has a lame right knee: as an infant he was injured during a raid. He can
walk a short distance . . . When he needs to go a long distance; men support him
on their arms. He is a favored man. [His] power came from God. God has made
him one of his servants.[31]

IBN KHALDUN AND THE OTTOMANS

Yet it was neither Timurlane nor his successors, the Timurids, who were destined to rule the Islamic Middle East in the coming decades. Instead, a relatively

obscure group of Turks in Asia Minor would successfully establish a new paradigm of imperial rule based on a combination of religious fervor, gun powder, well-oiled military might, and janissary power; break through Ibn Khaldun's cycle of history, of rapid rise and fall, of dependence on tribal *asabiyya*; and create the Ottoman empire, an empire that lasted until the First World War. Extraordinarily, although he had no idea of the future, spectacular success of the Ottomans, Ibn Khaldun encountered an emissary of one of their most important sultans: Bayezid I.

On his hasty return to Cairo from Damascus Ibn Khaldun and his caravan were attacked by pirates. Ibn Khaldun escaped to the coast and was able to board a ship that took him as far as Gaza. It was on this ship that Ibn Khaldun met the ambassador of Bayezid, the Ottoman sultan. Unfortunately, nothing was recorded of any conversation they may have had. Ibn Khaldun could have assumed only that, like the Mamluks, the Ottomans were under serious threat by Timurlane. In fact, in 1400, the Ottomans were almost completely crushed by Timurlane's forces. Even after the death of Timurlane, they would not begin their spectacular recovery for almost a decade. Even though the Mamluks stopped the Timurid expansion and Faraj was able to regain Syria, it would be the Ottomans who would rule the Middle East and turn the Mamluks into clients.

It was the Ottomans who preserved and studied Ibn Khaldun before his rediscovery by European scholars. Although Egyptian historians such as Al-Maqqari studied him, Ibn Khaldun was most useful to the Ottomans, whose new power, extending as it did to the borders of Algeria and Morocco, impelled them to learn about Arab and Berber government and history. Ibn Khaldun was mentioned in an early Ottoman encyclopedia, he was quoted and his manuscripts copied and interpreted by Turkish scholars such as Hajji Khalifa (d. 1657), also known as Katib Chelebi, who wrote in a period when Ottoman power was beginning to wane. Although still remarkably stable considering the fraught succession to the sultanate, the Ottoman empire no longer expanded and prospered as it had under Suleiman the Magnificent or under Mehmet who conquered Constantinople in 1453. The introduction to his treatise, 'The Rule of Action for the Rectification of Defects,' about the waning Ottoman power and the problems experienced by Ottoman dynasts cited Ibn Khaldun's theory of the cycle of history and the decline and fall of dynasties. He made an urgent call to avoid the problems and defects of a dynasty in decline as outlined in the *Muqaddimah*.[32] Naʾima (d. 1716), a student of Chelebi, said 'Above all there is the Arabic history of the Maghribi Ibn Khaldun . . . a work of which the introduction [*Muqaddimah*] . . . is a treasure house filled with gems of learning.'[33] Mehmed Sahib began, but then abandoned, an ambitious first translation of Ibn Khaldun into Turkish in 1725. Some Ottoman sultans even referred to Ibn Khaldun to explain the rise of Europe in the eighteenth century, ascribing a 'loss of virility' to the Ottoman empire and using Ibn Khaldun, once again, as a lightning rod for change and reform.[34]

Ibn Khaldun, of course, would never witness the rapid conquests of the Ottomans or their eventual fears of long-term decline, a decline that went through several cycles of revival and reform. He got off the ship at Gaza and made his way back to Cairo.

DISILLUSIONMENT AND LONELY DEATH

The Mamluks eventually defeated Timurlane. As the possibility of a new, unified caliphate under Timurlane faded away, Ibn Khaldun returned to the relatively routine and mundane politics of Cairo. He was nominated as chief Maliki judge in 1401 after his return from Damascus. Soon enough, corrupt officials and the intrigue of a certain Jamal al-Din Bisati, a type of legal operative who used his influence to gain favorable legal opinions for his clients, challenged him. Frustrated and feeling his age, Ibn Khaldun cried out 'May God confound them all!' He gave up the Maliki robe in December of that same year. Then the sultan revised his decision and reappointed Ibn Khaldun in February 1402. Again, Bisati conspired against him and again he was ousted. Bisati took Ibn Khaldun's position and used it to his advantage. Ibn Khaldun would be restored to office and ousted another four times. At the end of his autobiography all Ibn Khaldun could do to express his frustration was to proclaim, 'It is God who has the course of all things between his hands.' Ibn Khaldun died on March 17, 1406. He is buried at a Cairo Sufi cemetery; an appropriate burial for a man who practiced Sufism throughout his life and who often sought retreat from busy and seemingly fruitless political affairs.

NOTES

1 Unlike Ibn Khaldun's life in the Maghrib, his life in Cairo is more carefully documented and studied. Although he curiously leaves out the entire first half of Ibn Khaldun's life, Walter Fischel's, *Ibn Khaldun in Egypt* (Berkeley and Los Angeles, CA, 1967), remains an important source for Ibn Khaldun's time in the eastern Mediterranean.

2 For a discussion of population see Janet Abu-Lughod, *Cairo: 1001 Years of the City Victorious* (Princeton, 1971), 32–6. Compared with the relative paucity of studies of the medieval Maghrib in English, Cairo has received a great deal of attention from scholars. A comprehensive bibliography of Cairo's medieval history would be beyond the scope of this book. However, in addition to Abu-Lughod, the following are important, classic accounts. Gaston Weit, *Cairo: City of Art and Commerce*, trans. Seymour Feiler (Norman, OK, 1964); André Raymond, *Cairo*, trans. Willard Wood (Cambridge, MA, 2000). On the architecture of Mamluk Cairo, John Williams provided a scholarly assessment in

'Urbanization and monument construction in Mamluk Cairo,' *Muqarnas*, 2, 1984, 33–45. One of the most important Arabic accounts of Cairo dating to the time Ibn Khaldun was in Egypt was written by Ibn Khaldun's colleague Al-Maqrizi (d. 1442). A French translation exists: *Description topographique et historique de l'Égypte*, 3 vols., trans. Urbain Bouriant (Paris, 1895–1900).

3 *Al-Taᶜrif*, 246–7; *Autobiographie*, 162–3.

4 *Al-Taᶜrif*, 247; *Autobiographie*, 163.

5 From Al-Sakhtawi, *Al-Dawᵓ al-Lami ᶜli ahl al qarn al tasiᶜ*, quoted in Rosenthal, 'Ibn Khaldun in his Time,' 16.

6 Also from Al-Sakhtawi, quoted in Rosenthal, 'Ibn Khaldun in his Time,' 22.

7 For the importance of Al-Jubani, minister of war, see Walter Fischel, 'Ibn Khaldun's autobiography in the light of external Arabic sources,' *Studi orentalistici in onore di Giorgio Levi Della Vida*, 1, 1956, 297.

8 *Al-Taᶜrif*, 249–50; *Autobiographie*, 164.

9 According to Wilfred Madelung, this practice of appointing a chief judge to each of the schools, not just the Shafiᵓi school, was introduced in Cairo in 1265 AD. See his review of Ira Lapidus, *Muslim Cities in the Later Middle Ages*, in *Journal of Near Eastern Studies*, 29 (2), April 1970, 134.

10 Quoted in Charles Lindholm, *The Islamic Middle East: Tradition and Change*, 2nd edn. (Oxford, 2002), 164.

11 *Autobiographie*, 167; 'They did not fear God,' *Al-Taᶜrif*, 257.

12 Ira Lapidus, *Muslim Cities in the Later Middle Ages* (Cambridge, MA, 1984).

13 *Autobiographie*, 169. See Ibn Khaldun's description of the corrupt judges in *Al-Taᶜrif*, 253–60.

14 *Autobiographie*, 170.

15 *Al-Taᶜrif*, 259–60; *Autobiographie*, 171.

16 *Al-Taᶜrif*, 262; *Autobiographie*, 172.

17 *Al-Taᶜrif*, 330; *Autobiographie*, 211.

18 *Autobiographie*, 213. For Ibn Khaldun's entire poem in which he begs for absolution see *Al-Taᶜrif*, 331–5.

19 *Al-Taᶜrif*, 347; *Autobiographie*, 220.

20 *Al-Taᶜrif*, 365; *Autobiographie*, 232.

21 *Muqaddimah*, vol. II, 262.

22 *Muqaddimah*, vol. II, 262.

23 *Al-Taᶜrif*, 249–50; *Autobiographie*, 222.

24 Quoted in Walter Fischel, *Ibn Khaldun in Egypt* (Berkeley and Los Angeles, CA, 1967), 94.

25 On the various histories of Timurlane and his life see John Woods, 'The rise of Timurid historiography,' *Journal of Near Eastern Studies*, 46 (2), April 1987, 81–108.

26 Ibn ᶜArabshah, *Life of Timurlane or Timur the Great*, trans. J. H. Sanders (London, 1936), 295–99.

27 Fischel, *Ibn Khaldun in Egypt*, 101.

28 *Muqaddimah*, vol. 1, 93.

29 *Autobiographie*, 243. Ibn Khaldun's conversation is recorded in *Al-Taᶜrif*, 366–77.

30 *Autobiographie*, 244.

31 'It was God's will to make him one of his servants,' *Al-Taᶜrif*, 382–3; *Autobiographie*, 246.

32 Bernard Lewis, *Islam in History*, 2nd edn. (Peru, IL, 200), 233–4.

33 Quoted in Lewis, *Islam in History*, 235.

34 On the remarkable extent that Ibn Khaldun was discussed in Ottoman correspondence see Cornell Fleischer, 'Royal authority, dynastic cyclism and 'Ibn Khaldunism' in sixteenth century Ottoman letters,' in Bruce Lawrence (ed.), *Ibn Khaldun and Islamic Ideology* (Leiden, 1984), 46–68.

IBN KHALDUN'S METHOD

The countryside is the base and the reservoir of civilization and cities.

Ibn Khaldun, *Muqaddimah*

All sociology should be historical and all history sociological.

Bourdieu and Wacquant, *An Invitation to Reflexive Sociology*

It was Ibn Khaldun's stated ambition in the *Muqaddimah* to wash his hands of any 'blind trust' in 'tradition.'[1] This sort of statement from the pen of a fourteenth-century scholar seems radical, unexpected, and refreshing. Indeed, Ibn Khaldun spared few good words for the blind following of tradition that characterized the writings of his predecessors. Although there were exceptional Muslim historians who wrote faithfully about events, there were several who introduced 'untrue gossip' that was invented for political or personal gain. This corrupting of the historical record by unscrupulous writers led to a negative, compounding effect: later gullible historians simply repeated what myths they had heard with no critical inquiry into the truth of the information they mindlessly presented.[2] For Ibn Khaldun, the problem was one of erroneous repetition, especially blind repetition. Too many historians merely added glosses to earlier works by superior authors. Ibn Khaldun was quite satirical in his disparaging descriptions of these authors, reminding readers that the 'pasture of stupidity is unwholesome for mankind.' These so-called historians 'presented historical information about dynasties and stories of events from the early period as mere forms without substance, blades without scabbards, as knowledge that must be considered ignorance . . .'[3] Some, such as the chronologer Ibn Rashiq, went so far as to write nothing but lists of the names of kings and rulers with the length of rule.[4] Obviously, little was to be gained from such historical styles. Ibn Khaldun did, however, mention several exceptional historians who managed to create original and reliable histories: Muhammad al-Ishaq (d. 767/8), the author of Muhammad the Prophet's biography; ᶜUmar al-Waqidi (d. 823), the historian of the life of the Prophet and early Islamic conquests; Al-Masᶜudi (d. 956), author of the famed *Meadows of Gold*, an extensive and comprehensive history from deep in the pre-Islamic period. He barely even bothered to mention several prominent historians and predecessors whose simple, descriptive method he did not approve of, including giants of Arab historiography: Ibn Qutayba; Baladhuri; Yaᶜqubi.[5] He did not even recognize entire schools of history writing: he did not mention, for instance, the so-called 'Byzantine' school of Arabic historical and encyclopedic writing by chroniclers such as Nuwayri, ᵓUmari and Shafadi.[6]

Ibn Khaldun described an awakening, an awakening from the deep stupor of repetition and uncritical writing that characterized past histories: 'When I had read the works of others and probed into the recesses of yesterday and today, I shook myself out of that drowsy complacency and sleepiness.'[7] Even outstanding and scrupulous historians such as Al-Tabari (d. 923), the famed Persian historian from Tabaristan whose voluminous writings remain the main source for the history of the ᶜAbbasid caliphate, golden age of Arab and Islamic power, did not systematically interpret the significance, meaning, or patterns behind the events they described. Clearly Ibn Khaldun was the product of a long tradition of Arabic history writing, yet his approach was unique. Instead of simply describing events as Al-Tabari had, Ibn Khaldun proposed understanding the meaning behind events.

Ibn Khaldun's description of 'awakening' to the hidden truth, of finding meaning behind the surface of events, had parallels in the Sufism or Islamic mysticism that so inspired Ibn Khaldun's grandfather, father, and undoubtedly Ibn Khaldun himself. Ibn Khaldun's description of awakening to the necessity to probe the 'inner meaning' of history links his autobiography with his scholarship. Unlike some modern historians who, in an attempt to avoid bias, may try to erect a wall of distance between themselves and their subject, Ibn Khaldun freely claimed to find inspiration internally, finding the rules of logic in his own interior search for meaning, a search vividly described in his autobiography. This understanding of the internal logic of the individual spirit reflecting the logic of the world at large was written down in Ibn Khaldun's little-studied treatise on Sufism. Like the *Kitab al-ᶜIbar*, Ibn Khaldun's work on Sufism similarly attempted to search for the universal laws of mystical experience under the surface of mundane perception. In some instances the parallels were striking.

Just as history was dominated by cycles of rise and fall of dynastic power and tribal rebellion, so too was the universe of the mystic. For Ibn Khaldun, creation itself was circular, the universe going through complete changes, as if nature had gone through a new creation and organizes itself again. This process of being 'reborn' and 'recreated' was the same process that determined the mystical path as the adherent obeyed and submitted absolutely to the sheikh, the leader of the mystical community; his nature was completely reformed, recreated. Ibn Khaldun's constant personification of history, describing dynasties as human bodies, as lasting 'no longer than the life of the individual,' was no mere convenience but yet another expression of this universal rule of birth and death, decline and renewal, cause and effect, separation and unification that determined not only the external history of groups and dynasties but the interior workings of the spirit and the individual, of Ibn Khaldun himself.

It was this individual history that he laid bare in his autobiography. Ibn Khaldun's interior search, his realization through Sufism of the futility of superficial, material power and possession experienced in his life, and the science of history, the realization of the natural foundations of history in *ᶜasabiyya*, were parallel.[8] Ibn Khaldun's sudden inspiration came while he was holed up in Qalᵓat ibn Salama surrounded by the natural forces of society, the *ᶜasabiyya* of the Awlad ᶜArif, and the interior reflections inevitable to any thinker or mystic who might choose such a hermitage. In a very basic way Ibn Khaldun's inspired method involved the simple application of the logic of cause and effect. Indeed, the title to his work revealed this ambition.

Ibn Khaldun's attempt to decipher the universal laws of cause and effect, of general and particular in society, was stated explicitly in the title of Ibn Khaldun's universal history, *Kitab al-ᶜIbar wa diwan al-Mubtadaᵓ wa al-Khabar*. The most important parts of this title were two words laden with meaning: *mubtadaᵓ* and *khabar*. Some have translated these words as 'early and subsequent history,' while others have translated the words as 'antecedent and attribute' as subject and predicate.[9] In many respects, the concept of *mubtadaᵓ* was similar to Aristotle's notion of logical 'cause.' Ibn Khaldun was not simply seeking to describe universal rules but rather was seeking to distinguish the way the universal related to the particular, the way the specific manifestations of history related to general laws, both natural and divine.

LOGIC AND HISTORY

Ibn Khaldun's method involved the application of the rules of logic onto history. Every event, according to Ibn Khaldun, 'whether it comes into being in connection with some essence (rule) or (as the result of an) action, must inevitably possess a nature peculiar to its essence as well as to the accidental conditions that may attach themselves to it.'[10] Logic allowed the historian to distinguish between what was a general essence or pattern in history and what was merely acciden-tal. The main problem with previous histories, according to Ibn Khaldun, was the confusion of *mubtada'* and *khabar*, cause and effect, general and specific, the individual and universal, the legendary and the credible. For Ibn Khaldun the primary, natural cause of history was *ʿasabiyya* and the main and most power-ful manifestation of such group pride and solidarity were the tribes of the Arabs and the Berbers. *ʿAsabiyya* was a *mubtada'*, or essential cause of history, the specific characteristics of the dynasties supported by *ʿasabiyya* was the *khabar*. The ability of 'natural' social groups to overwhelm the artificial 'decadence' of the city, products of overcrowded and plagued human settlement in cities was simply a reflection of the logic of natural, first cause (*ʿasabiyya*) and second-ary effect (cities and urban life founded by *ʿasabiyya* and yet also destroyed by it). Natural causes even seemed to determine and precede manifestations of the divine. The only way for prophecy to be successful, according to Ibn Khaldun, was for it to rely on the natural support of *ʿasabiyya*, of the raw, natural vigor of tribes.

In his thesis, similar in some respects to the theorist Emile Durkheim's notion of the social basis of religious experience, *ʿasabiyya*, that is, 'natural society,' was not dependent on prophecy but the opposite. For Ibn Khaldun religion and politics were based on social organization. Both prophecy and other religious concepts such as *jihad*, or just struggle, were dependent on gathering a sufficient amount of support from those both fickle, awesome manifestations of natural human society: the Arab Bedouin and the Berbers. Later he would include the Turks and the Mongols as examples of *ʿasabiyya*. This did not mean that Ibn Khaldun negated the power of divine will. Rather, it was through the natural social force of *ʿasabiyya* that God approved of and supported manifestations of his will in prophecy. *ʿAsabiyya* as the natural cause of historical events, and the antecedent of events, of both prophets and of kings, was not the only example of Ibn Khaldun's basic logic of *mubtada'* and *khabar*. For Ibn Khaldun, it was also important to use logical methods in the mechanics of historical writing.

The Logic of Sea Monsters

Ibn Khaldun provided several examples of the mistakes of previous historians who did not employ logical methods or techniques, who did not distinguish *mubtada'* and *khabar* in their writings. Among the most entertaining examples of illogical history was that written by Masʿudi, a historian Ibn Khaldun both admired and criticized. Masʿudi declared that fierce sea monsters prevented Alexander the Great from building the port of Alexandria in Egypt. According to the account that Mas^cudi accepted without question, Alexander dove in a wooden container with a glass box to the bottom of the sea, drew the sea monsters and came back up to the surface. He then ordered metal replicas of the sea monsters to be fashioned, and when the monsters saw the replicas they fled. Ibn Khaldun dismissed this account because of his own understanding of logic. According to several essential rules, this event was not possible. First, rulers, according to Ibn Khaldun, would never put themselves in such risky situations. Second, Ibn Khaldun understood the process of drowning, that without enough air, one's 'spirit became hot.' Finally, *jinn* or sea monsters, according to Ibn Khaldun's 'scientific' understanding of the rules of nature, can change their shape at will. Thus, they would never have been able to be formed into a specific effigy.[11]

The important point here was not the validity of Ibn Khaldun's 'scientific' assumptions to us today. The last two assumptions are, for a modern mind, fabulous in many respects. Rather, it was the method of his reasoning that Ibn Khaldun claimed to be revolutionary. The natural laws of drowning, of the behavior of *jinn*, should be considered before simply recording the accidental, random claims of myth. Ibn Khaldun viewed history according to certain structural parameters determined not simply by the sequence of events but by natural causes. Other myths and legends Ibn Khaldun debunked were the legend of a city made completely of copper in the desert, the supposedly huge size of the ancient Israelite army and the existence of a lost city in the Arabian peninsula.

For Ibn Khaldun the more important work of a historian, however, was not simply to debunk myths and legends but to use a 'normative method for distinguishing right from wrong and truth from falsehood in historical information by means of a logical demonstration that admits of no doubts.' Ibn Khaldun believed he was establishing an 'original science,' a science that built upon, but exceeded what he learned from the Pseudo-Aristotle and other works by the 'Greeks.'[12] Rather than depending almost completely on the Greeks, he despaired at the destruction of the works of other great intellectual traditions, of the Persian sages, of the Copts and the Chaldeans. Unfortunately, 'The sciences of only one nation, the Greek, have come down to us . . .'[13] Rectifying this, Ibn Khaldun proposed a new science of history, an 'independent science' whose object was to explain the essence of 'human civilization and human organization.'[14] Whereas the Greeks had limited themselves only to urban organization, Ibn Khaldun aspired to understand the rules of history from the context of his own history. Ibn Khaldun's object was to formulate a new 'science of culture,' a science that could explain to his patrons in the Maghrib the interactions of the Arab Bedouin, the urban dwellers, and the Berbers in general ways.[15]

Ibn Khaldun's Inspirations

What specifically could have inspired Ibn Khaldun's method, his astounding idea to combine rational philosophy with history? Ibn Khaldun gave little direct credit to any particular reason for his new method. After all, he claimed to 'awaken' to a new science of culture and that he came to his conclusions in a sudden burst, a revelation of sorts that simply came to him. Although it may be tempting to take Ibn Khaldun at his word, and it was clear from his autobiography that extraordinary experiences had a profound effect on his view of the world, Ibn Khaldun was not a lone genius. He was inspired by his teachers, by a tradition of Islamic philosophy and rationalism, by his specific historical circumstances, and even by those historians whose methods he found lacking or, at best, incomplete. He was inspired both by rationalism and by Islamic theology. As the scholar Aziz al-Azmeh made clear, it would be historically inaccurate to assume that there were two distinct types of literati in Islamic culture, literati that took sides in a struggle between reason and belief.[16]

Despite Ibn Khaldun's dramatic epiphany claim, there were several previous influences on his work and several reasons why he would have been inspired to start writing an interpretive, philosophical history.

(1) Ibn Khaldun was ambitious. Unlike many of his predecessors and his contemporaries, Ibn Khaldun had the gumption to write a universal, world history, not a specific history of a single dynasty. World history was a subject that lent itself to comparative history and interpretation. There were other historians and intellectuals from the fourteenth century who had at least as much, if not more, knowledge of rational philosophy, the mundane and religious sciences, than Ibn Khaldun. Ibn al-Khatib, the great friend and rival of Ibn Khaldun mentioned earlier, was, in many ways the more refined intellectual. As head wazir at the court of Muhammad V of Granada, Ibn al-Khatib presided over the brilliant intellectual, literary, and cultural scene at the Alhambra. His poetry survives, carved into the walls of that beautiful but melancholy palace of the Banu Ahmar. Ibn al-Khatib noticed many of the same things Ibn Khaldun noticed. He studied under most of the same teachers and had at least as many qualifications and experiences to write a universal history of the known world. Instead, however, he chose local history. He wrote an impressive, multi-volume history of Granada and the Banu Ahmar, the clan that had ruled Granada since 1228.[17] As an ambitious wazir, and as a fully political man in the long tradition of Machiavellian, Andalusi wazirs, this choice to write local history made sense. All politics was local, especially in the midst the precarious circumstances of the Granada emirate. Writing a history of Granada would not only have enlightened Ibn al-Khatib of the many

motivations and purposes of his royal patrons, it pleased those patrons. Yet local history, especially of one's own locality, and especially of a locality over which one has official responsibility, comes with special hidden snares and dangers. These dangers prevented an author, especially an author as skittish and wary as Ibn al-Khatib, from straying too far from an established, royally sanctioned narrative. Ibn Khaldun wrote rather dire warnings that power and 'prestige lasts at best four generations in one lineage' and that prestige actually originates 'in the state of being outside . . . outside of leadership and nobility, and being in a vile, humble station devoid of prestige.'[18] Ibn Khaldun's relative independence, independence he could really have only in the turbulent and fractured political landscape of the fourteenth century, and his ambivalence about serving too eagerly in political positions, allowed him to step away from, if not out of, the local political firmament and write a 'universal' history. That did not mean that Ibn Khaldun did not have political motivations of his own.[19] His *Muqaddimah* directed readers to the conclusion that ᶜ*asabiyya*, especially the tribal ᶜ*asabiyya* to which he had direct access as negotiator with tribes, was a source of power. In so doing he linked his own position with the maintenance of dynastic power, not simply on a local level but as a key to the 'science of history.'

In contrast to his ambitious brother, Yahya ibn Khaldun, the younger brother of Ibn Khaldun, was a writer of more modest, explicitly panegyric, local, dynastic history. Although his life mirrored that of his older brother, his writing never approached the same level of generalization. Yahya worked as a wazir and advisor for a succession of sultans and would have been exposed to many of the same social changes experienced by Ibn Khaldun. Having studied under rationalists like Al-Abili, he would have known about the rational sciences and would have been exposed to the same methodology as his brother. Nevertheless, Yahya choose not to write a universal history, but rather a fairly constrained and limited history of the ᶜAbd al-Wadid dynasty, or the Zayyanids. As explained previously, the Zayyanids were the fairly weak, Zanata Berber dynasty that ruled the area that is now Algeria from the port city of Tilimsan. It would be perhaps unfair to say that Yahya was somehow less able than his brother. Yahya was murdered at Tilimsan in 1379 at a fairly young age.[20] His detailed and careful history of the Zayyanids and their accomplishments did not protect him; the intrigues and jealousies of court life under the fractious Zayyanid rulers had caught up with him, just as they had caught up with Ibn al-Khatib (d. 1374 AD). Perhaps Ibn Khaldun was just wily enough or just plain lucky enough to escape. It was remarkable that Ibn Khaldun thought of writing a universal history when those of equal or greater talent failed to do so. Perhaps there was something to Ibn Khaldun's claim to be suddenly inspired? This was certainly the conclusion of most European analysis of Ibn Khaldun as the lost modernist. As we saw above, this was also what Ibn

Khaldun wanted his readers to believe: that his work was the result of an exceptional, original awakening.

Yet unlike his friend, Ibn al-Khatib, and his brother, Yahya, Ibn Khaldun explicitly stated his ambition to write as a comparative, world historian. His objective was not to write a traditional, local dynastic history to one dynasty to which he was loyal in the main (like Ibn al-Khatib and Yahya ibn Khaldun) but to write a history that encompassed and compared all the dynasties and peoples of his world. By writing a comparative history Ibn Khaldun could avoid many of the pitfalls that could come from interpreting the history of a single dynasty. By claiming that general, not specific, aspects of universal, human and physical nature were the cause of events, Ibn Khaldun would avoid laying the blame on too many living rulers or their ancestors. It would be useless to speculate whether or not Ibn al-Khatib or Yahya ibn Khaldun could have written something exactly similar to the *Muqaddimah* because such a work would have been alien to their sentiments and ambitions as players of the poisonous political game. In this respect, Yahya was much more like his great grandfathers than his reclusive Sufi father. Ibn Khaldun had a little of both his father and great-grandfathers, both a hunger for power and a thirst for solitude. As stated above, one constant thread seems to link Ibn Khaldun's biography together: a sense of independence, even loneliness in this world. It was this combination of conflicting impulses in his character, a combination that grew out of a long life of experiences that may have helped to inspire Ibn Khaldun to write a universal history. He wanted to understand power, but not simply for its own sake or the sake of rulers. That said, Ibn Khaldun was not the first Arab historian to attempt a universal history.

(2) Ibn Khaldun read, studied and was heavily influenced by the *Meadows of Gold*, the universal history written by Al-Mas‘udi (d. 956 AD in Cairo).[21] Al-Mas‘udi's work would have been an important inspiration for him as Al-Mas‘udi was, like him, something of an interpretive historian. Al-Mas‘udi was one of Ibn Khaldun's preferred sources.[22] Although Al-Mas‘udi did not have a long and developed theory of human society as Ibn Khaldun, he did see the world as a comparative, historical whole.[23] Ibn Khaldun praised Al-Mas‘udi's work as a model and a reason for pursuing the *Muqaddimah*. He called him 'Imam of the Historians' and a mentor.[24] According to Ibn Khaldun, 'There is need at this time that someone should systematically set down the state of the world among all regions and races, as well as the customs and sectarian beliefs of their adherents as they have developed, doing for this age what Al-Mas‘udi did for his.'[25] Clearly, he saw Al-Mas‘udi as an important model; but there were others. Although he did not engage in the same depth of interpretation as Ibn Khaldun, Ibn Miskawayah (d. 1030 AD), the Persian philosopher of history, wrote a universal history that

explicitly sought to use all available sources. Some historiographers have proclaimed Ibn Miskawayah as at least as impressive as Ibn Khaldun in his historical methods if not in philosophical depth.[26]

The geographer and historian Al-Ya^cqubi also attempted a universal history that combined various geographical and social themes in his book entitled *History*.[27] Finally, Ibn Khaldun admitted to being influenced by Al-Turtushi (d. 1127 AD), the famed Andalusi lawyer and councilor for kings who, like Ibn Khaldun, emigrated to Egypt and became an important theologian and scholar there. Ibn Khaldun mentioned his *Mirror for Princes*, a handbook on how a prince should rule, as an important, if incomplete, inspiration for his work.[28] Ibn Khaldun's use of the *Mirror for Princes*, in fact, shows that he probably originally thought of the *Muqaddimah* as, at least partially, something of a guidebook for the Hafsid ruler, Abu al-^cAbbas and, later, for the Mamluk sultan, Barquq. However, unlike the somewhat limited scope of Al-Turtushi's work, Ibn Khaldun's *Muqaddimah* addressed issues beyond what was useful at court. Thus, Ibn Khaldun could not be justified in saying he was the first to think of writing a universal history in Arabic. He was not the first Arab historian to attempt a comparative approach toward history. He was, however, the first to attempt a profound analysis of the interactions between human society, geography, and political philosophy. As the esteemed scholar Margoliouth remarked:

> Ibn Khaldun's Prolegomena [introduction to the *Muqaddimah*] is unique in Arabic literature with few parallels in any that existed prior to the invention of printing . . . Both [Ibn Khaldun and Aristotle assumed] that there is a uniformity in human conduct comparable to the uniformity of nature: that certain modes of life develop certain tendencies; both eliminate so far as possible all elements that are exceptional and draw their inferences from normal occurrences, the repetition of which after the life antecedents justified them in formulating rules.[29]

Undoubtedly, Ibn Khaldun was an indirect student of Aristotle. Yet while Aristotle aspired to formulate the ideal state – his pupil Alexander the Great would make and transform the world – Ibn Khaldun did not believe in an ideal Atlantis or the progress of human history. In every rise of a dynasty were the seeds of its decline in decadence and, in his view since the plague, the literally unhealthy ways of urban life. Rather, Ibn Khaldun's concern was to distinguish between the cause and effect, between essence and existence, between general rules and patterns of history and specific events. In this respect, he followed the ideals of Greek logic but applied them to the rough and intemperate realities of history.

(3) Ibn Khaldun lived in a period of upheaval. Chapter 2 already described how the fourteenth-century plague and its decimation of North Africa had a profound influence on Ibn Khaldun. There was a need to write interpretive history. No longer could history be seen as a fulfillment of God's will. When God's plan seemed to be manifested, such as under the ᶜAbbasid caliphs, even if there were major challenges in the ᶜAbbasid period, at least the Islamic world was unified. A comparison between Ibn Khaldun, writing during the upheavals of the fourteenth century, and Al-Tabari, another equally ambitious, and equally independent historian, who wrote during the reign of the relatively stable ᶜAbbasids of Baghdad in the ninth and tenth centuries, reveals important differences between the world views of the two historians. A Persian aristocrat, somewhat insulated from political intrigues, Al-Tabari was able to avoid the interference of government authorities. From his elite perch and from the historical patterns found in his voluminous works, Al-Tabari had ample opportunity to become an interpretive historian. Yet unlike Ibn Khaldun, Al-Tabari did not necessarily have the need to explain the decline and fall of entire dynasties and governments. While many of the ᶜAbbasid caliphs he chronicled were less than salubrious, and while the ᶜAbbasid state was faced with several challenges from within and without, there was still a caliph and a continuity that existed when Al-Tabari was writing. Although there were times when the Islamic world seemed troubled, the hand of God still seemed to play a role in keeping chaos at bay. In the case of Ibn Khaldun, however, his world was defined by instability and discontinuities: the constant decline and rise of dynasties would have led him to consider the causes and meaning of events more closely.

(4) Ibn Khaldun's teachers, especially Al-Abili, steeped Ibn Khaldun in the traditions of rational philosophy and systematic theology. This training in rational philosophy, even though Ibn Khaldun rejected the pure study of philosophy for its own sake, would have equipped him with many of the same tools used by classical philosophers such as Plato and Aristotle.[30] He also had extensive access and knowledge of Arab predecessors such as Al-Farabi and Ibn Rushd, who wrote on political philosophy in the Arab context. Ibn Khaldun may have rejected many of the conclusions of Ibn Rushd as elitist and tinged by errors, but he would also have been able to use the same logical system as Ibn Rushd.[31] Nevertheless, he was fully aware of the intellectual tradition of rationalist thought that originated with the peripatetic philosophers of ancient Greece. According to one scholar, 'It is precisely because Ibn Khaldun used the logical apparatus and materialist assumptions of this rationalist tradition as the conceptual basis for his new historical science that he can be characterized as the last Greek historian.'[32]

(5) Ibn Khaldun's uniquely individualistic character, his desire for internal quiet contemplation – a desire often in conflict with his unavoidable, extroverted lust for authority, power, and recognition – would have certainly played a role in compelling him to write the *Muqaddimah*. Ibn Khaldun's writing was both intensely contemplative and deliberately public.

(6) The setting in which he wrote the *Muqaddimah*, the Qal°at ibn Salama, would have certainly allowed Ibn Khaldun some freedom to write. At least when he was writing at this retreat he was not under the same pressures as his predecessors had been to conform history and historical writing to the whim and will of a specific patron or sponsor. He did dedicate the *Muqaddimah* to the ruler of Tunis, yet at least the ruler and his court were not looking over his shoulder while he was actually writing. Also, by the time he started writing the *Muqaddimah* Ibn Khaldun had developed a well-worn repertoire of ways to escape the stranglehold of royal sponsorship.

(7) Although Ibn Khaldun was not completely devoted to mysticism like his father, the influence of Sufism on his thought should not be underestimated. After all, as was discussed in Chapter 1, it was the predictions of the Sufi saints that Ibn Khaldun used to justify his theories of the decline and fall of dynasties to Timurlane.

Ibn Khaldun usually described the Sufis in a positive light: 'The [Sufi] approach is based upon constant application to divine worship, complete devotion to God, aversion to the false splendor of the world, abstinence from the pleasure, property, and position to which the great mass aspires, and retirement from the world into solitude for divine worship.' In fact, he compared Sufis with the 'men around Muhammad and the early Muslims.' Sufis, according to Ibn Khaldun, really knew how to be Muslims whereas the great masses of Muslims in his own day were led astray. It was for this reason that Ibn Khaldun put so much trust in the predictions of Sufi sheikhs, or the heads of Sufi orders. He described the ecstatic experience of the Sufis, an experience that gave them a particular form of perception. In fact, his description of the superior perception of the Sufis was rather similar to his description of how he came to view history and human society. He described how Sufi exercises such as the *dhikr*, the repetitive remembrance of God's name, 'removed the veil of sensual perception.'[33] As he admitted to Timurlane, Ibn Khaldun's own perception and his analysis of human society were not simply the result of dry, rational method, but also the result of a higher state of perception. True Sufis, Sufis who had passed through all the necessary levels of spiritual discipline, could predict the future. By lifting the veil, rather as Ibn Khaldun had lifted the veil of ignorance that characterized past histories, Sufis could see 'existence as one' and could thus perceive what was otherwise impossible to perceive.[34] Ibn Khaldun was aware of the new wave of spiritual Sufi fervor that was sweeping through Al-Andalus and North Africa, a wave that would crest after his death with the establishment of Sufi saints as primary political and religious arbiters of North African society.[35]

Ibn Khaldun had not only found refuge at the shrines of important Sufis such as Abu Madyan, he vigorously defended Sufism and the mystical path as a legitimate and commendable pursuit. He condemned the infamous, extreme utterances of the Sufi Al-Hallaj (d. *c.* 874 AD) who publicly proclaimed, 'I am God!' But his condemnation was not against the notion that one could find unity with God, but only that such public displays confused the common people and caused the unwise mixing of the practical world with the spiritual world.[36] Although he was himself a jurist extremely well versed in the application of Islamic law, Ibn Khaldun disagreed with those jurists would found Sufism suspicious. The writings of these same anti-Sufi jurists formed the basis for Wahhabism, a vehemently anti-Sufi form of Islam practiced in Saudi Arabia today. According to Ibn Khaldun, 'many jurists and muftis . . . summarily disapproved of everything they came across in the [Sufi] path.' Unlike his assessment of the philosophers and logicians, whom he found dubious when they reduced theology to mere 'speculations,' Ibn Khaldun defended all of the Sufi practices.[37] He defended their ability to predict the future, their discussion of divine grace, and even the ecstatic utterances that most commonly provoked 'the censure of orthodox Muslims,' as long as these utterances were made by those 'removed from sense perception.'[38] Indeed, given the fact that Ibn Khaldun had such an intimate knowledge of the Sufi path, and the fact that he used almost no citations in his section describing the levels of mystical union with God, it would be reasonable to assume that Ibn Khaldun repeatedly practiced Sufi *dhikr* rituals, or 'remembrance' of the divine.

Was Ibn Khaldun a Sufi? In many respects, probably yes. He had to be Sufi, or at least to have had overt Sufi leanings to qualify in 1389 AD for the position of sheikh at the Sufi Baybarsiyya *khanqa*, or Sufi center of worship, in Cairo.[39] He praised the Mamluks for endowing so many of these *khanqas*, or convents for Sufi practice, hermitages for Sufi ascetics, and schools for the study of Sufism. Although he decried the corruption of these institutions, he claimed the establishment of these endowments would assure their benefactors of eternal rewards.[40] His respect for the predictions of Sufi saints, his general approach to perception and to reason, his frequent visits to the shrine of the Sufi saint Abu Madyan for spiritual retreat, and the influence of his father and his father's teachers, would all have turned Ibn Khaldun toward the waves of Sufism sweeping through the Maghrib. In other respects, however, Ibn Khaldun was certainly not a dedicated mystic who retreated from all worldly affairs. A lawyer, a judge, a councilor, and a man concerned with practical matters at least as much as spiritual ones, Ibn Khaldun was both of this world and aware of the spiritual world, a world that seemed to confirm God's existence despite the disunity, political disarray, and pestilence that characterized his era. In Ibn Khaldun's vision of the world it was not an ideal city of God, the vision of another famous North African named Saint Augustine (d. 430 AD), but the virtuous natural, if destructive, tribe that was the well-spring of civilization. In Sufism, one went through steps or levels to become closer to God, only to find the truth that was in front of one's face from the beginning. Similarly, tribalism, the basic and natural form of human organization, was the first and the last step, the beginning and the return of dynasties, governments and power. In fact, Sufism was clearly in his mind as he wrote the *Muqaddimah*. In 1374, immediately before writing the *Muqaddimah*, Ibn Khaldun completed a special treatise dedicated to Sufism, *Al-Shifaᵓ al-Saᵓil*, or the 'Answers for the Questioner.'[41]

Despite Ibn Khaldun's Sufi tendencies, the influence of his father, the visits to the shrine of Abu Madyan, the principal position at the Baybarsiyya Sufi *khanqa* in Cairo, some have identified Ibn Khaldun as anti-Sufi because of a peculiar *fatwa* attributed to him in which he lodged virulent attacks on illustrious Sufi masters. According to this alleged *fatwa*, dated to Ibn Khaldun's time in Egypt:

> Among those Sufis were Ibn ᶜArabi, Ibn Sabᵓin, Ibn Barrajan, and those who followed their steps and embraced their creed. They composed many works that they circulated among themselves. These [Sufi] works reek of downright unbelief and reprehensible innovation. [Any attempt to] explain their underlying meaning allegorically produces results that are as far-fetched as they are abhorrent . . . The judgment with respect to these and similar books is as follows: when found, they must be destroyed by fire or washed off by water, until the traces of writing disappear completely. Such an action is beneficial to the religion [of Islam] because it leads to the eradication of erroneous beliefs.

There are several major historical problems with this *fatwa* and its attribution to Ibn Khaldun. First, it was a quotation only attributed to Ibn Khaldun by a scholar from Fez who claimed to have met Ibn Khaldun in Egypt. This scholar, Taqi al-Din al-Fasi, was highly critical of the Sufis and especially Ibn ᶜArabi. He had every reason to misrepresent and even reformulate the position of the Qadi of Cairo, Ibn Khaldun, when he returned to Fez to write against the Sufis.[42] As an historical source, this *fatwa* was more useful as an indication of the esteem in which Ibn Khaldun was held and the extent to which those, like Al-Fasi, who wished to push for an agenda, attributed sayings to him, even if they wrote their opinions thousands of miles from Cairo. Second, even if this quotation was accurate, which is highly questionable since it does not make sense in the light of Ibn Khaldun's obvious affinity toward Sufism, he was probably only referring to the problem associated with the misunderstanding of Sufi knowledge by the masses and amateur novices who, in his description of Sufism, could become stuck in the ravine of 'combination' or *jam*^c, a false feeling of complete oneness with God which makes an adherent feel that he is, in fact, God.[43] Aziz al-Azmeh suggested that this passage could be explained by Ibn Khaldun's anti-eschatological position and anti-Shiite stance. Ibn Khaldun was mainly concerned with the political disruption caused by failed eschatological movements founded on false, mystical claims and related to Shiite doctrine.[44]

Even if this were a *fatwa* by Ibn Khaldun it may be explained by the division and potential rivalry between the 'high' Sufism practiced in the Sufi *khanqa*, or official, endowed institution such as the Baybarsiyya that Ibn Khaldun led, and their more popular, but poorer rivals, the *zawiyas*: small shrines built spontaneously and without a great deal of direction. In this context, Ibn Khaldun could simply be seen as doing his job as a protector of the established, 'high' practice of Sufism.[45] In fact, Ibn Khaldun's predecessors, including the esteemed elite scholar, Ibn al-Jawsi (d. 1200 AD) had criticized popular preachers who 'allegorically' misrepresented the ways of the Sufi masters. According to Al-Jawsi, the storytellers and popular preachers often used dubious tricks and employed 'lies' to increase their following. Ibn al-Jawsi claimed that none other than Al-Ghazali, whom Ibn Khaldun respected as the paragon Sufi jurist, similarly denounced the heretical teachings of popular preachers in Baghdad who, for example, depicted Satan as a 'true monotheist.' [46]

Ibn Khaldun was a Sufi, but he was also an elitist. Knowledge, whether philosophical or spiritual, was dangerous when put in the wrong hands. His elitism was distinct from Western notions of an urban-centered elite. Instead, he saw the tribes as holders of an elite prestige whose support was necessary for civilization.

CIVILIZATION OF AND FROM THE TRIBE

Following a dualistic logic of tribal versus settled, similar to his logic of a clash of East versus West, Samuel Huntington claimed that civilization was essentially, and could only really be, urban. Civilization was city life. In the Western historical tradition the *civitas*, the city on the hill, Aristotle's Atlantis, Augustine's City of God, was the telos, the goal and ideal of human civilization. More recently, Samuel Huntington suggested, 'Civilization began when agriculture and a definite form of organized village life became established.'[47] There were some Arab philosophers who thought that the urbane and the urban lifestyle were obviously superior to the lifestyle of the Bedouin. Averroes (Ibn Rushd), influenced so intensely by Aristotle and Plato, considered cities to be a higher, more developed, and essentially better, form of human organization than the 'barbarian' tribe.[48] For Ibn Rushd, 'prestige belongs to those who are ancient settlers in a town.'[49] Rather than seeing the tribe and the Bedouin as the antithesis of the civilized, or as a relic of a long-lost, primitive existence, the patronized 'noble savage,' Ibn Khaldun saw the tribe as civilization's constant and renewable source. There was tribal, Bedouin civilization as much as there was urban civilization. By expressing his theory that *ᶜasabiyya*, that primal social glue, was the basis for human society, Ibn Khaldun implicitly agreed with Aristotle's famous dictum that humanity was a social animal. Historically, there was probably substance to both Ibn Khaldun and Ibn Rushd's arguments. For, as Hodgson argued, it was an 'alliance of puritanical *faqihs* [trained] in the cities and relatively crude Berber pastoral tribesmen' that led to the rise of the great medieval Maghribi empires.[50] In his argument with Ibn Rushd, however, Ibn Khaldun was not judging the process or even necessarily the causes of the rise of urban dynasties, but rather their value, their morality, and prestige once they do rise. Even so, Ibn Khaldun's views of the countryside contradicted the established opinion contained in the works of the Greek philosophers.

Although he only had access to the book of Politics by a Pseudo-Aristotle, Ibn Khaldun was still exposed to the basic Greek philosophy of politics, if in altered form.[51] Unlike Aristotle, however, he did not propose that humanity developed in a linear fashion from a lower state of tribal barbarism to a necessarily morally higher state of urbanism. Although sedentary civilization may have been one of the 'goals of [urban] civilization' for Ibn Khaldun, this goal was not necessarily a good thing: 'it means the end of its lifespan and brings about its corruption.'[52] Nor did Ibn Khaldun negate the possibility that tribal peoples had their own form of civilization (*umran al bedu* in Arabic). After all, 'Bedouin are closer to being good than sedentary people,' their poetry was better, their manners, their way of speech, all of those notions that characterize what the word civilization originally meant in English, in French, and even in Arabic: *hadara*, the word Ibn Khaldun used for civilization did not simply mean cities and roads and bureaucracies. It also meant *politesse*, honor, poetics, and religious values; values that were often better held by tribal peoples.[53] All of these values could be associated with a basic aspect of tribal *ᶜasabiyya* that became lacking in cities: a sense of communal equality, a sharing not simply of economic goods and production necessary for survival in a precarious environment, but a sharing and sacrificing of individual will for the benefit of the honor of the tribe. In contrast, what an urban civilization gained though the division of labor, it necessarily lost in social solidarity and cohesion and even vulnerability to debilitating plagues.[54] Thus, he described the merchant as lacking in 'manliness' and honor.[55] The honor of the tribe meant more than the honor of any lone individual or urban economic community. This ideal of equality, this notion of common honor, founded on a primal human need, bred a fervent solidarity, transforming a tribe, or any society with strong tribal bonds, into something more akin to a single human body.

Ibn Khaldun did not come to this conclusion about tribes as the basis for human society, as the form from which other forms of civilization sprout, out of nothing. Rather, he spent a large amount of his adult life actually living with, or even defecting to, tribes and tribal peoples as an envoy of urbanized rulers. The Sufi sheikhs or the revered spiritual leaders of Sufi meeting houses in the countryside had a crucial role in negotiating and controlling feuds between tribal and kin groups in anthropologist Ernest Gellner's notion of Muslim society.[56] Similarly, Ibn Khaldun negotiated not only between tribes but also between dynasties ruling from cities and their rural tribal supporters. Although he had none of the *baraka* or spiritual charisma of a Sufi sheikh, Ibn Khaldun did have the pluck and ability to gain the respect of, and often manipulate, both restless tribesmen and manipulative rulers. What made Ibn Khaldun's philosophy unique was that it reflected his interesting position at the margins of both government and rule by pure *ᶜasabiyya*. Although he grew up in a fairly elite, urban context, Ibn Khaldun did not have the common prejudice of the urban intellectual who saw distance from the city as inversely proportional to intellect. In this respect, Ibn Khaldun described tribal society in ways that are similar to the way it has been described by postmodern scientists of human society who lived and worked closely with peoples remote from urban influence. The anthropologist and theorist Mary Douglas, for example, did extensive research on remote and isolated tribes as a way of understanding the origins of urbanized human societies and ritual. Like Ibn Khaldun, Mary Douglas assumed that the same rules of solidarity that applied in the tribe could be applied in the broader context of the city and dynasties.[57]

By no means could Ibn Khaldun think like a postmodern anthropologist. However, *ᶜasabiyya*, this central idea of Ibn Khaldun's, the idea that hunter-gatherers, tribal peoples, peoples usually considered on the fringes of society, are actually better off in many respects than settled people, has many chance similarities with the ideas of postmodern scholars, scholars who have not accepted modernism, urbanism, or typical Western views of progress uncritically. Ibn Khaldun claimed, for instance, how, even at the height of urbanized civilization, the people as a whole were actually most miserable, most vulnerable to pestilence, invasion, and destruction.[58] Of all people, Ibn Khaldun was certainly familiar with the ravages of disease, which killed off his family and most of his mentors, and the fact that the plague seemed to beset the city more than the country. Certainly, Ibn Khaldun acknowledged the apparently positive social effects of urbanism – monuments, institutions, the apparent outward wealth of urbanized existence – but he also saw these things as a source of their own destruction: a cancer of luxury and urban overstretch that brought about its own decline. For Ibn Khaldun, systematic agriculture, the source of settled life, was not necessarily an automatic good.[59] He saw, for instance, how Bedouin, hunter-gatherers, and those living in the countryside in small groups were often much better off than those in the cities, an observation that is repeated in the work of contemporary historical ecologists such as Jark Harlan, who observed, as did Ibn Khaldun, but with the tools of scientific analysis, some astonishing differences between large agricultural groups and smaller, hunter-gatherer groups:

> The ethnographic evidence indicates that people who do not farm do about everything that farmers do, but they do not work as hard . . . There is evidence that the diet of gathering peoples was better than that of cultivators, that starvation was rare, that their health status was generally superior, that there was a lower incidence of chronic disease and not nearly so many cavities in their teeth. The question must be raised: Why farm?[60]

Ibn Khaldun implicitly asked a very similar question: why farm, why settle? The consequences of farming, including the imposition of unjust taxes on farmers and the tyrannical rule that farming seemed to encourage, were condemned by Ibn Khaldun, not simply as socially harmful but as contrary to Islamic principles. The reason Muhammad proclaimed 'the hour will not rise until the charity tax becomes an (agricultural) impost,' according to Ibn Khaldun, was because too intense an occupation with agriculture inevitably leads to unjust rule, exploitation, overpopulation, famine and, ultimately, war and overthrow, thereby negating any beneficial effects agriculture may have had.[61] Why create cities and urban environments that only end up harming their inhabitants with plague, pestilence, luxury, and the loss of social cohesion? Indeed, for postmodernists such as Pierre Bourdieu, contemporary society, for all the benefits in lifespan and technology, has unbearable ills. Mega civilization, especially of the freewheeling, tyrannical, or neo-liberal kind, created, according to Bourdieu's theory, symbolic violence over the individual, the destruction of nature, and the loss of social bonds.[62] Ibn Khaldun, of course, was not even close to the intellectual context of Pierre Bourdieu, who, nonetheless, lived, like Ibn Khaldun, among the Berbers of Kabyle in Algeria. It is interesting to note that unlike Ibn Khaldun, who moved freely between sponsors and governments, Pierre Bourdieu, constrained by the same symbolic violence of paternal nationalism he later described, could not as easily give up his assignment as an ethnographer of Berbers for the French colonial state.[63] Whereas Pierre Bourdieu, inspired by the Berbers, explained the structural motivations for inequality in neo-liberal society, Ibn Khaldun saw the origins of the problem of urban civilization in its very inception. For Bourdieu, change was an illusion and social structures were essentially immortal. For Ibn Khaldun, change was real but it occurred in a spiral and in a universe determined as much by God's will as by man. For Ibn Khaldun there were at least two possible answers to the question of why humans choose a form of society that seemed to be against their immediate interests: religion, and/or the manipulation of tribal solidarity into super-tribal societies. In fact, the combination of religious inspiration and tribal solidarity was often an unbeatable mix: 'Dynasties of wide power and large royal authority have their origin in religion based either on prophecy or on truthful propaganda.'[64]

These apparent similarities between Ibn Khaldun and postmodernism (at least in the rejection of progressivism and the assumptions of the modernists) by no means allow us to call Ibn Khaldun a postmodernist. In many respects, Ibn Khaldun's relationship with tribes was richer and more pragmatically focused than that of the observer and the observed found in anthropology of the past century. He needed to be with, to negotiate with, and to live with tribes as part of his duty as a courtier, as part of the expectations society had placed upon him. He was as much a part of the dynamic of tribe and settled, the overthrow of old tribal dynasties to be replaced by fresher, new ones from the countryside, as he was an observer.

Yet even as he generalized about rural and urban life in the *Muqaddimah*, Ibn Khaldun did not describe all tribal peoples as the same. The North African portion of the Mediterranean was divided at the time into two major linguistic, ethnic and tribal groups: the Berbers and the Arabs. Ibn Khaldun worked for both Arabs, in Al-Andalus and in Cairo, and for Berbers, the rulers of Fez. He interacted at least as much with both Arabs and Berbers, often as an envoy between Bedouin tribes and urban rulers. Although both Arabs and Berbers were subject to the same universal, historical rules, in many ways the subtle and not so subtle tensions and differences between the two, especially after the devastating wave of invasions by the Arab Banu Hilal tribe beginning in the tenth century and described by Ibn Khaldun in detail, did much to confirm his theories about the importance of lineage and tribal solidarity. His description of the Berbers, for example, comprised perhaps the most important source on medieval Berber North Africa. This dedication to Berber history was ever the more incredible since Ibn Khaldun was such a staunch Arab.

IBN KHALDUN AND THE BERBERS

Ibn Khaldun claimed to be from pure, Arab stock. In his autobiography he traced his ancestors back in an unbroken line to Waʾil ibn Hujr from the Hadramawt region in Yemen, a famous Arab chief and companion of the Prophet Muhammad.[65] The Tunisian historian Muhammad Talbi even suggested that Ibn Khaldun was something of an Arab (and Andalusi) nationalist.[66] However, Ibn Khaldun's proud Arab ancestry did not keep him from writing extensively and, more importantly, with an open mind on the Berber population of the Maghrib. Indeed his *Muqaddimah* and the rest of the *Kitab al-ʿIbar* are some of the most important sources not only of Arab, but also of Berber history. It is for this reason that so much space is devoted to Ibn Khaldun's fascinating interaction with Berbers, an interaction that was not necessarily typical for an Arab of his background. This section will examine some possible reasons why Ibn Khaldun, a man born into an Arab intellectual elite with a family tied to Andalusia, ended up writing one of the most nuanced sources of Berber history available.

Ibn Khaldun's generally positive attitude towards the Berbers differed from most of his Arab contemporaries. Contemporary and near-contemporary Arab writers, especially those of the East, such as the twelfth/thirteenth-century historian from Mosul, Ibn al-Athir, often held unsympathetic views of the Berbers as barbaric and outside standard Arab, Islamic culture. Andalusi Arabs were often even more disparaging of Berbers, especially after Al-Andalus had been overtaken by the Berber Almoravids and Almohads. In the *Tauq al Hamama*, a peculiar pamphlet on courtly love by the literalist scholar Ibn Hazm, who belonged to the Arab aristocracy with its origins in Umayyad Syria that once ruled Spain, the Almoravid Berbers were described as fanatics, brutes, and hypocrites who were tricked by wily *faqihs*, or religious missionaries, and who had fallen quickly into debauchery. The Berbers were barbaric pillagers of his house in Cordoba.[67] Although from the same aristocratic Andalusi stock as Ibn Hazm, and although his ancestors would have similarly felt the blow of the Almoravid entry into Islamic Seville, Ibn Khaldun did not think to describe Berbers so disparagingly. Unlike Eastern and Andalusi historians, Ibn Khaldun had intense personal experience with the Berbers in their original environments. And as he worked for them and tried to please them, these personal contacts directly influenced his views on the Berbers and their history. Moreover, much of his theoretical historical concepts were based on his understanding of the history of the Maghrib, in which Berbers played such a prominent role. As written by Ibn Khaldun, the history of North African Berber dynasties, from the Almoravids to the Almohads to the Marinids and Hafsids, inspired Ibn Khaldun's overall model of history, a model based on the central role of tribes and group solidarity, *ʿasabiyya*, in the rise and fall of dynasties. As a consequence Berbers played a prominent role in his work.

In addition to his personal experience living with Berber and Arab tribes, Ibn Khaldun also worked for various Berber rulers. He praised the Hafsid Berber ruler Abu al-ᶜAbbas as the 'one to whom people turn their faces, and you are the great hope of all.'[68] This Hafsid ruler also became Ibn Khaldun's patron for the first version of the *Muqaddimah* – a later version was dedicated to the Mamluk sultan of Egypt, Barquq – and in his autobiography he writes: 'From my work I offer to your [Abu al-ᶜAbbas] grandeur precious pearls and stars that never set. I have created glory for your realm . . . You are able to see truth in all things, who could pretend to say anything false . . . God has accorded you a position higher than all others . . . You are the most equitable.'[69] Obviously, the Berbers had both a direct and indirect impact on the content of Ibn Khaldun's work. This was obvious even in Ibn Khaldun's explanation of the origin of the word Berber.

Read in isolation, Ibn Khaldun's oft-quoted explanation of the origins of the word 'Berber' seems to simply reiterate the notion that their name was adapted from the word 'barbarian': those who do not speak our language:

> Their language is not only foreign but of a special kind, which is why they are called Berbers. They say that when Ifriqish . . . invaded the Maghrib and Ifriqiya, they say to which he gave his name, killing Jurjis, the king, and building villages and towns, he encountered this strange race with its peculiar tongue, and struck with amazement exclaimed: 'What a barbara you have!' For this reason, they were called the Berbers. The word *barbara* in Arabic means a mixture of unintelligible noises, applied, for example, to the roaring of a lion.[70]

In fact, Ibn Khaldun called the history of Ifriqis an erroneous legend, and he used this legend as an example of how *not* to write history.[71] As Ibn Khaldun likely grasped, most Berbers probably would have called themselves not Berber (a label placed on them from the outside) but *Amazigh*: a word roughly translated as 'free man.'

Ibn Khaldun saw this natural state of 'freedom' as both a blessing and a curse. In the *Muqaddimah* Ibn Khaldun described the Berbers as constantly rebellious and incapable of 'obedience and submission' to the standard forms of Arab Islam. Although ᶜasabiyya was described by Ibn Khaldun as the source of new empires and civilizations, there was, in his view, almost too much ᶜasabiyya among the Berbers, too much tribalism and clannishness to form a long-lasting, authoritative state like the ᶜAbbasid empire. He writes in the *Muqaddimah*: 'Every time a tribe is pacified another takes its place, adopting the same attitude of rebellion . . .'[72]

Yet, even as he doubted the long-term sustainability of Berber dynasties in the Maghrib, he praised the purity, power, and aggressive potential of even the most remote Berber tribes. The Saskawa Berber tribe, one of the original Almohad tribes that still inhabits the Atlas Mountains south of Marrakech, for example, he described as 'Lovers of the hardy life, never adopting the ways of luxury . . . The mountain they inhabit forms the highest region of the Atlas and offers a better refuge than fortified castles. Impenetrable rocks and sheer peaks make it inviolable: it touches the celestial sphere and is covered in a veil of clouds, its peak crowned by stars.'[73]

Thus, in Ibn Khaldun's analysis, Berber tribes could be either a destructive or a creative force in history. In the *Muqaddimah* he used Berber North Africa as an example of a region that could 'rarely be submitted to a state in a durable fashion.'[74] The large number of tribes and clans in the Maghrib also led to 'disobedience and rebelliousness.' This contradiction between the creative and destructive power of tribes recurs in Ibn Khaldun's description of other races, such as the Arabs, Turks, and Mongols. In Ibn Khaldun's view, Timurlane was a barbarian but also potentially the new hope of the Islamic world, a unifier as well as a destroyer. Ibn Khaldun called Timurlane 'The man of the century in possession of an *ᶜasabiyya* to reunify the Muslim world and change the course of history.'[75]

Still, the Maghrib he viewed differently from the eastern parts of the Muslim world: 'The situation in Iraq and Syria was different . . . the population was largely from cities and villages. When the Muslim Arabs took over, they offered neither opposition nor resistance.'[76]

Berbers from the Maghrib, on the other hand, had fiercely resisted outside Arab rule. However, this did not mean that they were incapable of creating civilization and dynasties among their own ranks – far from it. In fact, those Berbers with the highest amount of *ᶜasabiyya* could emerge as rulers. This was especially true if *ᶜasabiyya* was combined with religion and a prophetic mission. In the section of the *Muqaddimah* dedicated to group solidarity and religious inspiration, Ibn Khaldun describes the Almohad and Almoravid Berber empires as his two examples of the power of *ᶜasabiyya* combined with religious inspiration. In both the Almoravid and Almohad cases, the Berbers did not submit to rule or domination by tribes or people from outside the Maghrib. Rather, they adopted a doctrine that would unite Berber tribes around a common prophetic ideal: 'Religion gives the state, at its beginning, a supplementary force in addition to *ᶜasabiyya.*'[77]

The apparent tension between Ibn Khaldun's description of Berber peoples as rebellious, incapable of long-lasting civilizations and government, but also in possession of the most noble qualities and capable of avoiding luxury and banding together to form new civilizations and empires is, in fact, a central feature of his work and theory. The most remote of peoples suddenly became the core of history and civilization. The urban center was constantly being invaded but also morally and socially renewed by the tribal frontier. And although Ibn Khaldun also studied other tribal peoples like the Arabs and Turks, the Berbers of North Africa form one of the main sources of inspiration for his cyclical theory of history.

BERBER IDENTITY

In the introduction to his description of the Berber tribes and dynasties in the *Kitab al-ʿIbar*, Ibn Khaldun praised the Berbers. In an extraordinary, long list of Berber achievements he sometimes seems to have become a panegyrist of Berber history, gushing at the 'talents of the Berber race, used both in ancient times and today, and their noble qualities for which they are elevated to the power and the rank of a nation.'[78] When he described the Berbers as divided by tribe, internal feuds, and blood, stubbornly against the rise of urban powers, Ibn Khaldun did not necessarily see this as a hindrance to their identity as a people, a nation. On the contrary, Ibn Khaldun recognized the power of Berber achievements and the strength of Berber identity despite centuries of Roman, Visigoth and Arab invasions and attempts to control them.

The history of the Arab invasions and the relationship between the Arabs and the Berbers was particularly important to Ibn Khaldun's theory of the strength of the Berber identity. He mentioned the strong resistance of the Berbers from the famous Dihyat al-Kahina who resisted the first Arab invasions and gained mythical status in the minds of all Berbers and the early North African Kharijites who resisted ʿAbbasid attempts to enslave the Berbers and treat them as second-class Muslims. He also referred to the establishment of Islamic empires based on Berber tribes: the desert Berbers of the Sahara who established the Almoravid Empire, and the mountain Berbers of the Atlas who established the Almohad Empire. And although Berber rulers and dynasties often adopted invented, Arab pedigrees that would link them to the Prophet Muhammad, they still, according to Ibn Khaldun, maintained their independent character: 'All of these pretensions are nothing but flatteries by those [genealogists] who wish to please their rulers.'[79] By adopting lineages linked to the Prophet and claiming descent from prestigious Arab tribes, Berbers could claim the legitimacy of Arab, Islamic rule without necessarily being ruled by outside, Arab tribes.[80]

For Ibn Khaldun, the history of the Berbers was a history defined by vigorous defiance and prideful resilience, an almost indescribable vigor rooted in the rough contours of the Berber experience. The main reason for the resilience of the Berbers, a resilience that lasted despite many attempts at controlling and taxing them, was their tribal solidarity. Berber success and Berber history was rooted in their ability to unite against external threats and in their ability to plant the seeds of new civilizations from simple, tribal beginnings.

Yet even as Ibn Khaldun praised the history of the Berbers, and dedicated so much of his work to the deeds of great Berber heroes and tribes, he lamented the loss of the Berber character in his own time. Compared with the great Berber dynasties of the past, the fourteenth century was generally a period of decline in Berber North Africa. The Berbers had 'fallen into decadence.' They had 'lost their solidarity and sense of spirit because of luxury.' They had grown used to 'domination.'[81] Even worse, they submitted to unlawful taxation by urban powers. They had become 'like slaves.'[82] By writing his history of the Berbers he wished to demonstrate the laudable qualities of the Berbers, to preserve their memory, to prove that the simple rural life of most Berbers did not preclude the ability to form great civilizations and honorable heroes. He asks the reader not to forget Berber history, not to forget, for example, the great Berber leaders like the chief Uzmar bin Sulat of the Zanata Berber confederation who nearly defeated the Arab armies and the powerful Katama tribe who expelled the ʿAbbasids and created the Fatimid dynasty.[83]

CYCLES OF HISTORY

The Berbers, like the Arabs, exemplified, for Ibn Khaldun, the theory that power was held not in the trappings of central, urban, organized authority, but in hardy tribes, in people often on the edge of survival, remote from the corruption and excess of urban life. For Ibn Khaldun, power must be seen across time, not simply in a single space. Future or potential power paradoxically rested in those tribes farthest away from power. Tribes that controlled the city quickly lost power to other tribes on the fringes. True power was like a mirage in a desert. Power, in a sense, could never be fully held; only attempts at authority and central control could exist, attempts that were quickly overturned by the rise of another tribal confederation, another religious leader, another idea backed by the potent force of tribal solidarity. For Ibn Khaldun the history of the Berbers was the history of this constant, but impossible, competitive race for illusive power. It was not power, which is essentially static, or illusory, but the race itself that defined Berber (and Arab) civilization, the cycle that brought about new and vigorous dynasties. In summary, these were Ibn Khaldun's stages in the dynastic cycle:

(1) Dynasties originate among virtuous tribes with enduring discipline. The first generation of rulers is successful because of their immediate connection to the glory and honor of the tribe.

(2) The second generation of rulers establishes itself in the city. Although there is a strong connection with the memories of the father and the first generation, the second generation begins adopting luxuries and other refinements that begin to isolate the ruler from tribal support. Nevertheless, the ruler is often able to harness enough loyalty and power to build impressive urban monuments or projects such as walls and mosques.

(3) In the third generation decline really begins to accelerate. The ruler has little connection with the original environment of the tribe, and the ease of urban life, so enriched by the previous generations of rulers, makes the ruler profligate and weak. Taxes increase and the people become restless.

(4) By the fourth generation a dynasty teeters on the brink of collapse. Unless saved by an unusual infusion of prophecy, economic windfalls, or popular complacency, a dynasty is usually doomed. Estimating the length of a dynasty at four generations, Ibn Khaldun limited the natural lifespan of dynasties to that of a human.

(5) In the fifth stage a new dynasty arrives, supported by the *ʿasabiyya* of a new tribe. Stages one through four could then repeat indefinitely.[84]

To illustrate this cycle, Ibn Khaldun described the Berbers and their history according to tribal confederation. He separated the Berbers into four main groups: the descendants of Butr, including the Nefzawa, the Luwata, and the Banu Fatan of Tunisia; the Sanhaja, including the famous Lamtuna tribes that established the Almoravid Empire; the Masmuda, who established the Almohad and Hafsid Empire; and the Zanata, who established the Marinid Empire. By dividing the Berbers according to branch or confederation, Ibn Khaldun was able to illustrate his thesis that power passed from one branch to another in a cycle. First, there were the Sanhaja, then the Masmuda, then the Zanata.

Yet Ibn Khaldun's cycle of history was not simply a cycle of 'rise and fall.' The supposed rise to power of a Berber tribal confederation was simultaneously the beginning of their fall into urban decadence, the death knell of tribal solidarity. 'Power was the end of tribal solidarity,' even as it was the beginning of decadence and decline.[85] Like the human body, the body of the state inevitably decayed. Achieving power could soon become the same as losing it. The fall of a dynasty or state meant the rise of tribal groups very similar to those who first established the state. Ibn Khaldun claimed that rural tribes, not cities, were the true reservoir of power, a reservoir that could break and overflow into ruinous luxury once power and urbanity seemed to be in hand: 'Only those tribes living in the countryside possess group solidarity';[86] and 'savage nations have the greatest amount of power.'[87]

By making the claim that true power was held in the potential force of tribal peoples, Ibn Khaldun disputed the assumptions of his eminent predecessors. One of these predecessors, the philosopher Ibn Rushd (d. 1198 AD), claimed that illustriousness and power was centered in the urban environment. Ibn Khaldun, in contrast, claimed that power could be sustained only by a new clan in power. The people of the city dominated by the tribe would even adopt the dress and ways of the tribe. According to Ibn Khaldun, the vanquished always imitate the victors. The tribe, not the urban aristocracy, was the source of authority, change, and culture. In Ibn Khaldun's view, Ibn Rushd was overly influenced by his urban upbringing. He 'grew up in a society and in a country not familiar with tribal solidarity.'[88]

Contrasting himself with Ibn Rushd, Ibn Khaldun used his own experience living with Berber tribes and working with Berber and Arab rulers as a primary source of his ideas, ideas not found in the customary, chronological histories of his predecessors. Ibn Khaldun's intuitions gained from constant exposure to Berbers as well as Arabs was part of the 'inner meaning' of history to Ibn Khaldun. Although he found much of his information in books and libraries, Ibn Khaldun seems also to have formed many ideas from his own experience, an experience heavily influenced by living with Berbers.

THE BODY POLITIC

The rise and fall of the Berber dynasties of North Africa also fitted Ibn Khaldun's idea that dynasties decay with a natural rhythm. Nature, the human body, and the attributes of the body, including growth and decay, corruption, mortality and luxurious desire, were inseparable from Ibn Khaldun's concept of civilization. The clockwork of the body and the clockwork of nature were the clockwork of society. He wrote for instance: 'When a man has reached the age of forty, nature stops growing for a while, then starts to decline. It should be known that the same is the case with [urban] civilization . . .'[89] Unlike the modern European state, with its vast divide between nature, the physical body, and distant, ideological, and institutional structures, Ibn Khaldun saw the nature of civilization as directly dependent upon, and perfectly conjoined with, the physical and spiritual body. Ibn Khaldun saw the human life cycle reflected in the life cycle of dynasties. Just as the tribe and the city were intimately connected, so were nature and society connected. What happened in nature, literally the 'body politic,' reflected what happened in human history. In this way, Ibn Khaldun categorized the rise and fall of dynasties and urban civilizations into cyclical stages.[90]

Ibn Khaldun's philosophy about the cyclical nature of urban civilization should not be confused with the pessimistic visions of later, European cyclical

theorists such as Oswald Spengler who, like Ibn Khaldun, saw luxury and imperial over-reach as the cause of decline. For Spengler, a society did not become
fully civilized until doomsday and decline were knocking at the gates.[91] For
Ibn Khaldun, however, the civilization of the over-ripe urban variety was by no
means superior or more developed than the culture of the original Bedouin who
had invaded the city years ago and had begun their dynastic rule, rooted in the
strength of the desert or the mountainside.

The history of Berber dynasties in North Africa from the eleventh to the
fourteenth centuries fit Ibn Khaldun's ideas about the natural lifespan of dynasties, the 'body politic.' Asia and Arabia and the East were a messy hodgepodge
of geographical, ethnic, religious, and political complexity. A massive tribal
invasion might come from deep in the steppe regions of Asia, seemingly from
nowhere. In the medieval Maghrib, in contrast, events were somewhat more predictable, more 'natural.' Ibn Khaldun's ideas about the natural lifespan of dynasties applied more easily to the fairly enclosed Berber North African context.
The rise and fall of the Almoravid dynasty in the eleventh century from their
Berber Saharan origins in about a century, the rise and fall of the Almohads in
the twelfth century from their Berber, mountain origins in about a century and
the rise and fall of the Marinids in the thirteenth century from their origins in
the oasis of Figuig, all fit into Ibn Khaldun's conceptual map of history. Berber
history in the medieval period was a clear and compelling model, an almost
rhythmic case study of Ibn Khaldun's ideas. Nevertheless, Ibn Khaldun's ideas
were themselves reflections of his historical context and should not be accepted
uncritically.

RE-THINKING IBN KHALDUN'S CYCLE

Ibn Khaldun's theory of the rise of dynasties through tribal, moral courage and
fall of dynasties into urban luxury has not been universally accepted by modern
historians of the medieval Maghrib. In fact, Ibn Khaldun's cycle of history was
at least as much a moral and philosophical vision, a vision certainly influenced
by Ibn Khaldun's life and interest, as a social theory supported by testable sup-
positions. Some authors have accused Ibn Khaldun of being too fatalistic, of
generalizing the muddle and complexity of social phenomenon into one 'homo-
geneous doctrine.'[92] Other critiques have used historical evidence to question
Ibn Khaldun's assumption that luxury, that is, urban consumption and urban rule,
necessarily led to the decline and fall of dynasties in medieval North Africa. R.
Messier, the archaeologist and historian of the medieval Maghrib, for example,
uses extensive evidence to show that the Almoravid Berber Empire declined
not because of urban waste and overspending on cities but because of overly

vigorous and expensive *jihad*, or holy war. The Almoravids were not seduced and brought down by the soft, luxurious ways of their urban conquests in Al-Andalus, but by their attempt to simultaneously wage *jihad* against Christians and the Almohads. The expense of *jihad*, not the expense of city living, forced the Almoravid ruler to raise 'unIslamic' taxes. This only increased the popularity of their Mountain Berber Almohad rivals, who rejected such taxes. They also failed to construct an adequate bureaucracy to run their empire. Messier concluded 'the lure of their arid homeland with its culture and ethos so utterly different from Spain, made them unwilling to struggle too hard to maintain an empire beyond the desert.' For Messier, it was lack of acculturation to urbanism, not the excesses of urbanism that led the Almoravids to 'return to the desert.'[93] In this sense, Messier had almost more confidence than Ibn Khaldun in the ability of the ruling tribe to maintain its identity and social cohesion – almost to the extent that it was a stumbling block. In any case, Messier implicitly supported Ibn Khaldun's chief argument about the importance of tribal *ᶜasabiyya*, even in the context of urban civilization.

CIVILIZATIONAL ASSUMPTIONS

Ibn Khaldun's views of the Berbers and other tribal peoples seemed ambivalent. At one moment he seemed to say that the Berbers were savage, incapable of urbanity or living in cities.[94] At another moment he seemed to suggest that Berbers were ranked highest among nations and civilizations. What explains this apparent contradiction in Ibn Khaldun's views? Why does he describe the Berber tribes as both the seeds of civilization and the source of decline? To answer this question, a paradigm shift is required – a shift away from the typical, Western emphasis on cities and urbanism as the basis for civilization.

Cities, urbanism, monuments, structures, and written institutions are what Western Europeans have assumed to be the prerequisite of true civilization. This Western bias for urbanism as a superior form of human organization has its roots deep in classical Athens and Rome. A closer reading and a better understanding of Ibn Khaldun's own life and context reveals, however, that he never put urban civilization on a pedestal. The European mind-set, perhaps since the rise of Athens in the fifth century BC, has insisted on urbanism and civilization being one and the same. In contrast, as discussed above, Ibn Khaldun described a concept that many in Western Europe might consider to be an inherent contradiction: the concept of 'rural civilization.' For Ibn Khaldun, rural civilization, a civilization characterized by tribalism and the rough condition of humans on little food or nourishment, constantly on the brink of annihilation by war, rivalry, or starvation, was not only an alternative form of civilization, it was the cause, the source of civilization itself. Even for medieval Andalusis who lived in cities, like Ibn Rushd, this is a difficult concept to digest. How could civilization exist in the most extreme conditions, at the brink of survival? Where could one find the seed for complex societies in Berbers, people who lived in simple, rural tribes? For Ibn Khaldun, however, civilization was more than the outward, superficial manifestations of power, more than the monuments, streets, palaces, even the written histories and glorified memories of rulers written by sycophantic poets. His observations of the Berbers and his original reading of their history confirmed what he understood as the hidden course of human history and the original source of civilizations in tribal or group *ʿasabiyya*. Berber history formed the model for his organic understanding of history as a process of birth from a tribal seed, decay, and then rebirth with another tribal dynasty emerging phoenix-like from the ashes. Although the Berbers were not that different from other tribal peoples like the Arabs and the Turks, whose history and civilization seemed to reflect Ibn Khaldun's ideas, the Berbers were the most readily available for his studies.

Ibn Khaldun, a scholar, diplomat, and minister for Berber rulers and Berber tribes, did not simply sit back and watch the course of events. Rather, he constructed a pattern in the North African, Berber society that surrounded him, a pattern that sparked his interest in the rise and fall of dynasties, a pattern that inspired him to look into the meaning of history.

Ibn Khaldun claimed to be a pure Arab, but his experiences, his patrons, his intellectual curiosity all led him to write probably the most important account of pre-modern Berber history available. And although the Berbers were not the exclusive inspiration for Ibn Khaldun's ideas, they were certainly one of the most important. The Arabs and the invasion of Arab tribes into North Africa were similarly an important example used by Ibn Khaldun. For most of his career before writing the *Muqaddimah*, Ibn Khaldun was a courtier to Berber rulers, not Arabs. It was thus without irony after all that a proud Arab should be the source of much of what is known about the medieval Berber past.

IBN KHALDUN AND THE ARABS

Ibn Khaldun recorded that in 1051 the Fatimid wazir in Egypt, Al-Yazuri, released a large group of nomadic Arabs, the Banu Hilal, and sent them to Tunis. According to Ibn Khaldun, he did this to punish Muʿizz bin Badis, the Zirid amir of Tunis who had switched his loyalty from the Fatimid caliph in Cairo to the ʿAbbasid caliph in Baghdad. Almost immediately, the Zirid amir was defeated by the overpowering force of various Banu Hilal tribes, including the Riyah and the Zughba, tribes that Ibn Khaldun would deal with as a negotiator centuries later. In fact, several historians have disputed this legendary migration commemorated in the *taghriba*, a series of famous Arabic epic poems boasting of their journey and conquests.[95] The historian Michael Brett, for instance, claimed that the Zughba Arabs had been in the region of Tripoli and North Africa decades before the alleged revenge of the Fatimids. In fact, much of Ibn Khaldun's depiction of the Arabs as a great horde, as the 'swarm of locusts,' but also as a redeeming force to overturn urban luxury – tough, triumphant and fierce warriors – was based on myth. This myth was, in fact, perpetuated by both the Banu Hilal and by Ibn Khaldun, the tribal negotiator, to increase their fierce reputation.[96]

Regardless of their origins, the increased prominence of Banu Hilal and Banu Sulaim Arabs in North Africa – the Banu Sulaim arrived in the thirteenth century – dramatically changed the situation of the Berbers in North Africa at least as much as the original Muslim conquests. While the initial Arab conquests put the Berbers under the weak, superficial control of the ʿAbbasids, they often successfully balked at Arab overlords and rebelled. The influx of camel-herding Banu Hilal in great numbers, however, added a completely new element to the rural dynamics of North Africa. In terms that are not especially sympathetic to his Arab cousins in North Africa, Ibn Khaldun described how, 'The Berbers, the original population of the Maghrib, have been replaced by an influx of Arabs [the Banu Hilal], that began in the eleventh century. The Arabs outnumbered and overpowered the Berbers, stripped them of most of their lands . . .'[97] Although some scholars have accused him of this, Ibn Khaldun did not subscribe to the zero sum notion of Berber versus Arab.[98] In fact, as described above, the ostensibly 'Arab' tribe that housed and protected Ibn Khaldun at the Qalʿat ibn Salama was itself associated with a branch of the Berber Banu Tujin. The dividing lines between Berber and Arab were set in sand, not in stone, even after the Banu Hilal invasion. In fact, according to the anthropologist Augustin Berque, the elder descendants of the 'Arab' tribe that hosted Ibn Khaldun at the Qalʿat ibn Salama while he wrote the *Muqaddimah* still spoke Berber as late as the Second World War.[99] Almost immediately after their influx into North Africa, in fact, the Arab chieftains intermarried with the rulers of North Africa; even the daughters of the defeated Badis were married to chiefs. They thus gained aristocratic prestige while generally maintaining their nomadic way of life. Through intermarriage and through their obvious military power, they become indispensable, if thorny and fickle, auxiliaries for the armies of Berber rulers.[100] Ibn Khaldun's many negotiations with the Arab Dawawida, Riyah, and Zughba showed just how important this relationship between Berber sultan and Arab tribes remained centuries later. Taken out of context, however, some of Ibn Khaldun's descriptions of the Arabs seem outright simplifications – this was particularly strange considering Ibn Khaldun's own self-described aristocratic Arab heritage.

Seemingly unaware of Ibn Khaldun's motivations for depicting the Arabs he negotiated with as frightening harbingers of doom to his Berber patrons such as Abu al-ᶜAbbas, the scholar E. F. Gautier used Ibn Khaldun's description of the Arabs and their invasion as evidence of an irreconcilable divide between the urban and the nomadic.[101] Ibn Khaldun, in fact, saw the seeds of civilization in the roughest of Banu Hilal Bedouin Arabs. Although the Arabs were 'unskilled at navigation, unfamiliar with crafts and sciences, unable to select proper sites for cities, and unwilling to subordinate themselves,' it was precisely this stubborn resistance to urbanized 'civilization' that made the Arabs such hearty and excellent conquerors of cities.[102] The Bedouin, like the Berbers, were a manifestation of the natural state of human society. Many of the same cycles, rules, and patterns he used to describe Berber history also appeared to describe the Arabs who were a new element, a new well of tribal ᶜ*asabiyya*, thrown into the mix of North African history. Ibn Khaldun's close relationship with the several Banu Hilal Arabs and the 'aristocratic' Dawawida, the powerful camel-herding clan of the Banu Hilal, in particular, must have influenced his description of the Bedouin as both frighteningly destructive and naturally pure. The more Ibn Khaldun portrayed the Bedouin as fearsome harbingers of the apocalypse – the Arabs as 'swarms of locusts' was actually a reference to the day of judgment (Qurᵓan 54:7) – the more important he became as a negotiator between rulers such as Abu al-ᶜAbbas and the Bedouin. In his autobiography, the Hafsid and Marinid and Zayyanid Berber sultans seemed almost subject to, or held hostage to the whims of the Dawawida, Riyah, and Zughba Arabs who could switch sides according to which sultan paid the most. In fact, the Arab nomads often fought between themselves for the honor and wealth of the sultan's patronage. The Arab Banu Muzni who hosted Ibn Khaldun at the walled oasis of Biskra, for example, paid the Dawawida taxes because the Hafsid sultan had chosen the Dawawida for his army. Eventually, as more and more Arabs settled down, more and more taxes could be levied by the Hafsid sultan. Instead of being fierce resisters of the Berber sultan, 'the tribes of the Banu Hilal and their successors flourished along the borderline between rulers and ruled as agents and as victims of the system.'[103]

Soon, the Banu Hilal would themselves be replaced by new migrations. As other Arab migrants, such as the Banu Sulaim, came into the Maghrib, competition for the sultan's favor and payment increased, as did competition for territory. The situation for the Banu Hilal Arabs and their traditional camel-herding livelihood was becoming increasingly perilous. As their numbers increased, the Arabs were forced to settle, to herd and, eventually, to use their prestigious genealogy and epic poetry as an asset. They become Marabouts, leaders who used claims of descent from the Prophet Muhammad to secure legitimacy and power.

NOTES

1 Ibn Khaldun, *Muqaddimah*, vol. I, 11.

2 *Muqaddimah*, vol. I, 6.

3 *Muqaddimah*, vol. 1, 9.

4 Ibn Khaldun referred to the lost *Mizan al'amal* or 'Dust Letters' of Hassan ibn Rashiq, *Muqaddimah*, vol. 1, footnote 23.

5 J. Berque, 'Ibn Khaldun et les Bédouins de Maghreb', in *Maghreb, Histoire et Société*, 1947, 59.

6 On the so-called 'Byzantine' school of Arab historiography see H. A. R. Gibb, *Arabic Literature*, 2nd edn. (Oxford, 1974), 144.

7 *Muqaddimah*, vol. I, 10.

8 In the title of his treatise Ibn Khaldun used the word *tahdhib* or 'method' of finding answers to questions about mystical matters. Ibn Khaldun *Shifa' al-Sa'il li Tahdib al-Masa'il*, M. Tawit al-Tanji (ed.) Istanbul, 1958. Jacques Berque mentioned the similarities between Ibn Khaldun's science of Sufism and science of history. 'Ibn Khaldun et les Bédouins de Maghreb,' 54.

9 See Franz Rosenthal's translation of the title as 'early and subsequent history' in the 1958 edition of *The Muqaddimah*. For 'antecedent and attribute' see J. Berque, 'Ibn Khaldun et les Bédouins de Maghreb,' 59.

10 *Muqaddimah*, vol. I, 72.

11 *Muqaddimah*, vol. I, 73.

12 Abdesselam Cheddadi claimed that Ibn Khaldun was inspired to formulate the outlines of a type of 'cultural anthropology.' *Actualité d'Ibn Khaldun* (Casablanca, 2005).

13 *Muqaddimah*, vol. I, 78.

14 *Muqaddimah*, vol. I, 77.

15 The phrase 'science of culture' comes from M. Mahdi's foundational study, *Ibn Khaldun's Philosophy of History* (Chicago, IL, 1957).

16 Aziz al-Azmeh, *Ibn Khaldun in Modern Scholarship* (London, 1981).

17 Ibn al-Khatib, *Al-Ihata fi Akhbar Gharnata*, 2 vols. (Cairo, 1901).

18 *Muqaddimah*, vol. I, 278.

19 As Waseem El-Rayes discussed in *The Political Aspects of Ibn Khaldun's Study of History* (Ph.D. diss., University of Maryland, July 24, 2008). Ibn Khaldun was concerned with specific, political objectives in his science of history.

20 Muhsin Mahdi, *Ibn Khaldun's Philosophy of History* (Chicago, IL, 1957), 52.

21 See Ahmad Shboul, *Al-Mas'udi and his World* (London, 1979) for a study of this influential historian. Also, on the many influences on Ibn Khaldun, admitted or not, see Franz Rosenthal, *A History of Muslim Historiography* (Leiden, 1968).

22 Walter Fischel, 'Ibn Khaldun's use of historical sources,' *Studia Islamica*, 14, 1961, 109–19.

23 Nevertheless, as the scholar Lenn Goodman remarked, 'Mas'udi advances the global perspective and thus the humanistic project of history writing.' *Islamic Humanism* (Oxford, 2003), 189. Lenn Goodman referred to several universal histories written before Ibn Khaldun, pp. 161–211.

24 Goodman, *Islamic Humanism*, 205.

25 Quoted in Fischel, 'Ibn Khaldun's use of Historical Sources,' 117.

26 See the introduction to Ibn Miskawayah, *Kitab tajarib al-umam wa ta'aqub al-himam*, 7 vol., trans. D. S. Margoliouth, *The Eclipse of the Abbasid Caliphate* (Oxford, 1921).

27 Chase Robinson, *Islamic Historiography* (Cambridge, 2003), 136–37.

28 Ibn Khaldun cited Al-Turtushi in *Muqaddimah*, vol. I, 83, where, although he admitted using the *Mirror for Princes*, he complained that 'He does not verify his statements or clarify them with the help of natural arguments. The work is merely a compilation of transmitted material . . .' Also see *Muqaddimah*, vol. II, 87 and *Muqaddimah*, vol. III, 17.

29 D. S. Margoliouth, *Lectures on Arabic Historians* (New York, 1972), 155.

30 Ibn Khaldun displayed a detailed knowledge of the life and work of Aristotle and Plato. *Muqaddimah*, vol. III, 114.

31 Ibn Khaldun described the influence of the work of Al-Farabi, Ibn Sina, Ibn Rushd, Abu Bakr ibn al-Saigh or Avempace. They 'surpassed their predecessors in the intellectual sciences,' *Muqaddimah*, vol. III, 116.

32 Stephen Dale, 'Ibn Khaldun: the last Greek and first Annaliste Historian,' *International Journal of Middle East Studies*, 30 (3), 2006, 431–51.

33 *Muqaddimah*, vol. III, 81.

34 *Muqaddimah*, vol. III, 90.

35 The history of the rise of the Sufi saints in North Africa is described in expert detail by Vincent Cornell, *Realm of the Saint: Power and Authority in Moroccan Sufism* (Austin, TX, 1998). He discussed the role of Sufi saints in the fourteenth-century North African political context in which Ibn Khaldun worked.

36 *Muqaddimah*, vol. III, 102.

37 Contrast his 'Refutation of philosophy and corruption of the students of philosophy,' *Muqaddimah*, vol. III, 246 with this remarkably favorable discussion of Sufism.

38 *Muqaddimah*, vol. III, 99–101.

39 Walter Fischel believed that Ibn Khaldun may have pretended to become a Sufi simply to seem qualified for this position. In fact, as my description of Ibn Khaldun's activities at the shrine of Abu Madyan and his father's influence has shown, Ibn Khaldun was certainly fully qualified for the position and did not need to feign his Sufi credentials. 'Ibn Khaldun's autobiography in the light of external sources,' *Studi orientalistici in onore di Giorgio Levi Della Vida*, 1, 1956, 293.

40 *Autobiographie*, 179. On his direction of the Baybarsiyya see *Al-Ta'rif*, 312–13.

41 Ibn Khaldun, *Shifa' al-Sa'il li Tahdib al-Masa'il* (*Treatise on Mysticism*) M. al-Tanji (ed.) (Istanbul, 1958). Ibn Khaldun was responding in this treatise to the question of whether or not a Sufi adherent could dispense with a spiritual master or guide. Alexander Knysh, *Ibn 'Arabi in the Later Islamic Tradition: The Making of a Polemical Image in Medieval Islam* (New York, 1999), 186.

42 Alexander Knysh, in fact, refers to Al-Fasi's virulent anti-Sufi criticism of Ibn 'Arabi in his book, *Ibn 'Arabi in the Later Islamic Tradition*; it seems odd that he does not, however, question the authenticity of Al-Fasi's quotation of Ibn Khaldun's supposed fatwa. For Al-Fasi's criticism of Sufism see Knysh, pp. 74–5, 247–8. Also, see Al-Fasi in Arabic: *Al-'Iqd al Thamin fi Ta'rikh al-Balad al-Amin*, 8 vols., Muhammad al-Faqi *et al.* (eds.) (Cairo, 1958–69).

43 *Muqaddimah*, vol. III, 92.

44 Aziz al-Azmeh, *Ibn Khaldun: An Essay in Reinterpretation* (Budapest, 2003), 6, note 8.

45 See Leonor Fernandes, *The Evolution of a Sufi Institution in Mamluk Egypt* (Berlin, 1998).

46 From *Kitab al-Qassas*, 57, 170–1, 177–96, quoted in Boaz Shoshan, 'High culture and popular culture in medieval Islam,' *Studia Islamica*, 73, 1991, 84.

47 Samuel Huntington, *Clash of Civilizations and the Remaking of World Order* (New York, 1996), 574.

48 This can be seen in Ibn Rushd's commentary on Plato's Republic, *Averroes on Plato's Republic*, trans. Ralph Lerner (New York, 2005).

49 Ibn Rushd, *Rhetoric*, quoted by Ibn Khaldun in *Muqaddimah*, vol. I, 275. For the original Arabic see Ibn Rushd, *Talkhis al Kitabah*, ᶜAbd al-Rahman Badawi (ed.) (Cairo, 1960), 41.

50 M. G. S. Hodgson, *Venture of Islam*, vol. 2 (Chicago, IL, 1972), 270.

51 This Pseudo-Aristotle's book of politics was entitled the *Sirr al-Asrar*, or *Secret of Secrets* and was translated from the Greek by Yahya bin al-Bitriq. See Mahmoud Manzalaoui, 'The Pseudo-Aristotelian Kitab Sirr al-Asrar: facts and problems,' *Oriens*, 23, 1974, 147–257. There were several versions of this book used in Europe as well.

52 *Muqaddimah*, vol. II, 291.

53 *Muqaddimah*, vol. II, 253.

54 Ibn Khaldun described the division of labor in the urban environment as 'the various ways and means of making a living,' *Muqaddimah*, vol. II, 315–27.

55 *Muqaddimah*, vol. II, 343.

56 Ernest Gellner, *Muslim Society* (Cambridge, 1983).

57 Mary Douglas, *The Lele of Kasai* (Oxford, 1963). Yet, unlike Ibn Khaldun, who saw social virtues originating in the tribe, Mary Douglas saw social ills. She claimed this was a study in 'economic backwardness.' Mary Douglas saw and described these tribes as backward economically and socially. Her later work would take on a more relativistic tone.

58 'There is an abundant civilization at the end of dynasties, and pestilences and famines frequently occur then,' *Muqaddimah*, vol. II, 135.

59 *Muqaddimah*, vol. II, 335, 'Agriculture is a way of making a living for weak people and Bedouin in search of subsidence.'

60 John Harlan, *Crops and Man* (Madison, WN, 1992), 92. See Felipe Fernandez-Armesto's useful synthesis of contemporary debates about the origins of agriculture in *Civilizations* (New York, 2001, 174–87).

61 *Muqaddimah*, vol. II, 336.

62 Pierre Bourdieu, 'Social space and symbolic power,' *Sociological Theory*, 7 (1), Spring 1989, 14–25.

63 Experience with Berber tribes, however, did not always mean clear understanding. In 'The proverbial Bourdieu: habits and the politics of representation in the ethnography of Kabylia,' Jane Goodman criticized Pierre Bourdieu's apparent naive understanding tribes and the favoring of certain accounts in the context of wartime. *American Anthropologist*, December 2003, 782–93.

64 *Muqaddimah*, vol. I, 319–22.

65 Ibn Khaldun, *Le Livre des Exemples*, ed. and trans. Abdesselam Cheddadi (Paris, 2002), 51.

66 Muhammad Talbi, *Ibn Khaldun: The Mediterranean in the 14th Century* (Seville), 366–80.

67 Ibn Hazm, *Le Collier du Pigeon*, trans L. Bercher (Algiers, 1949), 272–3. G. von Grunebaum described Ibn Hazm's attitude toward the Berbers in *Unity and Variety in*

Muslim Civilization (Chicago, IL, 1955), 220. Ibn Hazm also defended the aristocracy of the Arabs and Andalusis in *Kitab Fadl al Andalus* and attacked Almoravid doctrine in *Masaᵓil usul al fiqh* and *Kitab al- usul wa al-furuᶜ*, see G. von Grunebaum, 229, note 24.

68 Ibn Khaldun wrote this poem to dedicate the sultan's new library, a library that Ibn Khaldun undoubtedly would have found useful. *Al-Taᶜrif*, 240–1; *Autobiographie*, 159.

69 *Al-Taᶜrif*, 240–1; *Autobiographie*, 159.

70 As quoted in Michael Brett and Elizabeth Fentress, *The Berbers* (Oxford, 1997), 124. The quotation is substantially different, however, from that found in Rosenthal's translation of the *Muqaddimah*. See note 71 below.

71 It should be remembered Ibn Khaldun used this story of the origins of the word Berber as an example of bad historical scholarship. It is surprising that Michael Brett and Elizabeth Fentress in their otherwise useful book on the Berbers (*The Berbers*, Oxford, 1997, 124) identify this as Ibn Khaldun's own definition and as an example of Ibn Khaldun's negative attitude towards Berbers. Ibn Khaldun did not look down on the Berbers. Rather he suggested the legend was bogus. This passage in context, and as translated by Rosenthal, is found in *Muqaddimah*, vol. I, 21–2.

72 *Le Livre des Exemples*, 'Muqaddimah,' 452.

73 Ibn Khaldun, *Histoire des Berbères*, vol. II, trans. William de Slane, Mohand Oulhadj (ed.) (Algiers, 2001), 119.

74 *Le Livre des Exemples*, '*Muqaddimah*,' 431.

75 Tahir Hamami, 'Ibn Khaldun: life and political activity,' *Ibn Khaldun: The Mediterranean in the 14th Century*, 314.

76 'Muqaddimah,' *Le Livre des Exemples*, 432.

77 'Muqaddimah,' *Le Livre des Exemples*, 422. *Muqaddimah*, F. Rosenthal trans., vol. 1, 320.

78 *Histoire des Berbères*, vol. I, 137.

79 'Muqaddimah,' *Le Livre des Exemples*, 387. *Muqaddimah*, F. Rosenthal trans., vol. 1, 267–8.

80 *Le Livre des Exemples*, 'Muqaddimah,' 386. *Muqaddimah*, F. Rosenthal trans., vol. 1, 267–8.

81 *Histoire des Berbères*, vol. I, 137.

82 *Histoire des Berbères*, vol. I, 138.

83 *Histoire des Berbères*, vol. I, 138.

84 See the *Muqaddimah*, vol. I, ch. 2–3 for Ibn Khaldun's full discussion of his cycle of history.

85 *Le Livre des Exemples*, 396. *Muqaddimah*, F. Rosenthal trans., vol. 1, 284

86 *Le Livre des Exemples*, 380. *Muqaddimah*, F. Rosenthal trans., vol. 1, 261.

87 *Le Livre des Exemples*, 404. *Muqaddimah*, F. Rosenthal trans., vol. 1, 282

88 *Le Livre des Exemples*, 'Muqaddimah,' 390.

89 *Muqaddimah*, vol. II, 291.

90 Noting the influence of Ibn Khaldun's ideas on modern scholars such as E. Gellner (d. 1995) and Richard Tapper, a specialist on Afghanistan and Iran, anthropologist Dale Eickelman summarized these stages succinctly in *The Middle East and Central Asia: An Anthropological Approach* (Upper Saddle River, NJ, 2002), 23–4.

91 Oswald Spengler, *The Decline of the West*, H. Werner (ed.) (Oxford, 1991).

92 B. A. Mojuetan, 'Ibn Khaldun and his cycle of fatalism: a critique,' *Studia Islamica*, 53, 1981, 93.

93 R. Messier and R. A. Messier, 'Rethinking the Almoravids, re-thinking Ibn Khaldun,' in J. Clancy-Smith (ed.), *North Africa, Islam and the Mediterranean World* (London, 2001), 58–80.

94 Ibn Khaldun, 'There are few cities and villages in Africa and the Maghrib.' *Le Livre des Exemples*, 'Muqaddimah,' 725.

95 There are several version of this epic, which is still being recited today. See A. Ayoub, 'The Hilali epic: material and memory,' *Revue d'Histoire Maghrébine*, XI (35–6), 1984, 189–217. For a beautiful translation of some of the poem with parallel text see *Histoire des Beni Hilal*, M. Galley and A. Ayoub (eds.) (Paris, 1983).

96 The Zughba had already conquered Tripoli in 1037 AD. Michael Brett, 'The way of the nomad,' 258. Also see Michael Brett, 'Ibn Khaldun and the Arabisation of North Africa,' *Maghrib Review*, 41, 1979, 9–16. Jacques Berque similarly called the 'destruction' of the Banu Hilal a myth. See 'Du nouveau sur les Bani Hilal?,' *Studia Islamica*, 35, 1972, 99–111.

97 *Muqaddimah*, vol. I, 64.

98 E-F. Gautier, *La passé de l'Afrique du Nord: les siècles obscurs* (Paris, 1952).

99 See J. Berque's reference to Saint Augustine's idenification of the Suwayd 'Arabs' as originally Berbers in 'Ibn Khaldun et les Bédouins de Maghreb,' *Maghreb: Histoire et Société*, 1947, 51. Also, Augustin Berque made similar conclusions in, *L'Algerie, terre d'art et d'histoire* (Algiers, 1937).

100 Michael Brett, 'The way of the nomad,' 262.

101 *La passé de l'Afrique du Nord.*

102 All of these descriptions of the Arabs are chapter sub-headings devoted to the characteristics of Arabs in the *Muqaddimah*, vol. I, 304, vol. II, 353, 377, 230, 247.

103 Michael Brett, 'The way of the nomad,' 266.

MODERNITY

Il faut Manger!

Habib Bourguiba (d. 2000 AD)

IBN KHALDUN AS A MODERN MYTH

Ibn Khaldun's face appears prominently on that heavily used unit of Tunisian currency: the 10 dinar note. His statue occupies center stage on the main Avenue Bourguiba in the capital, Tunis. The Ibn Khaldun Hotel is a landmark building in the city. A popular Tunisian stamp features his image: he is framed by traditional Tunisian architectural motifs and seems to look confidently into the future. He represents continuity between tradition and innovation. He represents Tunisia's modern, national ambitions: the pursuit of innovation that simultaneously preserves an authentic Tunisian identity. His name adorns innumerable institutes, government buildings, and schools, not only in Tunisia, but also throughout the Islamic world. It may at first seem ironic that this fourteenth-century author of a universal history should himself come to embody the universal claims of a modern nation. Indeed, the universalism of Ibn Khaldun seems to be unique among historical figures represented by the modern, Islamic state. Ibn Khaldun is unlike other famous medieval or even early Islamic figures, such as Ibn Rushd or Ibn Sina, whose names seem most appropriate for specific venues, hospitals, or clinics associated with their most famous work. Ibn Khaldun, however, seems to have been universalized as appropriate for nearly any place, situation or venue. His name is conveniently appropriate for almost any situation that calls for some sort of intellectual or social authenticity. Ibn Khaldun has become the inspiration for an acceptable, modern-day *ʿasabiyya* of nationalism.

It is particularly ironic, for instance, how Ibn Khaldun's name is commonly used for modern academic and school buildings, when he and his teacher, Al-Abili, stated their distaste for formalized educational institutions. They saw formal madrasas, in fact, as instruments of indoctrination, not of learning, and praised their own method of seeking out individual teachers for instruction and receiving their *ijaza*.[1]

Admittedly, there is little in common between medieval Hafsid Tunis and modern Tunisia. Ibn Khaldun's medieval world, a world dominated by the claims of Arab and Berber tribes, rocked by instability, by the threat of plague and Mongol invasion, could not be more different from the comparative stability of modern national borders and identities. Ibn Khaldun was born in Tunis in 1332 and lived there most of his childhood. He also worked for Hafsid dynasts such as Abu al-ᶜAbbas. He dedicated his first edition of the *Muqaddimah* to the Hafsid amir. His sense of being 'Tunisian,' or Maghribi, however, was very different from the modern sense of being Tunisian. There were no real, inviolable national borders. The machinery of modern state institutions and media were not in place. Nevertheless, Ibn Khaldun as distinctly Tunisian has become an integral part of that modern Tunisian identity. In his recent book, *Myth of Nations*, Patrick Geary wrote convincingly about the ways in which modern European states have appropriated heroes of the medieval past and have written nationalized narratives that fit the modern configurations of the state.[2] A similar, if unstudied, phenomenon happened in the Middle East and North Africa, Ibn Khaldun being probably the most popular 'appropriated symbol' for several reasons.

First, the potential symbolism of Ibn Khaldun is highly plastic or elastic. Unlike perhaps any other medieval Muslim intellectual, the very name Ibn Khaldun has become, in the word used by Clifford Geertz, 'thick' with more national and modern meaning than with historical meaning, thick with meaning for different modern, social and national agendas and groups within Tunisia and the Islamic world at large.[3] Although no image of Ibn Khaldun survives from the fourteenth century, this has not stopped the production and promulgation of his apparent likeness in statues, stamps, currency, school books, and, most importantly, in the imagination of modern Tunisians. The most prominent and one of the most well-known examples of Tunisian Ibn Khaldunania is the almost monumental Ibn Khaldun statue erected in 1978 at the western end of the Avenue Habib Bourguiba.

Ibn Khaldun and Bourguiba

The year 1978, the year the Ibn Khaldun statue was erected, was a critical year for the authoritarian reformist Habib Bourguiba and for Tunisian politics. Habib

Bourguiba, the mercurial and strong-willed president of Tunisia since 1957, was voted 'president for life' in 1975. A social reformer, he pushed for family planning, women's rights, and the development of infrastructure. He did not allow Islamic traditions or rituals to stand in his way, famously drinking orange juice in the middle of the day during the traditional fast of Ramadan. He ordered restaurants to remain open throughout the day and said, *Il faut Manger* – 'One must eat!' Ramadan, according to Bourguiba, decreased the economic productivity of the nation. A popular way to resist Bourguiba's regime was to fast in defiance.[4]

The Prime Minister, Hedi Nouira, introduced a controversial five-year reform plan in 1977 that raised tensions between the government of Bourguiba and Tunisian union organizations. On January 26, 1978, the unions scheduled a general strike and demanded both economic security and political reform, and protests flared up throughout the country. Although the numbers are disputed, scores of Tunisians were killed in clashes with police and security forces. These protests have since been called 'Black Thursday.'[5]

It was thus in the context of one of the most serious challenges to the Bourguiba regime that he erected the statue of Ibn Khaldun, scrolling his name on a marble plaque directly below the name of the philosopher and pointing the statue to face an even larger statue of Bourguiba riding triumphantly on a horse at the eastern end of the Avenue Bourguiba. The Equine Bourguiba, four tons of bronze and 5 meters high, was erected on January 17, 1978, in the Place d'Afrique, the same place where the 'humiliating' statue of Jules Ferry (d. 1893) once stood.[6] Jules Ferry was the French Prime Minister who vigorously supported the expansion of French colonialism in Africa. The Tunisian press agency proclaimed the statue yet another 'symbol of fidelity,' an indication that the Tunisian people were 'of the same opinion that [Bourguiba] never errs. . .'[7]

Instead of facing the old medina, the old city of Tunis with its traditional rhythm and traditional ways, Ibn Khaldun's statue faces outward toward Bourguiba Avenue, the broad, modern 'Champs Elysee' of Tunis, with his back to the past. In fact, a new suburban development, 'Ibn Khaldun city,' had been named in his honor.[8] The message was clear. The Ibn Khaldun of Bourguiba was no longer a fourteenth-century scholar who wrote about the perils of urban luxury and the distance between rulers and their people. Rather, the Ibn Khaldun of Bourguiba was an Ibn Khaldun draped in bournous and a jalaba, sternly focused on the future, a traditional figure from the past used to justify the politics of reform. Neither Islamist nor Western but clearly a universally recognized icon of Tunisian national pride, Ibn Khaldun became an idealized and aggrandized symbol of Habib Bourguiba's remaking of Tunisian society.

The Ibn Khaldun statue was originally intended to be erected on June 1, 1978, on the anniversary of Habib Bourguiba's return to Tunis after years of French colonialism. Although the official commemoration by the 'supreme combatant' Bourguiba did not occur until July 3, the official press releases sent to both Arabic and French newspapers by the TAP (the official Tunisian Press Agency) made the connection between Bourguiba and Ibn Khaldun clear. Although 3.5 meters tall, 1.5 meters shorter than the equine statue of Bourguiba, the Ibn Khaldun statue 'indicates from top to bottom the constant progress towards the grandeur of wisdom . . . It is our own, a homage to Arab and Muslim thought.' As the Tunisian intellectual, Ahmed Kedidi, wrote on March 17, in commemoration of the death of Ibn Khaldun in 1406, 'our pride as Tunisians is legitimate. He is none other than our compatriot . . . The very same narrow streets between Darb Ibn Abdessalam and the Zitouna Mosque one can traverse today were frequented by the great scholar . . .' Kedidi then went so far as to compare Ibn Khaldun with the Prophet himself. Remarking on Ibn Khaldun's ability to write and think and create in solitude, Kedidi remarked that 'so too had the prophets transformed solitude into triumph.'[9] Ibn Khaldun was a nationalized, intellectual prophet of Tunisia.

Like the Bourguiba statue replacing the monument to Jules Ferry, Ibn Khaldun would also replace a remnant of the colonial past: it would be in the same location as the tomb of the unknown French soldier. According to the official presses, when Bourguiba arrived at 11:10 on Saturday, June 3, to inaugurate the statue, lines of people crowded into the two lanes of the Avenue Bourguiba shouting 'Vive Bourguiba!' As he cut the ribbon, the supreme combatant indicated that solicitude should be 'accorded to all those who give their insight and intellectual power in the service of the fatherland . . .' The place chosen for the Ibn Khaldun statue across from that of the Statue of the Supreme Combatant Habib Bourguiba is itself symbolic. It indicates the will of the Tunisian people to continuously defend their character, to support their civilization and to safeguard their authenticity. As he made a tour of the statue, the crowds erupted into applause. The Supreme Combatant then 'departed in triumph.'[10]

There are no surviving portraits of Ibn Khaldun from the fourteenth century. What most modern images of Ibn Khaldun, such as the statue on Avenue Bourguiba and the portrait of Ibn Khaldun on the 10-dinar note, represent are not simply the Ibn Khaldun of the fourteenth century but the Ibn Khaldun of modern concerns. In this way the name and image of Ibn Khaldun today means something very different from what they meant in his own historical context. Although his writings remain important among the intellectual elite, the name and image of Ibn Khaldun have become a national, popular evocation of modernization or innovation within 'legitimate' or, in the words of the Tunisian official press, 'authentic' traditional bounds, both an evocation and a legitimization of new, national identities and of collective innovations. This use of Ibn Khaldun as a legitimization of Tunisian national goals and identity provides a uniquely acceptable, somehow uniquely comfortable, part of Tunisian national history. He fits into the ideology of Arab nationalists, Islamic nationalists, nationalists of the 'Greater Maghrib,' and even the small, Tunisian Berber minority who claim him as their own. Yet even as he is a hero of all these nationalisms, he is also considered to be fully Tunisian. He is thus one of those rare and precious links between these more universal nationalisms of the Islamic world and the nationalism of the Tunisian state. It is this fully Tunisian but also fully Islamic, fully Arab, even fully Berber and Maghribi, identity of Ibn Khaldun that forms an alternative to the demands of groups who claim legitimization almost solely in the context of a limited seventh- and eighth-century Arabian milieu. The representation of Ibn Khaldun as Tunisian national hero thus contrasts with the agenda of Islamism. There is some evidence that even Islamist actors have attempted to appropriate Ibn Khaldun as a stern enforcer of traditional values, focusing, for example, on his conservative role as Qadi of Cairo where he rooted out corruption and punished 'libertines.'[11] In fact, Ibn Khaldun's stay in Cairo from 1382 to 1406 has inspired an equally fervent reaction among modern Egyptians. Unlike Tunisia, however, where he is largely portrayed in uncontroversial ways and as a source of national pride, Egyptian academics have used Ibn Khaldun to promote the cause of reform and academic freedom.

A CONTENTIOUS EGYPTIAN NATIONAL SYMBOL

Like Tunisia, Algeria, Morocco, and even modern Spain, which hosted a major Ibn Khaldun international event at Seville in 2006, Egypt also lays a national claim to Ibn Khaldun as part of their Islamic intellectual heritage. There have been repeated attempts to locate Ibn Khaldun's precise place of burial as well as numerous attempts at creating public memorials to claim Ibn Khaldun as an Egyptian. The public intellectuals of Egypt, led by the fiercely nationalist Ahmed Zaki Pasha, called for a similar statue and tomb in Egypt. While recognizing Ibn Khaldun as a pan-Arab and pan-Islamic figure, it was just as important to claim him as an Egyptian. As one reader commented in a letter to the editor, if 'our Tunisian brothers have moved to revive the memory of that great man . . . We must roll up our sleeves and earnestly set to work in order to make Egypt the home for commemorating this man who rests in [Egyptian] soil, the pride of Islam and master of historians.' It was Ahmed Zaki Pasha who instigated the search for Ibn Khaldun, declaring in *Al-Ahram* with an explicit cry of nationalist fervor:

> If Tunisia can take pride in the fact that it was the country in which Ibn Khaldun saw his first glimmer of light . . . if the Maghrib jubilates in the fact that Ibn

Khaldun had visited their capitals and courts; if the Tartars claim credit because their tyrant Timurlane, who had decimated every stretch of land before him, had spared Ibn Khaldun . . . if France never tires of pointing out that in 1858 its presses in Cairo's Boulaq [district] published the *Muqaddimah* in Arabic . . . then it is the right of the city of Cairo to raise its head up high, for it has *surpassed* its peers with a distinction no others can rival and thus has greater claim to take eternal pride [by creating a] day to boast its patronage of Ibn Khaldun. (emphasis added)'[12]

Ahmed Zaki Pasha, often called the dean of Arabism, was a pan-Arabist (if loyal to Egypt first), and first secretary general of the Oriental League. As leader of the Nadha, or modern renaissance of Egyptian scholarship in the first half of the twentieth century, it only made sense to manufacture Ibn Khaldun into a symbolic forefather of that modern renaissance.[13] His feverish search for Ibn Khaldun's grave was recorded in several articles in the *Al-Ahram* newspaper and transmitted around the country, and around the Arab world, as a type of 'national detective hunt.' The quest for Ibn Khaldun's tomb was as much a quest for recognition of the intellectual achievements of the new flowering of Arab intellectualism as it was a quest for the specific place that Ibn Khaldun was buried.

ISLAMIC MODERNISM

In a letter to the newspaper, a student of Muhammad ᶜAbduh (d. 1905), architect of Islamic modernism, claimed that his teacher had written extensive comparative notes on Ibn Khaldun's *Muqaddimah*. These notes for a comparative work described 'the differences in circumstances and conditions between the present and Ibn Khaldun's times.' Ibn Khaldun, a father of Arab history, was thus directly associated with a father of modern pan-Arab nationalism. A seamless link of nationalist pride was created across centuries. Unfortunately, the letter explained that much of Muhammad ᶜAbduh's writings on Ibn Khaldun had mysteriously 'gone missing,' a loss ᶜAbduh apparently lamented greatly. In fact, the letter was true. It is now known that Muhammad ᶜAbduh's draft on Ibn Khaldun was among his works confiscated by the state and destroyed in 1879.[14]

Rashid Rida, Muhammad ᶜAbduh's disciple, found Ibn Khaldun's elevation of ᶜasabiyya over religious inspiration offensive. Rida saw ᶜasabiyya as the embodiment of racism, ethno-centrism, tribalism, and prejudice that distracted Muslims from obedience to the *sharia*. Rida's opponent, Ali ᶜAbd al-Raziq, defended Ibn Khaldun as a rationalist whose logical methodology liberated the mind from reductionism and scholasticism. Al-Raziq used Ibn Khaldun's notion of the state of political expedience to justify the power-based states of the modern world. In south Asia the reformist and poet Muhammad Iqbal used Ibn Khaldun's description of the fall of the caliphate to justify Ataturk's abolition of the moribund Caliphate. Ataturk, like Ibn Khaldun, was accepting reality, reconciling Islam with 'the hard logic of facts.' [15]

While prominent nationalist intellectuals such as Rashid Rida and Al-Raziq read and debated Ibn Khaldun, some ordinary Cairenes took the call to find Ibn Khaldun's grave quite literally. On reading the articles, several middle-class, literate Egyptians took upon themselves the task of finding the grave. Mohamad al-Hariri, for example, a senior clerk for the Helwan district court, claimed that the grave could be found near the Bab al-Nasr area of Cairo near an ancient Sufi meetinghouse or *khanqa* called Said al-Suᵓada. South of this mosque was the burial ground where members of the Sufi order were buried. Al-Hariri's speculations may not be that far off the mark. After all, a contemporary of Ibn Khaldun, Ibn Hisham al-Ansari, a philologist, was buried in that cemetery. Although little conclusive evidence for the grave of Ibn Khaldun was found, the most important mission, according to Ahmed Zaki Pasha, was to instill Egyptians with a knowledge of Ibn Khaldun's work. An Ibn Khaldun Society was formed and an Ibn Khaldun library was proposed, as was a commemorative edition of Ibn Khaldun's work.

DEMOCRACY

In present-day Egypt, however, Ibn Khaldun is a symbol of a certain defiance towards the brutalities of the nation-state. His name has been attached to a center dedicated to civil society and development. The Ibn Khaldun Center for Development Studies, founded by Saad Eddin Ibrahim in 1988, has frequently encountered government interference and intimidation. In June 2000, Saad Eddin Ibrahim and twenty-seven of the center's researchers were arrested and tried before Egypt's state security courts. They were sentenced to years of hard labor. These sentences were ultimately overruled by Egypt's high court in 2003.[16] Although his sentenced was overturned, Saad Eddin is currently living in exile in Doha, Qatar, under the auspices of Sheikh Hamid bin Khalifa al-Thani.[17]

Due to the official crackdown on its activities, and the publicity that the farcical trial in the state security courts generated, this center and its name, Ibn Khaldun, has received a tremendous amount of attention in the press, both inside and outside the Arabic speaking world. According to former UN Secretary General Kofi Annan, 'the very name [Ibn Khaldun] evokes the age of intellectual brilliance in Islamic history.'[18] By attaching the name Ibn Khaldun to the center, Ibn Khaldun's 'intellectual brilliance' is placed in contrast to the supposed dearth of intellectual activity in the modern world. While the medieval period in the West is still popularly seen as a time of darkness, the medieval period in the Middle East is thus identified as time of brilliance. What these simplified views of Middle Eastern history lead to is a rather problematic logic: while the West is free to move blithely forward, the only way the Middle East can look forward is to look back. While the West is set free on its progressive agenda to ignore the 'medieval past' and view its history in patronizing terms of culture and heritage, preserving the past in the safe dust bins of archives, sanitized museums, and politically correct high school text books, the Middle East has no option but to look back, not forward, to look back to a mythical brilliance that once was. Thus, by over-emphasizing the brilliance of a medieval, Muslim past, popular Western views of medieval Islam and the medieval Middle East ironically deny the Middle East of today the possibility of the future. What simplified, if well-intentioned, Western images of Ibn Khaldun and a mythologized 'age of intellectual genius' ignore, or are simply not aware of, are the specific historical context, the tremendous difficulties and challenges faced by Ibn Khaldun and other intellectual 'geniuses' of the medieval Islamic world. As this book has explained in detail, mythologized views of an Islamic golden age ignore those aspects of Ibn Khaldun's thinking that are decidedly unmodern. But why should one expect Ibn Khaldun to be modern in the first place? Taking major historical figures like Ibn Khaldun out of historical context has consequences beyond the rather limited concerns of the specialized historian. Just as several modern Western historians have been tempted to identify Ibn Khaldun as a unique 'modern' mind, the use of Ibn Khaldun as symbol of a former age of intellectual brilliance denies the complexities of both past and present and clouds the possibility of a future.

Just as Ibn Khaldun has been projected as a symbol of Tunisian nationalism, the historical Ibn Khaldun is similarly ignored or re-written by those who wish to paint him as a symbol of progress. He becomes the image and symbol of a once-brilliant modernism, of democracy and civil society connecting East and West. This use of Ibn Khaldun has led to well-intentioned but seriously problematic, Western rhetoric of a 'lost Islamic golden age.' Yet the reliance on Ibn Khaldun as a symbol of 'modernism' has been exploited by right-wing organizations in the West in virulently anti-Muslim websites such as *Jihad Watch*. Selectively quoting a passage by Ibn Khaldun on *jihad*, a passage that ignores the many conditions that Ibn Khaldun put on *jihad*, let alone the fourteenth-century context in which this passage was written, the fear-mongering website condemns even Saad Eddin Ibrahim and the Ibn Khaldun Center.[19] A similar game of mixed historical standards could be played with American symbols such as Thomas Jefferson, owner of slaves. Immediately, however, the blanket of historical context can defend Western, American historical symbols. Middle Eastern historical symbols, such as Ibn Khaldun, in contrast, are somehow expected to follow and live up to impossible, modern standards.

This is not to suggest that the Ibn Khaldun Center in Cairo should change its name or that the members of the Ibn Khaldun Center are themselves unaware of the differences between the contemporary world and Mamluk Cairo. Rather, the problematic nature of Ibn Khaldun as 'symbol for the West' is emblematic of a much more systematic problem with the cursory understanding of Middle Eastern history in the West. Edward Said famously identified the political consequences of Western orientalism, or views of the Middle East as an exotic other that embodied everything the West did not want to be.[20] Yet there is another, much more subtle, form of sympathetic orientalism that develops when the well-intentioned West views the 'brilliant past' of Islam, but is then unreasonably disappointed to find out that those living in the 'brilliant past' were not as modern as they should be. Scholars, such as Aziz al-Azmeh, have already discussed the misuse of Ibn Khaldun as an orientalist Western fantasy.[21] The temptation to extract Ibn Khaldun from his historical context leads to a double misrepresentation, first by Western orientalists attempting to discover the 'lone Western thinker' and then by Muslims and Middle Easterners themselves who may view Ibn Khaldun not as he was, but as a reaction to Western demands to prove the modernism of Islamic tradition.

LEARNING FROM IBN KHALDUN AND THE FOURTEENTH CENTURY

Clearly, temptations to view Ibn Khaldun as either a national or an orientalist symbol of a past, apparent modernity have existed in both Europe and the Near East. After all, according to Bruce Lawrence, 'nineteenth-century Europe, or rather textual scholars intent on discovering the foundations of non-European civilizations created Ibn Khaldun.'[22] This European rediscovery and 'recreation' of Ibn Khaldun almost immediately led to comparisons between Ibn Khaldun's thought and the positivist, reformist sociological theories developing in Europe. There are several problems that arise when Ibn Khaldun is taken out of context, given the label of modern thinker, and expected to hold modern standards. Nevertheless, Ibn Khaldun's ideas and his context are still quite relevant and important for modern concerns. Just as it would be arbitrary to extract Ibn Khaldun from his context and put him in another, modern one, it would be equally arbitrary to declare that the modern world is completely separated from the concerns Ibn Khaldun encountered in the fourteenth century. Far from it. The issues of the fourteenth century discussed in the *Muqaddimah* – political disunity, plague, tribal rebellion and the radical power of religious inspiration – are issues that continue to resonate today. Nevertheless, Ibn Khaldun viewed these issues through a perspective that is most often ignored or misunderstood by the 'modern' West. A solution that preserves Ibn Khaldun's historical context but that still allows his ideas to live and frame modern thinking is to use and apply Ibn Khaldun's ideas to modern concerns while recognizing both his ideas and Ibn Khaldun himself as conditioned by their context. A problem arises not when Ibn Khaldun's ideas are used to enlighten and compare with some aspect of a modern concern, but rather when those ideas, and Ibn Khaldun himself, are expected to be modern in themselves.

In many ways, Ibn Khaldun crossed over social and geographic barriers that a modern person, surrounded and packaged into the structures and assumptions of modern development and progress, would never have the chance to traverse. As such, his insights are significant because they fuse together so many disciplines and perspectives that even a modern person would be unlikely to encounter. Ibn Khaldun crossed over not only the varied physical geography of the Mediterranean but also over the varied spiritual and intellectual geographies of the inner sea. He was not only a courtier for kings, princes, sultans, and rulers in the city, but also a negotiator for remote but hearty tribes with powerful aspirations. He was not only versed in Greek rational philosophy and the abstract methods of logical deduction, but also in the specific, down to earth knowledge of history as it was written at that time. While Greek philosophers rejected history as a series of irrelevant specific events, Ibn Khaldun combined the abstractions of philosophy with the details of history. He was not only a rather stern enforcer of Islamic law and norms, but also a Sufi mystic, interested in understanding the spiritual realm and the 'hidden meaning' of all things. Unlike most modern individuals, trapped by specific national identities, by a narrow sense of civilization and progress, and by an obsession with the avoidance of contradictory affiliations, Ibn Khaldun moved freely between roles and identities. It was through the combination of his many roles and experiences as philosopher, as mystic, as functionary, as link between rural tribes and urban dynasty, as religious judge that Ibn Khaldun was able to attempt a universal view of history, a view that that not only crossed over geographic boundaries but conceptual boundaries as well.

Ibn Khaldun wrote down the *Muqaddimah* as a series of lessons, observations, or proscriptions culminating from this fusion of spiritual, philosophical, rational, and religious influences on his life and thought. At least ostensibly, these lessons were aimed at a specific audience: rulers such as Abu al-ᶜAbbas or Sultan Barquq of Egypt. Although intended for an elite audience in the context of the fourteenth century, Ibn Khaldun's ideas remain important reflections for today, not because they are modern, but because they are different from modern thinking and assumptions about the Middle East and North Africa. There has been much discussion about whether Ibn Khaldun can be considered a 'precursor,' an 'alternative,' or a 'founder' of modern sociology and social sciences or whether Ibn Khaldun is a historical relic who can only be limited to his historical context.[23] While focusing on the importance of seeing Ibn Khaldun in context, this book has not precluded the possibility of comparing both Ibn Khaldun *and* his context with contemporary assumptions about the Middle East and North Africa. Listed below are several ways Ibn Khaldun's thought and the conditions of his historical context challenges common modern assumptions and misconceptions about the Middle East.

(1) Societies cannot be easily divided into arbitrary categories of barbaric and rural or civilized and urban

The Western historical imagination is dominated by the notion of struggle between civilization and barbarism. The Greeks were most certainly considered barbaric by the highly advanced civilization of the Persians. From the Western historical perspective, however, the Greeks have been promoted as heroes of civilized life who defeated the Goliath, oriental menace of the Persian empire. The history of the fall of Rome was the most explicit example of the construction of an epic struggle between urban civilization and barbarism.

Ibn Khaldun, living in both magnificent cities such as Cairo and in the remotest corners of North Africa, had little such notion of an irreconcilable division between the settled, urban life and the nomadic or semi-nomadic life of the mountain and desert. Civilization could apply to the Bedouin Arab way of life or to the Berber mountain way of life as much as it could to urban civilization. In fact, Bedouin and Berber civilization, both usually based on the immediate, face to face bonds of *ʿasabiyya*, was much more durable than urban civilization, and in that sense was a better, more moral form of human society.[24] Urban civilization was subject to corruption and decay on its own accord, a corruption perpetuated by the creation of ruling classes and other divisions in society. Rural, nomadic tribes were a better source of recruits for the army than the cities. The cause of the fall of urban-centered civilization was not the invading barbarous tribes, but the corrupting force of impersonal power in the cities. The internal policies of the city and the ruling dynasty over a series of generations, became more and more distant from the people and more and more vulnerable to invasion from Bedouin or Berber tribes. For Ibn Khaldun tribalism was not the problem, but rather the inherent corruption and luxury of the city. If anything, the periodic fall of dynastic power and urban civilization could be a good thing: it cleared out the rot and prepared a blank slate. Prosperous urban rulers had to reach out to the surrounding tribal regions and maintain the loyalty and following of those outside their immediate control.

First, there were deep, informal, and unexpected links between those living in the cities and those living in the countryside. Tribal affiliations did not disappear after settlement, but remained largely in force. Urban dwellers often assumed their neighbors were blood kin.[25] Also, most rulers and ruling dynasties came not from the cities but from powerful tribes in the countryside. These tribal dynasties eventually decayed in the morass of corrupt urban power, only to be replaced by a new, more vigorous tribal dynasty. 'Like the silkworm that spins and then, in turn, finds its end amidst the threads itself has spun.'[26]

Thus, as real threats to the ruling dynasty, rural tribes have often been a check on corruption and mismanagement in the city. Tribes, unlike urban power, were often founded on consensus, not absolute force. Tribes can even remain and persist within the most urbanized of environments. The cities of Kufa and Marrakech were founded around quarters designated for different tribes. Even Paris in the 1960s, according to a survey by the scholar, Louis Massignon, was divided into quarters corresponding to the tribal identities and clans of the Algerian Kabyle Berber immigrants living there.[27] Westerners, steeped in the ideal notion of government in the service of people, often fail to realize that tribes justifiably see urbanization and settlement and classic notions of development as the loss of their freedom. Development and institutionalization is often seen, sometimes quite justifiably, as an incursion by the state. Even education, if controlled and monitored by the dynasty in power such that doctrine was forced upon the student and taught without context or room for debate about religious matter, could be an instrument of pacification and corruption. Unless the corruption of the urban establishment is curtailed, almost nothing can convince a society based primarily on tribal lineage to trust the state, to give up their lineage in favor of a wider sense of national unity.

(2) Actual lineage may not matter; the appearance of lineage matters a great deal

According to Ibn Khaldun's reading of Greek philosophy, humans are naturally social animals with a social instinct: 'Human social organization is something necessary. The philosophers expressed this fact by saying Man is 'political' by nature'[28] However, humans are able to manipulate their social instinct, their *ʿasabiyya*, through words, communication, and the manipulation of the emotions. Religion and religious prophecy was the most powerful way to manipulate and mold natural social instincts. On a fundamental level, all societies are dependent on group feeling, on *ʿasabiyya*:

> Blood ties are something natural among men, with the rarest exceptions. It leads to affection for one's relations and blood relatives. One feels shame when one's

relatives are treated unjustly or attacked, and one wishes to intervene between them and whatever peril or destruction threatens them. This is a natural urge in man, for as long as there have been human beings.[29]

This natural social instinct, this *ʿasabiyya* at the heart of Ibn Khaldun's theory of history, however, need not be based on real lineage. Most often it is not. The appearance or the feeling of a common lineage was just as good as the real thing: 'When the things which result from [common] descent are there it is as if [common descent] itself were there . . . In the course of time, the original descent is almost forgotten.'[30] Ibn Khaldun provided numerous examples of kings and rulers attempting to gain nobility by adopting the lineage of the Prophet or by claiming to be of a particular tribe. Also, whole groups of people with a common enemy will often construct a common lineage as a way of solidifying a useful alliance. This was typical not only in North Africa but throughout much of mountainous central Asia. Gene Garthwaite, in his study of the Bakhtiyari confederation of Iran, demonstrated the essentially illusory nature of the tribes' 'unity.'[31] Tribes may also split. One faction may end up as two even if successfully defeated or eliminated by a rival.[32] Blood is fluid even as it appears to be fixed.

(3) Tribal affiliations change

In a stereotypical view of the blood ties of the Bedouin and the Berbers, relations are determined patrilineally. In modern American and European genealogy, the graph of one's ancestry becomes progressively larger as both male and female branches expand out from a single individual. In patrilineal, or father-based, genealogy, however, the pyramid is upside down with an individual identifying with a progressively smaller number of common male ancestors until the ancestry dissolves into pure fancy and myth with claims of descent from Moses, Cain, or Ishmael.[33] Yet this was not always the case, even for an elite Arab such as Ibn Khaldun, who was expected to use mainly patrilineal affiliations. Certain matrilineal, or mother-based, ties that were important and useful were emphasized, whereas those patrilineal ties that that were shameful or irrelevant were forgotten. Ibn Khaldun constantly affirmed his family's matrilineal ties to the Hafsids through the marriage of a Galician slave girl to the Hafsid ruler in the 1230s AD. Although this was not even a direct blood bond, and it was a bond on his mother's side of his ancestral history, Ibn Khaldun held it out as a highly significant ancestral tie, a tie to the powerful Hafsids, a tie that he even used to justify his fraternizing and possible conspiring with a Hafsid exile against Abu ʿInan, Marinid ruler of Fez. Certain ties that are important and useful could be emphasized, whereas those that were shameful or irrelevant were forgotten.

Ibn Khaldun stated repeatedly in his writings that tribal affiliations are not immutable. The unexpected flexibility of blood relations has several implications. First, tribal affiliation should never be seen as an ancient or a dead identity. Tribes cannot be precisely mapped out as if they were fixed geographic landmarks, the valleys or mountains of human, rural society. In fact, as part of survival, a tribe must make full use of its ancestral identity to maximize strategic alliances even as it protects the independence of the group and avoids domination and taxation by the urban dynasty. The modern tendency to categorize groups minutely by tribal affiliation may not reveal the intimate, hidden associations between tribes and tribal coalitions that flux according to economic, political, and religious circumstances. Just as the British recording of the Indian caste system solidified what was a more traditional dynamic, the categorizing of tribe and clan with a specific geographic area imposes an artificial systemization on tribes, imprisoning them within an artificially set identity determined from the outside. As the anthropologist Richard Tapper pointed out, 'Administrators – and many academics – still take a highly positivist view of tribes in the Middle East. They expect them to be mappable, bounded groups with little membership change, and they want an exact terminology for classificatory and comparative purposes.'[34] This desire to map out tribes into a manageable human taxonomy has continued in full force in both Afghanistan and Iraq. Ironically, without an understanding of the almost unlimited flexibility and responsiveness of tribal identity to political and economic change, however, these modern taxonomists may be subverting their very mission of 'nation building.'

(4) Negotiation provides advantages for both tribes and urban powers

In his book *Yemen Chronicle: An Anthropology of War and Mediation*, Steven Caton, the Harvard anthropologist who spent several long stretches living with Yemeni tribes, explained the Yemeni view of force:

> Force, or rather the threat of force, should always be used in a dialectical relationship with mediation and negotiation . . . Understanding the use of force in this way entails working patiently with partners in highly complex situations, accepting the vulnerability that comes with such partnerships, and perhaps, most important of all, the negative possibility of uncertainty and contingency.[35]

Ibn Khaldun knew the complexity of such partnerships first hand. It was certainly in Ibn Khaldun's personal interest to advocate negotiation with the Arab Dawawida tribes, or the Berber Banu Marin. Unlike the modern gulf between the mechanized state and the poor and localized tribe, there was not much difference between the rulers of the cities that he represented and the chiefs of the tribes whose mercenary support he sought. It was Ibn Khaldun's ability to negotiate and secure alliances and partnerships with tribal chiefs that assured the success or failure of his urban patrons. Similarly, the success or failure of modern governments in places dominated by 'traditional' tribal societies may also depend on a willingness to negotiate directly with tribes despite the 'vulnerability' that can come with such relationships.

NOTES

1 Ibn Khaldun, *Le Livre des Exemples*, trans. A. Cheddadi (Paris, 2002), 1073–81.
2 Patrick Geary, *Myth of Nations* (Princeton, 2003).
3 Clifford Geertz, 'Thick description: toward an interpretive theory of culture,' in *The Interpretation of Cultures* (New York, 1973). As an example of the use of Ibn Khaldun's image as a representation of distinctly 'Muslim' cultural notions of democracy as opposed to 'Western' norms one need only mention the Ibn Khaldun Center for Democracy in Cairo established by Saad Eddin Ibrahim. Likewise, Ibn Khaldun has been appropriated to represent the stability and confidence of the state.
4 Fred Halliday, 'The politics of Islamic fundamentalism: Iran, Tunisia and the challenge to the secular state', in *Islam, Globalization and Postmodernity*, ed. Akbar Ahmed and Hastings Donnan (eds.) (London, 1994), 104.
5 Kenneth Perkins, *A History of Modern Tunisia* (Cambridge, 2004), 165–6.
6 *La Presse Tunisienne*, January 17, 1978, p. 1. The equine statue of Bourguiba has since been moved from Place d'Afrique and replaced with a clock tower. The statue now rests in a far less prestigious setting: the industrial town of La Goulette on the other side of Lake Tunis.
7 *La Presse*, January 19, 1978, p. 1.
8 *La Presse*, 'A la cité Ibn Khaldoun,' February 10, 1978, p. 2.
9 *La Presse*, 'Autrement Dit,' March 16, 1978, p. 3.
10 *La Presse*, 'Bourguiba Inaugre la statue d'Ibn Khaldoun,' June 4, 1978, pp. 1 and 2. Also *Le Temps*, 'Bourguiba Inaugre la statue d'Ibn Khaldoun,' June 4, 1978, pp. 1 and 2. The same article appeared in the Arabic newspaper *Al-ʿAlamon* the same day.
11 Franz Rosenthal, *Islam in the Modern National State* (Cambridge, 1965). See his description of how modern Islamist movements have attempted to use Ibn Khaldun to legitimate their positions, pp. 16–27.
12 Quoted in Yunan Labib Rizk, 'A diwan of contemporary life (509)' in *Al-Ahram*, August 23–September 3, 2003, Issue 653. Available on-line at: http://weekly.ahram.org.eg/2003/653/chrncls.htm, accessed March 31, 2009.
13 Arthur Goldschmidt, *Biographical Dictionary of Modern Egypt* (Cairo), 236–7.
14 Bruce Lawrence, 'Ibn Khaldun and Islamic Reform,' in *Ibn Khaldun and Islamic Ideology*, B. Lawrence (ed.) (Leiden, 1984), 80.
15 Lawrence, 'Ibn Khaldun and Islamic Reform,' 82.
16 http://www.eicds.org/about1.html, accessed April 3, 2009.
17 I met Saad Eddin Ibrahim in Doha during my year of teaching at Qatar University, 2007–8.

18 See former UN Secretary General Kofi Annan's remarks on the Center at: http://www. unis.unvienna.org/unis/pressrels/2003/sgsm8766.html, accessed April 2, 2009.

19 Available online at: http://www.*jihad*watch.org/archives/000250.php, accessed April 2, 2009.

20 Edward Said, *Orientalism* (New York, 1979).

21 A. al-Azmeh, *Ibn Khaldun in Modern Scholarship. A Study in Orientalism* (London, 1980).

22 Lawrence, 'Ibn Khaldun and Islamic Reform,' 69.

23 This was a major theme of the Second International Ibn Khaldun Society Conference in Istanbul, Turkey: 'Ibn Khaldun: Precursor or Alternative.' Also, see F. Alatas, 'Ibn Khaldun and contemporary sociology,' *International Sociology*, 2006, 21(6), 782–95.

24 *Muqaddimah*, vol. I, 252–4.

25 Charles Lindholm, *The Islamic Middle East: Tradition and Change* (Oxford, 2002), 54.

26 *Muqaddimah*, vol. I, 297.

27 'Cartes de répartition des kabyles dans la region Parisienne,' in *Opera Minora* (Beirut, 1963), vol. 3, 569–74.

28 *Muqaddimah*, vol. I, 89.

29 *Muqaddimah*, vol. I, 264.

30 *Muqaddimah*, vol. I, 267.

31 'The Bakhtiyari Ilkhani: an illusion of unity,' *International Journal of Middle East Studies*, 8, 1977, 145–60.

32 Ibn Khaldun's notion of the dynamism of tribal affiliation is confirmed by modern scholarship on the period. See Patricia Crone, *Slaves on Horses*, (Cambridge, 1980), 233, 'clearly, had one [medieval] faction succeeded in eliminating the other, it would have split in two itself.'

33 There are a wealth of discussions and debates in the anthropological literature about the usefulness of graphing patrilineal 'segmentary' alliances. The segmentary system was first convincingly presented by E. E. Evans-Pritchard in *The Sanusi of Cyrenacia* (Oxford, 1949). The segmentary model has been the focus of a great deal of debate among anthropologists. Several, including Henry Munson Jr., have rejected the value of the model. Others, including the expert on Moroccan tribes, D. M. Hart, have defended the validity of segmentary systems in real, observed, circumstances. See 'Rejoiner to Henry Munson Jr., "On the Irrelevance of the Segmentary Lineage Model in the Moroccan Rif,"' *American Anthropologist*, 91(2), 1989, 386–400.

34 R. Tapper, 'Anthropologists, historians and tribespeople on tribe and state formation in the Middle East,' in P. Khoury and J. Kostiner (eds.), *Tribes and State Formation in the Middle East* (Berkeley and Los Angeles, CA, 1990), 54–5.

35 Steven Caton, *Yemen Chronicle: An Anthropology of War and Mediation* (New York, 2005), 339.

ON BEING IBN KHALDUN

The outward man is the swinging door; the inner man is the still hinge.

Meister Eckhart (d. 1328)

As this biography has shown, Ibn Khaldun had an unusually individualistic character. It is ironic, therefore, that Ibn Khaldun's view of history did not seem to allow much room for the agency or free will of the individual. For Ibn Khaldun even the charisma of an individual leader must be sanctified by divine prophecy.[1] Although he described the lives of great sultans, chiefs, prophets, and mahdis in great detail, there was rarely the sense in his philosophy of history that individuals could break through inevitable patterns and cycles. Unlike many previous historians who strung together biographies of great rulers and personalities and called it history, Ibn Khaldun saw events systematically. Individuals were subjected to events, events were subject to social or tribal solidarity, to *'asabiyya*, to divine inspiration, and to the irreversible cycle of the rise and fall of dynasties. Individuals could attempt to slow down the inevitable course of events, but they were ultimately subject to the cyclical laws of history.

In vivid contrast to this apparent determinism, Ibn Khaldun's autobiography, an autobiography that described a great deal of individual will, of decisiveness and initiative on his own part, seemed to contrast with this wider view of history as an inevitable social process – the inevitable death and rebirth of social bodies. In fact, before he published the book as an independent volume, Ibn Khaldun wrote the autobiography as marginal text, a separate chapter in his *Muqaddimah*.[2] It was as if his life as an individual literally moved concurrently and parallel to the text of his philosophy. This striking contrast between Ibn Khaldun's wider view of history and his own role in it, however, need not be seen as an irreconcilable contradiction. It was as if Ibn Khaldun went through an individual 'metamorphosis' in his identity and voice.[3] His autobiography was often personal and full of agency. After all, as described above, he came to his conclusions out of his own efforts in a eureka moment. His historical writing, in contrast, seemed decidedly more deterministic.[4]

BETWEEN DETERMINISM AND FREE WILL

It was in Ibn Khaldun's description of the Sufi path, a path that he ostensibly attempted to take, that a reconciliation of the determinist and the autobiographical might be found. In his varied, encyclopedic account of Sufism in the *Muqaddimah*, Ibn Khaldun warned against the error of 'combination,' an error common among Sufi initiates in which they confuse themselves with the world, in which they feel a sense of cosmic universalism but get stuck there, unable to find true union with the divine. According to Ibn Khaldun, this sense of 'combination' comes from what he thought was a baseless theory, the notion that 'only the primeval God has real existence.' According to this 'erroneous' theory, 'human perception' is what creates the notion of differences between God and creation. Human beings are necessary for the 'particularization' of existence. Without humans, 'existence would be simple and one.'[5] Ibn Khaldun rejected this notion of human perception. There was more to what we see than mere perception. In fact, a Sufi novice must progress out of an elementary state of combination (*jam*ᶜ), out of a deterministic sense of oneness, and into a higher level of differentiation, an awareness of the separateness of the divine. Ibn Khaldun called the determinist oneness of this stage of combination a 'ravine' and stated that there was a danger that an adherent could get stuck there. Ironically, it was by blowing apart this sense of combination, by understanding God and the universe as separate from the individual but still fully within it that a Sufi could achieve the final stages of understanding. A similar, but logically argued, notion of the individual and the world existed in ashᶜari theology, an influential theology with a wide following in Ibn Khaldun's time. In this case, however, ashᶜari theology was not responding to a mystical experience but to the challenge posed by the following question: should humans be held responsible for their actions if God is all powerful?[6] For the Ashᶜaris, humans could be responsible and God could be omnipotent simultaneously. To explain how this was possible, Ibn Khaldun referred to the theological theory of the medieval scholar Fakhr al-Din al-Razi.

Ibn Khaldun wrote a treatise on the ostensibly determinist doctrine of Fakhr al-Din al-Razi when he was still a very young man. According to Al-Razi, humans are not the creators of acts, but God is. Only an omniscient being, who knew all the details and conditions of life, could act.[7] Nevertheless, the perception of motivation still existed. The modern scholar of Muslim theology Fazlur Rahman claimed that Sufism and even rationalist philosophers also advocated determinism at this time. This combination of mystical, theological, and philosophical determinism created 'a giant theoretical wheel of Medieval Islam revolving around the axis of determinism.' According to Fazlur Rahman, this deterministic axis was the result of similarly determinist notions of political despotism: 'increasing despotism both sustained and was sustained by this [determinist] theoretical attitude.'[8] As the autobiography and the writings of Ibn Khaldun revealed, however, in actual practice one could live as if one had motivations, even if those motivations and that will were ultimately determined by God in some theoretical way, or more practically, by whomever happened to be in power. In fact, Islam in the medieval period was, according to the scholar Marshall Hodgson, quite tolerant 'at the personal level.' While the guilds and class hierarchies of the occident mitigated against social mobility and freedom of movement, in Islam 'there remained wide personal liberty for a man to make his own choice within a reasonably predictable framework and in a range that was relatively broad . . . Such freedom was essential for a further sort of freedom of action – freedom of historical action, freedom to initiate new ideas and teach them . . .'[9]

The life of Ibn Khaldun, in many respects, was an example of this 'relative freedom' described by Hodgson. Although he often complained of the unjust acts of rulers, neither political despotism nor theological determinism contained Ibn Khaldun's thoughts or his travels. For just as he knew that dynasties must ultimately rely on the support of tribal *ʿasabiyya*, a rudimentary form of social freedom outside the boundaries of 'despotism,' so too could Ibn Khaldun, the individual, think and act, even if that thinking and acting was ultimately controlled by God. While dynasties may be subjected to a determinist cycle of history, it did not necessarily appear deterministic to those dynasties. Also, as scholars such as Steven Caton have observed, Ibn Khaldun's model of history only appears deterministic. In fact, his model also includes room for the 'charismatic personality, in the guise of either the desert chieftain or the prophet.'[10] Although he emphasized *ʿasabiyya*, the particular sayings and doings of particular prophets and chiefs were essential to the successful foundation of states.

Ibn Khaldun was interested in the content of history, in the meticulous facts and details of events listed and spread out in the massive history of the world in the *Kitab al-ʿIbar*, as much as in the patterns of history examined in the *Muqaddimah*. Ibn Khaldun could write an autobiography, an act that is in itself an implicit statement of free will, even if God determined that free will in some imperceptible way. Likewise, Ibn Khaldun's Sufism was not a Sufism of 'monistic determinism' as Fazlur Rahman described medieval mysticism,[11] but rather of 'differentiation' as the 'station of the competent Gnostic.'[12] Ibn Khaldun's ideas were not simply his own but the opinion of those mountaintops of Sufi scholarship: Al-Harawi, Ibn al-ᶜArabi and Najm al-Din 'the Israeli,' among others.[13] It was not as if Ibn Khaldun was lost in a sea of determinism, a sole believer in differentiation, in the relevance of human perceptions of free will. Rather, it is more likely the case that observations about medieval Islam as governed by an unbreakable 'wheel of determinism' created by the closing of the 'gates of *ijtihad* (interpretation)' needs serious reconsideration.

THE ORIGINALITY OF IBN KHALDUN'S AUTOBIOGRAPHY

Ibn Khaldun's autobiography was not a mere list, an unoriginal entry or addendum, the afterthought of a determinist, medieval Muslim automaton. With the rather cursory examination it has often been given, Ibn Khaldun's autobiography has been wrongly stuffed into the category of typical Arabic autobiography described, rather dismissively, by the influential Arabis Gustave von Grunebaum as 'Much of Arabic autobiography is limited to the listing of significant dates: birth, study, public appointments. The personality behind the events remains shrouded . . .'[14] Yet, as previous chapters have demonstrated, Ibn Khaldun did reveal a great deal of his personality in his autobiography. Although he did provide long lists of appointments, teachers, and dates, he also provided intriguing glimpses into the internal workings of his mind and the consequences of his own choices and initiatives. Ibn Khaldun's autobiography revealed not only how much he was able to accomplish as an individual, but how he, an orphan, rose to the highest offices mainly on his own initiative, becoming minister to sultans and grand Qadi of Cairo. Instead of traveling to Fez to work with the Marinids, an act that launched his travels throughout the Mediterranean, he could have followed his brother's advice and chosen to stay in Tunis. Ibn Khaldun could not help but make clear it was cunning, not luck – his request for a pilgrimage to Mecca, for example, to get out of his service to the Hafsid caliph, Abu al-ᶜAbbas – that helped him to escape the entreaties of sultans who wanted to confine his movements and keep him locked away in their courts. He emphasized the fact that most of his learning was self-taught, not the result of the government-run madrasas that he despised. Both the autobiography and the *Muqaddimah* described his writing of and his philosophy of history as wholly individual and original. He described how he had to retreat from all distractions, from all political events, to write the *Muqaddimah*. Nevertheless, the autobiography was ultimately framed by events, political conditions, and acts of God completely outside his control. His reaction to these fateful events – the plague, the death of his family at sea, his imprisonment in Fez, the bickering and conniving of rivals who appeared as friends – was poetry, silence or, towards the end of his life, a tired conster-nation. Throughout the book there are intriguing glimpses on what seem to be admissions of fault or, at least, overzealousness in the pursuit of political gain. When, for instance, one of his close friends became the *de facto* ruler in Marinid Fez, the young Ibn Khaldun assumed that he would be promoted to high posi-tion. In the course of time, the friendship turned out to be meaningless, and Ibn Khaldun yet again found himself on the wrong side of the political game. At this stage, the older Ibn Khaldun, writing later in his life, rebuked his younger self, saying, 'Youthfulness brings about excess. I aspired constantly to always achieve a higher position considering my old friendship with him.'[15] There are several moments of self-remonstration such as this. Most poignant, perhaps, was the way Ibn Khaldun framed himself in opposition to the memories of his Sufi father and his more humble older brother, Muhammad. Also, Ibn Khaldun's insertions of poetry and florid, formalized correspondence with colleagues into his autobiography were not meaningless diversions; they demonstrated an aware-ness of self and experience, an experience expressed more symbolically than the simple self-reflective, historical narrative between the poems. He wrote poems in prison, he wrote to his friend Ibn al-Khatib and to various amirs, but it was not merely the purpose of the poems and letters that Ibn Khaldun wanted the reader to remember. Rather, poetry was a window into deeper feeling, even personal angst. Although Ibn Khaldun pre-emptively professed a lack of poetic acumen, his autobiography was a stage constructed to display his mastery of the poetic form. The reader of Ibn Khaldun's autobiography could thus periodically dip into the poetic realm that revealed the undercurrents of seemingly concrete events and happenings. Yet even though it is suffused with modes of self-expression, Ibn Khaldun's autobiography does not, as the literary critic of autobiography Phillippe Lejeune cautioned, collapse completely into fiction. In many respects, Ibn Khaldun's autobiography was also very much a historical project of sources, not just experiences. The collections of letters from Ibn al-Khatib or Ibn Zamrak he did not write were included rather haphazardly into the autobiographical nar-rative even as they interrupt the narrative stream, making the original version of his autobiography quite difficult to read. He referred to his life 'in history' and he urged the reader to consult his historical research on the dynasties and the persons with whom he worked, research that employed both self-referential information as well as the perspectives of other historians and ministers.[16]

AUTOBIOGRAPHY AND ALLEGORY?

As the scholar Tawit al-Tanji suggested, Ibn Khaldun wrote his autobiography not only to list the events in his life but also to self-consciously preserve the way he wanted to be viewed.[17] As his expressions of regret demonstrate, Ibn Khaldun wanted to be seen not only as an important statesman and thinker but also as learning from the excess of his ambition. Ibn Khaldun wrote his autobiography not simply as a register of his experiences but as an allegory, a lesson for readers about how to live in the world and how not to fall into the same traps he fell into as a youth. In this respect the autobiography could be viewed, in some respects, as a Sufi document. As Ibn Khaldun repeatedly made clear, the only way he was able to come to his revelations about history was to retreat into himself, to engage in the same silent study that characterized the pursuits of his politically unambitious, mystic father. At the same time, it was his engagement in the world, his futile and frustrating attempts to change the world, to shape the minds of rulers, that allowed him to see the truth of his contemplations first hand. A similar autobiographical allegory, although different in form and much more profound in its theological implications for the Islamic world as a whole, was written by the great theologian Al-Ghazali (d. 1111 AD), whose writings Ibn Khaldun had studied since his youth.[18] Ibn Khaldun knew his work on the reconciliation of mysticism and Islamic law; in fact, he constantly referred to Al-Ghazali as a pre-eminent theological authority. It was more than likely that he also must have known Al-Ghazali's autobiography.[19] As discussed earlier, Ibn Khaldun especially admired Al-Ghazali's viewpoints on, and defense of, Sufism, the mystical form of Islam practiced by Ibn Khaldun's father, and privately by Ibn Khaldun himself. Like Ibn Khaldun, Al-Ghazali also seemed to live a double life, or at least a political life at odds with his deepest thoughts and mystical experiences of the divine. After an initial period of alternating political success and disillusionment, Al-Ghazali retreated into a life of individual circumspection, of mystical revelation that separated him from the world. He then returned, wrote down his thoughts and achieved a renewed engagement with the world, even though that engagement accepted the inevitable fate imposed by God's hand. Ibn Khaldun recognized Al-Ghazali's work as that essential point when Sufi mysticism and *sharia* legalism were, if not fully reconciled, at least redirected toward similar ends. Yet Al-Ghazali's autobiography exemplified another important reconciliation: between the individual and his or her world, between political engagement and personal, moral ideals, a reconciliation that Ibn Khaldun was, if not explicitly, implicitly expressing in his own autobiography.

In addition to Al-Ghazali, Ibn Khaldun also had access to a rich body of autobiographical literature available on which to model his work.[20] Sufism influenced much of this autobiographical literature. Autobiographies were written as a guide for future adherents to a particular school of Sufism. Ibn Khaldun was intimately aware of the work of the Sufi writer Al-Muhasibi (d. 857 AD), an early mystic who wrote a famous autobiography about his conversion to mystical life.[21]

PRECURSORS

The tradition of Arabic political autobiography, fairly well established by the fourteenth century, was another influence on the autobiographical style of Ibn Khaldun, such as the often poignant autobiography by the exiled Zirid emir of Granada Ibn Buluggin (d. after 1094 AD), for example. Written in an apologetic mode, Ibn Buluggın attempted to justify his ultimately fruitless decisions and attempts to thwart the takeover of Granada by the Almoravids. He described his exile in Aghmat, the ancient Almoravid capital just north of the Atlas Mountains, in intimate detail.[22] Like Ibn Khaldun, Ibn Buluggin expressed the ultimate futility and burden of political power. Ibn Khaldun would have likely known about Ibn Buluggin and his work during his stay in Granada. Ibn Khaldun's colleague and friend, Ibn al-Khatib, claimed to consult the original version of Ibn Buluggin's work.[23] Clearly, Ibn Khaldun's decision to write an autobiography with introspective elements was not completely unique.

Although some, often in an attempt to characterize Ibn Khaldun as modern, have seen Ibn Khaldun's autobiography as the first 'true' autobiography, the examples cited above, especially of Al-Ghazali and Ibn Buluggın, show that autobiography as an Arabic literary form was fairly well developed by the time Ibn Khaldun was writing.[24] In some superficial respects only did Ibn Khaldun's autobiography follow the tradition of the *tarajim*, the somewhat formulaic biographical and autobiographical writing dedicated to the lives of poets, thinkers or, originally, the transmitters of the sayings of the Prophet Muhammad. In parts of the autobiography, he did simply list his teachers and qualifications and the basic dates of his life.[25] Viewed as a whole, however, Ibn Khaldun's autobiography betrayed a great deal of personal information and even psychological awareness, even if that information was hidden either between the lines, in letters, in bouts of remorse, vulnerability and homesickness, or in the poetic verse dispersed throughout the work.

NOTE ON MANUSCRIPTS AND SOURCES

The surviving manuscripts of Ibn Khaldun's autobiography show that the work developed in at least three stages.[26] The editor, Tawit al-Tanji, used manuscripts from all three of these stages in what remains an authoritative Arabic version of Ibn Khaldun's autobiography.[27] As Tawit al-Tanji and the Moroccan scholar A. Cheddadi make clear, the earliest manuscripts were an integral part of the *Kitab al-ᶜIbar*, his book on North African history, a book prefaced by the *Muqaddimah* and presented to the Hafsid caliph Abu al-ᶜAbbas in 1382. This version of the autobiography was appended to these first version of the *Kitab al-ᶜIbar*. There are at least four extant manuscripts of this earliest version of the autobiography and also, hence, of the *Muqaddimah*: a manuscript in the Al-Azhar mosque in Cairo, and three other manuscripts in Egypt that are nearly identical. The second stage of development in Ibn Khaldun's autobiography occurred after he left Tunis for Egypt in 1383. Ibn Khaldun dedicated a second version of the autobiography to the Mamluk ruler of Egypt, Al-Zahir Barquq, a version that reflected his work in Egypt. Perhaps unexpectedly, there are several copies of this manuscript preserved in Moroccan libraries and dated somewhat later (1724–5 AD).

There are two original manuscripts of the last and most complete version. The most famous is the Hagia Sofia manuscript 3200, located under the Hagia Sofia, the magnificent cathedral built by Justinian and transformed into a mosque after the Ottoman conquest of Constantinople in 1453 AD. Unlike earlier versions attached to the *Muqaddimah*, the Hagia Sofia version of the autobiography was a separate volume, revealing Ibn Khaldun's final intention for the work: that it should be read separately for its own sake. The existence of this magnificent manuscript, an original complete volume in separate form, reveals that Ibn Khaldun did not intend his autobiography to be read as merely a list of accomplishments and qualifications. Instead, by the time he finished his final version, he saw the autobiography as an independent work in its own right. There is also the Manuscript Ahmed III. This manuscript does not seem to vary significantly from the Hagia Sofia manuscript, but has not been comprehensively studied.[28]

In fact, the very extensiveness of Ibn Khaldun's autobiography, as well as biographical references in his *Muqaddimah*, posed a historical challenge for writing this book. While Ibn Khaldun's autobiography provided a rich, detailed record of his political activities, most of the biographical information on Ibn Khaldun and his life written by his contemporaries was scanty and brief at best and historically quite dubious at worst. Perhaps his friend and colleague, Ibn al-Khatib, minister for the amir of Granada, Muhammad V, wrote the most important external account of Ibn Khaldun's life. Yet this account no longer exists in the original writings or manuscripts of Ibn al-Khatib.[29] Also, it was rather brief and not nearly as enlightening about the relationship between Ibn al-Khatib and Ibn Khaldun as that revealed in the letters from Ibn al-Khatib preserved, perhaps selectively, by Ibn Khaldun in his autobiography. It simply mentioned Ibn Khaldun's intellectual achievements and qualifications when he first starting working for Ibn al-Khatib, including his commentaries on religious poems, mathematics, the philosophy of Averroes, and important theological works.[30]

Nevertheless, there are important biographical references found in several Arabic sources from the fifteenth century that do vary in some respects from Ibn Khaldun's account of his own life.[31] These variations often occur at those points in Ibn Khaldun's career when he reached a position of great political significance. The Caiene historian Ibn Qadi Shuhba mentioned Ibn Khaldun's five daughters and two sons, Muhammad and ʿAli, who, unlike their sisters and mother who died in a shipwreck, arrived in Cairo on a separate boat. There are also references to Ibn Khaldun's second marriage in Cairo, something he did not feel was relevant enough to mention in his autobiography.[32] There are also accounts of Ibn Khaldun's teaching style and interpretations of legal questions by his students and assistants in Cairo.[33] There are also striking omissions about the favors provided to Ibn Khaldun by important friends such as Amir al-Jubani (d. 1390 AD), a powerful military commander who opened doors for Ibn Khaldun shortly after his arrival in Cairo. Perhaps his friendship soured with Amir, or perhaps Ibn Khaldun wanted to give the impression that his successes in Cairo were mainly of his own making.[34] Ibn Khaldun also failed to clarify his specific role in signing a *fatwa* against the Sultan Barquq during a rebellion against him in 1389.[35] When Sultan Barquq returned to power he forced Ibn Khaldun from his important and lucrative position as sheikh of the Sufi Baybarsiyya *khanqa*. Although Ibn Khaldun could have refused to sign, just as his colleague the judge Shams al-Din Muhammad al-Rakraki did, Ibn Khaldun gave the impression in his autobiography that he was forced to sign the *fatwa* against his patron.[36] Nevertheless, Ibn Khaldun made no mention of Shams al-Dın Muhammad al-Rakraki and his brave refusal. The incident, in fact, as discussed previously, forced Ibn Khaldun to retire from public life for about a decade. He did not fill any major position in Cairo until he was finally forgiven by Sultan Barquq and installed as Qadi in 1399 AD.

The scholar Walter Fischel lamented, 'it would be wrong to assume that with the complete text of his Autobiography now at our disposal we would be in possession of a comprehensive and complete biography of Ibn Khaldun.' He claimed that the autobiography merely contained 'long historical excurses and surveys which have no relationship whatsoever to his personal life.'[37] In fact, as this book has shown, these historical surveys and excurses, on the Hafsids or on the Dawawida tribal confederation for example, provided the historical context needed to make a historical biography rich and relevant. Ibn Khaldun's autobiography was not simply an extended *curriculum vitae*. It betrays a form and personal references not found in the abbreviated versions of earlier autobiographies and shares a great deal with the Sufi autobiographical form.

Ibn Khaldun was intimately involved in the complex political milieu of both the western and eastern Mediterranean. Nevertheless, and despite its many lacunae and the historiographic challenges involved in writing the history of his life, no other source on Ibn Khaldun matches the autobiography's remarkable depth of description and even self-reflection. Ibn Khaldun did not completely avoid difficult or shameful occurrences in his life. In fact, it was these occurrences that made the autobiography such a remarkable document, intended not merely to praise its own subject but to show the trials and tribulations of public life, even as he so often longed for peace and contemplation. Although Ibn Khaldun's life was full of apparent contradictions – between the pursuit of Sufi mysticism and political advancement, between longings for both solitude and influence, between the heterogeneous geography of his North African home-land and the settled and sophisticated urban culture of Mamluk Egypt where he died, between a trust in the predictions of the saints and a new science of history – these contradictions never paralyzed him. Rather, these very contradictions added yet more richness and complexity to the life of a person who reflected his own period of history, a person who wrote big history, a history of the world, but also a history of his own life in the world.

NOTES

1 Steven Caton summarized the importance of charisma in Ibn Khaldun's writing in 'Anthropological theories of tribe and state formation in the Middle East: ideology and the semiotics of power,' in *Tribes and State Formation in the Middle East*, ed. P. Khoury and J. Kostiner (eds.) (Berkeley and Los Angeles, CA, 1990), 75–108.

2 Ibn Khaldun published the autobiography as a separate text after his encounter with Timurlane. For a discussion of different versions of Ibn Khaldun's biography see Walter Fischel, *Ibn Khaldun and Timurlane* (Berkeley, CA, 1952).

3 On the idea of metamorphosis and identity in the medieval world see C. W. Bynum, *Metamorphosis and Identity* (New York, 2001).

4 On Ibn Khaldun's fatalism see B. A. Mojuetan, 'Ibn Khaldun and his cycle of fatalism: a critique,' *Studia Islamica*, 53 (1981), 93–108.

5 *Muqaddimah*, vol. III, 86, 90. Instead, 'we know for certain that a country which we have quit on our travels or to which we are traveling, exists, despite the fact that we do not see it any more.'

6 Like the Christian Protestant and Catholic traditions, questions of predestination and free will have a long and contentious history in Islam. For a good primer on the question see Montgomery Watt, *Free Will and Predestination in Early Islam* (London, 1948).

7 For a summary of determinist philosophy in medieval Muslim theology see Fazlur Rahman, *Islam* (Chicago, IL, 1979), 98–9. Ibn Khaldun's commentary on Al-Razi, *Lubab al-Muhssal fi Usul al-Din* (*Treatise on Metaphysics*), R. Rubio (ed.) (Tetuan, 1952).

8 F. Rahman, *Islam*, 99.

9 Marshall Hodgson, *Rethinking World History*, Edmund Burke III (ed.) (Cambridge, 1993).

10 See Steven Caton, 'Anthropological theories,' 89–90 and Muhsin Mahdi, *Ibn Khaldun's Philosophy of History* (Chicago, IL, 1957), 89, 91.

11 Rahman, *Islam*, 99.

12 *Muqaddimah*, vol. III, 90.

13 *Muqaddimah*, vol. III, 92.

14 Gustave von Grunebaum, 'Self expression: literature and history,' in *Medieval Islam: A Study in Cultural Orientation* (Chicago, IL, 1956), 270.

15 *Al-Taʿrif*, 77; *Autobiographie*, 95.

16 On the use of various narrative devices in Autobiography and the importance of switching between voices see Philippe Lejeune, *On Autobiography*, trans. Katherine Leary (Minneapolis, MN, 1995); Jared Poley, *Decolonization in Germany: Weimar Narratives of Colonial Loss and Foreign Occupation* (New York, 2007).

17 *Al-Taʿrif*, Introduction, i.

18 Marshall Hodgson considered Al-Ghazali as the only true, pre-modern Arab autobiographer: *Venture of Islam* (Chicago, IL, 1972), vol. II, 180. For the autobiography of Al-Ghazali and a discussion of his life see Montgomery Watt, *The Faith and Practice of Al-Ghazali* (London, 1953).

19 *Muqaddimah*, vol. III, 29, 32, 52–4, 75.

20 Due to recent, extensive research on the history of the autobiographical form in Arabic literature, it is now possible to account for these influences. For recent important research on the historical development of autobiography in Arabic see *Interpreting the Self: Autobiography in the Arabic Literary Tradition*, D. Reynolds (ed.) (Berkeley, CA, 2001).

21 *Muqaddimah*, vol. III, 80. Ibn Khaldun cited Al-Muhasibi as a main source for 'laws governing asceticism and self-scrutiny.' For a translation of Al-Muhasibi see K. Schoonver, *Muslim World*, XXIV, 1949, 26–35, also Margaret Smith, *An Early Mystic of Baghdad* (London, 1977).

22 Amin T. Tibi, *The Tibyan: Memoirs of ʿAbd Allah b. Buluggin: Last Zirid Amir of Granada* (Leiden, 1986).

23 *Interpreting the Self*, 85.

24 In identifying Ibn Khaldun with the modern, the famed Egyptian writer and minister of education Taha Hussein claimed that Ibn Khaldun, *pace* M. Hodgson, was the first 'real' autobiographer in *ʿIlm al ʿijtima'*, vol. VIII in *Al-Majmuʿa al kamila li-muʾallafat T. Husayn* (Beirut, 1973), 27. Several scholars have made contrasting judgments about when the 'birth' of Arabic autobiography occurred. Some even claimed that T. Husayn himself was the true first true Arab autobiographer. See *Interpreting the Self*, 72.

25 A. Cheddadi suggested that, in some important respects, Ibn Khaldun's autobiography was in the formulaic *tarajim* tradition in *Le Livre des Exemples*, 1275.

26 Muhammad Tawit al-Tanji, *Al-Taʿrif*, introduction. According to Muhammad Tawit al-Tanji, there were several different complete names used for the book, Although *Al-Taʿrif Ibn Khaldun Rihlatu Gharban wa Sharqan*, or 'The Life of Ibn Khaldun and his voyages from the West to the East' is the title he used for his edition, it is only one version. There was also, for example, the title *Kitab Rihla ibn Khaldun bi Khata, Rahmatu Allah wa Taʾala*, or 'The book of the Voyage of Ibn Khaldun, May God Preserve Him.' For a more recent discussion of the different versions of Ibn Khaldun's autobiography see A. Cheddadi's bibliographical essay in *Le Livre des Exemples*, pp. 1276–8.

27 Ibn Khaldun, *Al-Taʿrif bi Ibn Khaldun rihlatuhu gharban wa sharqan*, Muhammad Tawit al-Tanji (ed.) (Cairo, 1951). For his discussion of the original manuscripts used in his edition and the placement of the *Taʿrif* in relation to the *Kitab al-ʿIbar* see his introduction, (waw) ii. This work is the basis for the Moroccan scholar A. Cheddadi's authoritative translation as well as the present biography.

28 *Le Livre des Exemples*, 1277.
29 The book *Al-Ihata bi-akhbar Gharnata*, a '*History of Granada*,' by Lisan al-Din Ibn al-Khatib, 2 vols. (Cairo, 1901), is an important source for the history of Al-Andalus. Unfortunately, the surviving or known manuscripts do not seem to contain the biographical reference to Ibn Khaldun. Instead, a very brief biographical reference was attributed to Ibn al-Khatib by a much later writer, Al-Maqqari (d. 1632 AD), *Nafh al-Tib*, 8 vols. (Beirut, 1968).
30 According to Ibn al-Khatib, he wrote on the works of the important theologian Fakhr al-Din al-Razi (d. 1209 AD); on the *Burda*, a poem praising the Prophet Muhammad and the *Lubab al-Muhassal fi Usul al-Din*, R. Rubio (ed.) (Tetuan 1952), vol. 1. For an English translation of Ibn al-Khatib's account see Franz Rosenthal, *Muqaddimah*, vol. I, xliv.
31 In Arabic these include, but are not limited to, the following sources, most of which make passing references to Ibn Khaldun: Ibn al-Furat (d. 1404), *al-Tarikh* (Beirut, 1936–8), vol. IX; Maqrizi (d. 1442), *Kitab al-Suluk*, MS. Paris No. 1728 and *al-Khitat* (Cairo, 1853); Ibn ⁿArabshah (d. 1450), *ʿAjaʾib al-maqdur*, Manger (ed.) (Leeuwarden, 1767) (this account is especially interesting as it provides another brief perspective on Ibn Khaldun's encounter with Timurlane); Al-ⁿAini (d. 1451), *ʿIqd al-Juman*, MS Paris No. 1544; Ibn Taghri Birdi (d. 1469), *al-Manhal al-Safi*, MS Paris No. 2069-71, Al-Nujum al-Zahira, W. Popper (ed.) (Berkeley, CA) vol. V, 1932–6 and vol. VI, 1915–23; Al-Sakhtawi (d. 1497), *al-Dauʾ al-Lamiⁿ*, 12 vols. (Cairo, 1934); Ibn Iyas (d. 1524), *Badaʾiʾ al-Zuhur*, 3 vols. Cairo, 1893–4; Ibn Qadi Shuhba (d. 1448), *al-Dhail ʿala Tarikh al-Islam*, MS Paris Nos. 1598–9.
32 Fischel, 'Ibn Khaldun's Autobiography,' 291.
33 Fischel, 'Ibn Khaldun's Autobiography,' 292.
34 Fischel, 'Ibn Khaldun's Autobiography,' 298–9.
35 Fischel, 'Ibn Khaldun's Autobiography,' 304.
36 Fischel, 'Ibn Khaldun's Autobiography,' 305.
37 Fischel, 'Ibn Khaldun's Autobiography,' 288.

BIBLIOGRAPHY

Although an updated, scholarly Ibn Khaldun bibliography is past due, it is not my ambition to produce one here. The literature on Ibn Khaldun and the use of his ideas in disciplines as diverse as economics, pedagogy and poetry is too vast and could fill a volume on its own. Also, many of these studies would only be tangentially related to a biography of Ibn Khaldun. Only the sources I consulted while writing this book are listed below.

Aberth, J., *The Black Death, The Great Mortality of 1348–1350* (Boston and New York, 2005).

Abulafia, D., *The Western Mediterranean Kingdoms, 1200–1500* (London, 1997).

Abulafia, D., *Italy, Sicily and the Mediterranean, 1100–1400* (London, 1987).

Abulafia, D., *Commerce and Conquest in the Mediterranean, 1100–1500* (Aldershot, 1993).

Abu-Lughod, J., *Before European Hegemony: The World System A.D. 1250–1350* (Oxford, 1989).

Abu-Lughod, J., 'The World System Perspective in the Construction of Economic History,' *History and Theory*, 34, 1995, 86–98.

Agius D. and I. Netton (eds.), *Across the Mediterranean Frontiers: Trade, Politics, and Religion, 650–1450* (Turnhout, 1997).

Ahmed, Z., *The Epistemology of Ibn Khaldun* (London, 2003).

Alatas, F., 'Ibn Khaldun and contemporary sociology,' *International Sociology*, 21 (6), November 2006, 782–95.

Arkoun, M., *Pour une critique de la raison islamique* (Paris, 1984).

Asatrian, M., 'Ibn Khaldun on magic and the occult,' *Iran and the Caucasus*, 7 (1–2), 2003, 73–123.

Ashtor, E., *Social and Economic History of the Near East in the Middle Ages* (Berkeley and Los Angeles, CA), 1976.

Ashtor, E., *East–West Trade in the Medieval Mediterranean* (Aldershot, 1986).

Ayalon, D., *Gunpowder and Firearms in the Mamluk Kingdom, a Challenge to a Mediaeval Society* (London, 1956).

Al-Azmeh, A., *Ibn Khaldun in Modern Scholarship. A Study in Orientalism* (London, 1980).

Al-Azmeh, A., *Ibn Khaldun: An Essay in Reinterpretation* (London 1982).

Al-Azmeh, A., *Ibn Khaldun: An Essay in Reinterpretation* (Budapest, 2003).

Baali, F., *Society, State and Urbanism: Ibn Khaldun's Sociological Thought* (New York, 1988).

Belkhodja, M. H., 'Hazim al-Qartajani' in *Institute des Belles Lettres Arabes a Tunis (IBLA)*, 1966, 341–70 and 1967, 117–49.

Bennison, A., 'Liminal states: Morocco and the Iberian frontier between the twelfth and nineteenth centuries,' in Julia Clancy-Smith (ed.), *North Africa, Islam and the Mediterranean World* (London, 2001), 11–29.

Berque, A., *L'Algerie, terre d'art et d'histoire* (Algiers, 1937).

Berque, J., 'Ibn Khaldun et les Bédouins de Maghreb,' *Histoire et société* (Argel, 1947), 48–64.

Berque, J., 'Du nouveau sur les Beni Hilal,' *Studia Islamica*, 36, 1972, 99–111.

Blair, Sheila, 'Sufi saints and shrine architecture,' *Muqarnas*, 7, 1990, 42.

Boswell, J., *The Royal Treasure: Muslim Communities Under the Crown of Aragon in the Fourteenth Century* (New Haven, CT, 1977).

Bourdieu, P., 'Social space and symbolic power,' *Sociological Theory*, 7 (1), Spring 1989, 14–25.

Bowsky, W. M., *The Black Death: A Turning Point in History?* (Huntington, NY, 1971).

Brett, M., 'Ibn Khaldun and a dynastic approach to local history: the case of Biskra,' *al-Qantara*, 12, 1991, 157–70.

Brett, M., *Ibn Khaldun and the Medieval Maghrib* (Aldershot, 1999).

Brett, M., and Elizabeth Fentress, *The Berbers* (Oxford, 1997).

Brunschvig, R., *La Berberie orientale sous les Hafsides* (Paris), vol. III and XI, 1940 and 1947 of 'Publications de l'Institut d'Études Orientales d'Alger.'

Bulliet, R., *Islam: The View from the Edge* (New York, 1994).

Bynum, C. W., *Metamorphosis and Identity* (New York, 2001).

Caton, S., 'Anthropological theories of tribe and state formation in the Middle East: ideology and the semiotics of power,' in *Tribes and State Formation in the Middle East*, P. Khoury and J. Kostiner (eds.) (Berkeley and Los Angeles, CA, 1990), 75–108.

Chabane, D., *La penseé d l'urbanisation chez Ibn Khaldun* (Paris, 1998).

Cheddadi, A., 'À propos d'une ambassade d'Ibn Khaldun auprès de Pierre le Cruel,' *Hespéris-Tamuda*, 20–1, 1982–3, 5–23.

Cheddadi, A., *Ibn Khaldun et le Science de la Civilisation* (Paris, 2006).

Cheddadi, A., *Ibn Khaldun revisité* (Casablanca, 1999).

Clancy-Smith Julia (ed.), *North Africa, Islam and the Mediterranean World* (London, 2001).

Cornell, Vincent, *Realm of the Saint* (Austin, TX, 1998).

Cornell, Vincent, *The Book of the Glory of the Black Race: al-Jahiz's Kitab Fakhr as-Sudan ᶜala al-Bidan*, trans. and ed. Vincent Cornell (Waddington, NY, 1981).

Cornell, Vincent, *The Way of Abu Madyan: Doctrinal and Poetic Works of Abu Madyan Shuᵓayb ibn al-Husayn al-Ansari*, trans. and ed. Vincent Cornell (Cambridge, 1996).

Crone, Patricia, *God's Rule* (New York, 2004).

Crone, Patricia, *God's Caliph* (Cambridge, 2003).

Crone, Patricia, *Slaves on Horses: The Evolution of an Islamic Polity* (Cambridge, 1980).

Crone, Patricia, *Medieval Islamic Political Thought* (Edinburgh, 2005).

Dale, Stephen, 'Ibn Khaldun: the last Greek and first Annaliste historian,' *International Journal of Middle East Studies*, 30 (3), 2006, 431–51.

Doumerc, B., *Venise et l'émirat hafside de Tunis (1231–1535)* (Paris, 1999).

Dufourcq, Charles, *L'Espagne catalane et le Maghrib aux XII et XIV siècles* (Paris, 1966).

Eickelman, D., *Moroccan Islam: Tradition and Society in a Pilgrimage Center* (Austin, TX, 1976).

Eickelman, D., *The Middle East: An Anthropological Approach* (Englewood Cliffs, NJ, 1981).

Eickelman, D., 'The art of memory: Islamic knowledge and its social reproduction,' in Juan Cole (ed.), *Comparing Muslim Societies: Knowledge and the State in a World Civilization* (Ann Arbor, MI, 1992).

Eickelman D. and James Piscatori (eds.), *Muslim Travelers: Pilgrimage, Migration, and the Religious Imagination* (Berkeley and Los Angeles, CA, 1990).

El Rayes, W., *The Political Aspects of Ibn Khaldun's Study of History*, Ph.D. Dissertation, University of Maryland, College Park, July 24, 2008.

Fernandes, Leonor, *The Evolution of a Sufi Institution in Mamluk Egypt* (Berlin, 1998).

Fischel, Walter, 'Ibn Khaldun's 'Autobiography' in the light of external Arabic sources,' *Studi Orientalistici in onore di G. Levi Della Vida* (Rome, 1956), I, 287–308.

Fischel, Walter, *Ibn Khaldun in Egypt* (Berkeley and Los Angeles, CA, 1967).

Fischel, Walter, *Ibn Khaldun and Timurlane: Their Historic Meeting in Damascus, 1401 AD* (Berkeley and Los Angeles, CA, 1952).

Fischel, Walter, 'Ibn Khaldun's sources for the history of Jenghis Khan and the Tatars,' *Journal of the American Oriental Society*, 76 (2), April–June 1956, 91–9.

Fromherz, A., *The Almohads: Rise of An Islamic Empire* (London, 2010).

Fromherz, A., 'North Africa and the twelfth century Renaissance: Christian Europe and the Almohad Islamic empire,' *Islam and Christian–Muslim Relations*, 20 (1), 43–59.

García Arenal M., and M. J. Viguera (eds.), *Relaciones de la Península Ibérica con el Magreb* (Madrid, 1988).

Garthwaite, G., 'The Bakhtiyari Ilkhani: an illusion of unity,' *International Journal of Middle East Studies*, 8, 1977, 145–60.

Gates, W. E., 'The spread of Ibn Khaldun's ideas on climate and culture,' *Journal of the History of Ideas*, 28, 1967, 415–22.

Gellner, Ernest, *Muslim Society* (Cambridge, 1991).

Gellner, Ernest, 'From Ibn Khaldun to Karl Marx,' *Political Quarterly*, XXXII, 1961, 385–92.

Gibb, H. A. R., 'The Islamic background of Ibn Khaldun's political theory,' *Bulletin of the School of Oriental Studies*, 7 (1), 1933, 23–31.

Goitein, S. D., *A Mediterranean Society*, 6 vols. (Berkeley, CA, 1967–98).

Goitein, S. D., *Studies in Islamic History and Institutions* (Leiden, 1968).

Goodman, Lenn, *Islamic Humanism* (Oxford, 2003).

Grunebaum, G. E. von, *Medieval Islam* (Chicago, IL, 1953).

Guzman, Gregory, 'Were the barbarians a negative or a positive factor in ancient and medieval History?,' *The Historian*, 50 (1), August 1988, 558–72.

Harlan, J., *Crops and Man* (Madison, 1992).

Hillenbrand, Carole, *The Crusades: Islamic Perspectives* (Chicago, IL, 1999).

Hillenbrand, Robert, *Islamic Architecture: Form, Function and Meaning* (New York, 1994).

Hocquet, J. C., *Le sel et la fortune de Venise* (Lille, 1982).

Hodgson, M., and M. G. S. Hodgson, *Venture of Islam*, 3 vols. (Chicago, IL, 1972).

Hodgson, M., *Rethinking World History*, Edmund Burke III (ed.) (Cambridge, 1993).

Hopkins, Nicholas, 'Engels and Ibn Khaldun,' *Alif*, 10, 1990, 9–18.

Hourani, Albert, *Arabic Thought in the Liberal Age, 1798–1939* (Oxford, 1992).

Hourani, Albert, *A History of the Arab Peoples* (Cambridge, MA, 1991).

Ibn ᶜArabshah, *Timurlane or Timur the Great Amir: From the Arabic Life by Ahmed Ibn ᶜArabshah*, trans. and ed. John H. Sanders (London, 1936).

Jegel, G., *l'Italie et le Maghreb au Moyen Age* (Paris, 2001).

Kably, Mohamed, *Société, Pouvoir et Religion au Maroc à la fin du 'Moyen-Age'* (Paris, 1986).

Kennedy, Hugh, *Muslim Spain and Portugal: A Political History of Al-Andalus* (London, 1996).

Kennedy, Hugh, *Mongols, Huns and Vikings: Nomads at War* (London, 2003).

Lapidus, I., 'Tribes and state formation in Islamic history,' in P. Khoury and J. Kostiner (eds.), *Tribes and State Formation in the Middle East* (Berkeley and Los Angeles, CA, 1990), 25-47.

Lapidus, I., *Muslim Cities in the Later Middle Ages* (Cambridge, MA, 1984).

Laroui, A., *History of the Maghreb* (Princeton, 1977).

Latham, J. D., 'Towards a study of Andalusian immigration and its place in Tunisian History,' *Les Cahiers de Tunisie*, 1957, 203–52.

Lawrence, B., (ed.), *Ibn Khaldun and Islamic Ideology* (Leiden, 1984).

Lejeune, Philippe, *On Autobiography*, trans. Katherine Leary (Minneapolis, MN, 1995).

Lewis, Bernard, *Islam in History*, 2nd ed. (Peru, IL, 2001).

Lindholm, Charles, *The Islamic Middle East: Tradition and Change* (Oxford, 2002).

Mahdi, M., *Ibn Khaldun's Philosophy of History* (Chicago, IL, 1957).

Manz, B. F., *The Rise and Rule of Timurlane* (Cambridge, 1989).

Messier, R. A., 'Rethinking the Almoravids, rethinking Ibn Khaldun,' in J. Clancy-Smith (ed.), *North Africa, Islam and the Mediterranean World* (London, 2001), 58–80.

Messier R. A. (ed.), *The Journal of North African Studies Special Edition: The Worlds of Ibn Khaldun*, 13 (3), September 2008.

Mojuetan, B. A., 'Ibn Khaldun and his cycle of fatalism: a critique,' *Studia Islamica*, 53, 1981, 93–108.

Nassar, N., *La pensée réaliste d'Ibn Khaldun* (Paris, 1967).

Nwya, P., *Une Mystique Prédicateur a la Qarawiyyin de Fes: Ibn ᶜAbbad de Ronda (1332–1390)* (Beirut, 1961).

Pederson, J., *The Arabic Book*, trans. Goeffrey French (Princeton, 1984).

Perkins, K., *A History of Modern Tunisia* (Cambridge, 2004).

Peretie, M. A., 'Les Medersas de Fes,' *Archives Marocaines*, 18, 1912, 257–372.

Picard, Ch., *L'Océan Atlantique musulman de la conquête arabe à l'époque almohade* (Paris, 1997).

Poley, Jared, *Decolonization in Germany: Weimar Narratives of Colonial Loss and Foreign Occupation* (New York, 2007).

Powers, D., *Law Society and Culture in the Maghrib, 1300–1500* (Cambridge, 2002).

Premare, A. L., *Maghreb et Andalousie au XIVe siècle: les notes de voyage d'un Andalou au Maroc (1344–1345)* (Lyon, 1981).

Rabie, H., *The Financial System of Egypt AD 1169–1341* (London, 1972).

Rahman, F., *Islam* (Chicago, IL, 1979).

Robinson, Chase, *Islamic Historiography* (Cambridge, 2003).

Rosenthal, E., 'Ibn Khaldun: a North African Muslim thinker of the fourteenth century,' *Bulletin of the John Rylands Library*, 24, 1940, 307–20.

Rosenthal, Franz, *A History of Muslim Historiography* (Leiden, 1968).

Rosenthal, Franz, *Knowledge Triumphant: The Concept of Knowledge in Medieval Islam* (Leiden, 1970).

Rosenthal, Franz, 'Ibn Khaldun in his time' in Bruce Lawrence (ed.), *Ibn Khaldun and Islamic Ideology* (Leiden, 1984), 14–26.

Ruggles, D. F., 'Mothers of a Hybrid dynasty: race, genealogy, and acculturation in al-Andalus,' *Journal of Medieval and Early Modern Studies*, 34 (1), Winter 2004, 65–94.

Sacerdoti, A., 'Il Consolato veneziano del regno Hafsida di Tunis (1274–1518), *Studi Veneziani*, 1969.

Schmidt, N., *Ibn Khaldun: Historian, Sociologist and Philosopher* (New York, 1930). (Note: this book came out before the publication of several important sources by Ibn Khaldun, including the complete autobiography.)

Sebag, P., *Tunis: Histoire d'une Ville* (Paris, 1998).

Shatzmiller, M., 'Les premiers Mérinides et le milieu religieux de Fès: l'Introduction des Médersas,' *Studia Islamica*, 43, 1976, 109–18.

Shatzmiller, M., *The Berbers and the Islamic State: The Marinid Experience in Pre-Protectorate Morocco* (Princeton, 2000).

Shboul, Ahmadm, *Al-Mas ͨudi and his World* (London, 1979).

Stowasser, B., *Religion and Political Development: Some Comparative ideas on Ibn Khaldun and Machiavelli* (Washington, DC, 1983).

Talbi, M., *Ibn Khaldun et l'histoire* (Tunis, 2005).

Tapper, R., 'Anthropologists, historians and tribespeople on tribe and state formation in the Middle East,' in P. Khoury and J. Kostiner (eds.), *Tribes and State Formation in the Middle East* (Berkeley and Los Angeles, CA, 1990), 48–73.

Tibi, A., (trans), *The Tibyan: Memoirs of ͨAbd Allah b. Buluggin: Last Zirid Amir of Granada* (Leiden, 1986).

Tuchman, B., *A Distant Mirror: The Calamitous 14th Century* (New York, 1978).

Udovitch, A. L. (ed.), *The Islamic Middle East, 700–1900* (Princeton, 1981).

Valencia, R., 'La emigración sevillana hacia el Magreb alrededor de 1248,' in *Andalucía entre Oriente y Occidente, 1236–1248* (Cordoba, 1988), 31–6.

Wallerstein, I., *World-Systems Analysis: An Introduction* (Durham, NC, 2004).

Watt, M., *The Faith and Practice of Al-Ghazali* (London, 1953).

Watt, M., *Free Will and Predestination in Early Islam* (London, 1948).

White, H., 'Ibn Khaldun in world philosophy of history,' *Comparative Studies in Society and History*, 2 (1), 1959, 110–25.

Williams, John, 'Urbanization and monument construction in Mamluk Cairo,' *Muqarnas*, 2, 1984, 33–45.

Woods, John, 'The rise of Timurid historiography,' *Journal of Near Eastern Studies*, 46 (2), April 1987, 81–108.

Sources in Arabic

Al- ͨAini (d. 1451), *ͨIqd al-Juman*, MS Paris No. 1544.

Ibn ͨArabshah (d. 1450), *ͨAja ʾib al-maqdur*, Manger (ed.) (Leeuwarden, 1767).

Abu Bakr Muhammad al-Baqillani, *Kitab al-Bayan ͨan al-firaq bayna al-mu ʾjizat wal al karamat*, R. McCarthy (ed.) (Beirut, 1958).

Ibn Taghri Birdi (d. 1469), *al-Manhal al-Safi*, MS Paris No. 2069–2071.

Taqi al-Din al-Fasi, *Al-ʿIqd al Thamin fi Tarikh al-Balad al-Amin*, 8 vols., Muhammad al-Faqi *et al.* (eds.) (Cairo, 1958–69).

Ibn al-Furat (d. 1404), *al-Tarikh* (Beirut, 1936–8, vol. IX).

Ibn Iyas (d. 1524), *Badaʾiʾ al-Zuhur*, 3 vols. (Cairo, 1893–4).

Ibn Khaldun, *Al-Taʿrif bi Ibn Khaldun wa rihlatuhu gharban wa sharqan*, (autobiography), Muhammad Tawit al-Tanji (ed.) Cairo, 1951). Also cited in this book as 'Autobiographie' the updated scholarly translation by A. Cheddadi in *Le Livre des Exemples* (Paris, 2002), 52–248.

Ibn Khaldun, *Lubab al-Muhassal fi Usul al-Din* (*Treatise on the Metaphysics of Al-Razi*), R. Rubio (ed.) (Tetuan 1952).

Ibn Khaldun, *Kitab al-ʿIbar* (The Book of Forms or Examples, with Muqaddimah and Autobiography), 7 vols. Y. A. Dagir (ed.) (Beirut, 1992). The more widely available, but incomplete French translation is cited in this book as *Histoire des Berbères*, 4 vols., trans. Le Baron de Slane, ed. Paul Casanova (Paris, 1956).

Ibn Khaldun, *Shifaʾ al-Saʾil li Tahdhib al-Masaʾil* (*Treatise on Mysticism: The Solution for One Who Asks for the Improvement of their Questions*) Ignace-Abdo Kalifé (ed.) (Beirut, 1959).

Ibn Khaldun, *Mazil al-Malam ʿan Hukkam al-Anam*, Ms. 1899–1, (attributed to Ibn Khaldun), Asad Effendi Library (Turkey); Ms. Koprulu (Turkey), No. 1587–7, F. al-ʿAbd al-Munʾim Ahmad (ed.) (Riyadh, 1996–7).

Ibn Khaldun, *Tadkir al Sahwan* (attributed to Ibn Khaldun), Ms. 1899–2, Asad Efendi Library (Turkey).

Al Maqqari (d. 1632), *Nafh al-Tib*, 8 vols. (Beirut, 1968).

Maqrizi (d. 1442), *Kitab al-Suluk*, MS Paris No. 1728 and *al-Khitat*, Cairo, 1853.

Ibn Miskawayh, *Kitab tajarib al-umam wa taʾaqub al-himam*, 7 vols., trans. D. S. Margoliouth, *The Eclipse of the Abbasid Caliphate* (Oxford, 1921).

Muhammad Ibn al-Qadi, *Judhwat al iqtibas* (Rabat, 1973–4).

Muhammad al-Sakhawi, *al-Dawʿ al-lami*, 12 vols. (Cairo, 1934).

Ibn al-Shamma, *Al-adilla al bayyina al nuraniyya ʿala mafakhir al dawla al hafsiyya*, O Kaak (ed.) (Tunis, 1931).

Ibn Qadi Shuhba, *al-Dhail ʿala Tarikh al-Islam*, MS Paris Nos. 1598–9.

Ibn Qadi Shubba, *Description topographique et historique de l'Égypte*, 3 vols., trans. Urbain Bouriant (Paris, 1895–1900).

Ibn Qadi Shubba, *Al-Nujum al-Zahira*, W. Popper (ed.) (Berkeley, CA), vol. VI, 1932–6 and vol. V, 1915–23.

Al-ʿUmari, *Masalik al-absar fi mamalik al amsar*, trans. M Gaudefroy-Demombynes (Paris, 1927).

INDEX